THE

MINISTRY

How Japan's Most Powerful

Institution Endangers

World Markets

■

Peter Hartcher

HARVARD BUSINESS SCHOOL PRESS
Boston, Massachusetts

Printed in the United States of America

02 01 00 99 98   5 4 3 2 1

Library of Congress Cataloging-in-Publication Data

Hartcher, Peter.
    The Ministry : how Japan's most powerful institution
endangers world markets / Peter Hartcher.
        p.   cm.
    ISBN 0-87584-785-4 (alk. paper)
    Includes bibliographical references.
        1. Finance, Public—Japan.   2. Japan. Ōkurashō.
    3. Japan—Economic policy—1945–   I. Title.
    HJ1394.H383   1998
    336.52—dc21   97-27489
                                                            CIP

The paper used in this publication meets the requirements
of the American National Standard for Permanence of
Paper for Printed Library Materials Z39.49–1984

For Helen

CONTENTS

大蔵省

Acknowledgments   *vii*

Introduction   THE OKURASHO   *1*

1   THE CLUB   *8*

2   REWARDS AND PUNISHMENTS   *31*

3   A SUPERPOWER IN MIRAGE   *60*

4   THE MIRAGE DISSOLVES   *95*

5   JAPAN BECOMES THE RISK   *123*

6   THE RISING PRICE OF FAILURE   *158*

7   A CRISIS OF IDEAS   *185*

8   THE SACRED MISSION   *203*

9   A WORLD APART   *223*

10   TIME FOR CHANGE?   *236*

Glossary   *261*

Notes   *265*

Index   *295*

About the Author   *311*

ACKNOWLEDGMENTS

大蔵省

Helen, my partner, provided the moment of inspiration for this book. She also supplied the years of unswerving support that necessarily followed. So while I may have put the words on the page, she put the idea in my head and kept my eyes focused on the screen. This book is as much hers as mine—and perhaps even more. To Kate, Dylan, and Nina, thanks for your patience and understanding on all those days when I was too busy to play.

For the precious gift of time, I am deeply grateful to the enlightened management of Gregory Hywood, editor in chief and publisher of *The Australian Financial Review*, an unfailing and generous source of support.

And my thanks go to the world's most efficient researcher, my assistant, Midori Kai. No detail was ever too small, no request ever too difficult, no problem ever insurmountable. For valuable ideas and for selfless support, I am indebted to two of the most relentlessly logical and extraordinarily dynamic people on either side of the Pacific, Kenichi Ohmae and David Hale.

I thank the many officials at the Okurasho, those still serving and those who have descended from heaven, who gave me their time and assistance in researching the institution. Although some of the more enlightened and less orthodox will be pleased at the disclosure and analysis in this book, many others will not appreciate the final product. I make no apology, however, for honesty. The contributions of some officials are noted throughout the book. Others preferred to remain anonymous.

To the friends who probably didn't realize the contributions they made to this venture, my thanks. The ideas, the discussion, the dialectic, the enthusiasm, and the friendship of Shunsuke Motani, Nobuya Nemoto, Greg Dodds, and Richard McGregor, were invigorating and valuable. And finally, to William Miller and Junzo Sawa in Tokyo and John Thornton in New York, my gratitude for extraordinary patience and kindness in initiating me into the mysteries of the world of book publishing.

THE OKURASHO

In 1994 the U.S. President Bill Clinton made a public attack on one of America's staunchest postwar allies—Japan. He did not criticize the country or its leaders. Instead, he chose two government institutions. Japan, Clinton suggested, was a premodern protectionist state, and the engineers of the system were the Ministry of International Trade and Industry (MITI) and the Ministry of Finance.

Mr. Clinton named the trade and finance ministries as "the permanent government agencies [in Japan] that have dominated policy for years and years, for decades." They had created an economy with "low unemployment and high savings rates, big exports and no imports—and they want to keep it [that way]." According to Clinton, these two arms of the public service were responsible for impeding Japan's emergence as "a fully modern state with fair and open trade."[1]

Clinton's claim was tantamount to accusing the two ministries of international economic sabotage on a grand scale. But Tokyo did not retaliate with an outraged rebuttal or a Chinese-style denunciation of U.S. meddling in the internal affairs of a sovereign nation. In fact, the government made almost no public response.

This is because Clinton's comments were simply a public confirmation of what Japan's prime minister at the time, Morihiro Hosokawa, was saying privately. The main point of departure was that Mr. Hosokawa was little concerned with that favorite of foreign forensics, MITI, long examined by the West as a potential model for interventionist industry policy. He was preoccupied with the Ministry of Finance, the center of real bureaucratic power in Japan's economy, the second biggest in the world.

Mr. Hosokawa was the most popular Japanese leader since the invention of the opinion poll, a reformer who conjured a vision of a delightful new Japan where consumers had more choice and producers less privilege, where workers had more dignity and their bosses less power over them, where citizens had sovereignty and vested interests lost their veto.

But to give body to this vision, Mr. Hosokawa knew that he had to break down a vast array of laws, ordinances, and customs. And this meant breaking the power of bureaucracy, or somehow turning its power to his own purposes. He was determined to "bring Japan out of the Reign of the Bureaucracy and back into the Reign of Representative Politics."[2]

But by April 1994, a few months after Clinton's speech, the bureaucracy was still intact, and it was Hosokawa who had been broken. A few days after announcing his intention to resign, the outgoing Prime Minister of Japan confessed morosely during dinner with two political intimates: "I tried to manipulate the power of the Ministry of Finance, but in the end it was the ministry that manipulated me."[3]

Japan's Ministry of Finance is much more than an office of government. It is a political, economic, and intellectual force without parallel in the developed world. It enjoys a greater concentration of powers, formal and informal, than any comparable body in any other industrialized democracy. In Japan, there is no institution with more power.

Japan's Constitution, imposed by the U.S. occupation forces in the aftermath of World War II, stipulates that the parliament, or Diet, is the highest organ of state power. It makes no reference to the Ministry of Finance. Yet the ministry lays claim to origins that predate the Constitution by 1,269 years, to principles of national duty that transcend the Constitution, and to the exclusive right to the budget powers, without which the entire structure of government would be meaningless.

On induction into the Finance Ministry, recruits are told that its earliest known incarnation dates from at least A.D. 678, when the ancient imperial court comprised three main components: an inner shrine for the gods, an outer shrine for the man-god (the emperor), and the treasure-store, or *Okura*. It is from this term that the Ministry of Finance takes its Japanese name, the Okura*sho*—literally, great storehouse ministry. And so it is that in Japan, after the deities of heaven and earth comes that of the Ministry of Finance.

The U.S. occupation of Japan from 1945 to 1952 made only a glancing impression on the Ministry of Finance. General Douglas MacArthur and his command purged some 210,000 officials from the military, politics, the *zaibatsu* industrial conglomerates (Japan's biggest, most influential companies) and the bureaucracy, the often huge network of government offices staffed by unelected officials! But their bureaucratic targets were concentrated in the armed forces and the Ministry of Home Affairs.

The Finance Ministry lost just nine officials to the purge. Its prewar personnel and principles were essentially untouched. There was a time when a U.S. president could have had a profound impact on the institution and its operations. Bill Clinton was half a century too late.

While history is one of the foundations of the Okurasho's claim to privileged status, pragmatism is another. If the Okurasho did not keep national spending in check, who would?

The Okurasho works under the assumption that politicians represent special interests; it is left to the bureaucracy to represent the national interest. And among the various ministries that make up that bureaucracy, the Finance Ministry is chief. The other ministries, which preside over particular sectors of society, are tainted by their interest in the health of their constituent industries. Only finance claims to be servant to none but the nation. As its members are fond of saying, it is the "ministry of ministries."

So while the politicians clamor for cash to pay for pork-barrel projects and the other ministries secure funds for their private-sector friends, the Okurasho tallies the cost to the national debt and the implications for Japan's fiscal soundness and sovereign strength. Constitutionally, there is nothing to prevent an irresponsible government from spending its way into a debt trap. But what the edicts of the Constitution do not supply, the Okurasho claims to have imposed by sheer force of will and assertion of power. In its cam-

paign to achieve a conservative national budget balance, the ministry has been instrumental in the downfall of at least two postwar
prime ministers. Tetsu Katayama was prime minister from 1947 to
1948, and Morihiro Hokosawa held that office from 1993 to 1994.
Its proudest claims are that it has held pork-barrel politicking in
check and curbed bureaucratic growth to keep government small.
The Ministry of Finance takes credit for rebuilding Japan's sovereign strength following World War II. A nation that had forfeited
its independence when vanquished by force of arms just half a century ago is now robustly independent, a nation with little natural
wealth is now ranked as the wealthiest in the world through its
holding of overseas assets.

And if the Okurasho has no political master, neither does it bow
before the god worshipped by the financial authorities of lesser
lands, the almighty market. The Finance Ministry acknowledges the
usefulness of the market in providing for the efficient allocation of
goods and capital, but it invokes a higher power. The national good
is not necessarily served by the most efficient outcome, and only the
elite servants of the nation—officials of the Finance Ministry—are
qualified to decide when that is the case.

Japan's policy makers have escaped the excesses of neoclassical or
purist free-market economics because the government in general
and the Okurasho in particular are wary of its missionaries—the
economists. The ministry employs a relative handful of these true
believers, and they are kept in careful check. Unchecked, economics
could undermine naturalism in Japan's policy-making class.
Efficiency and perfect market outcomes do not respect the demands
of nation building and nationalists.

The prevailing philosophy in postwar Japan—and for centuries
before the war—holds that no principle, practice, or people should
be allowed to take precedence over the wealth and welfare of the
nation. The Okurasho, high priest of modern nationalism, is not
about to allow itself to be hypnotized by the imported heresy of a
supreme market.

So Japan's stock market is forbidden to fall to its natural point of
resistance, no matter how overvalued it may be, and its financial
industries are exempted from the full play of the forces of gravity, no
matter how heavy they happen to be. The giant life insurance com-

panies are protected from the forces of competition, no matter how harsh or vast, and the banks are permitted to collude in setting interest rates, no matter how great the loss to ordinary bank depositors.

And again, the Okurasho can claim some successes. The deliberate tolerance of such inefficiencies detailed above has given Japan one of the lowest unemployment rates among the world's wealthy nations. Partly as a consequence, Japan has less violent crime, too. The country rejected the abrupt, convulsive, and costly Anglo-American approach to deregulating markets and unleashing free competition, instead spending fifteen years carefully dismantling controls over interest rates to prevent sudden dislocations in the system. Even now some hidden measures persist to keep the forces of competition in check.

In Western countries, where church elders or seers once enjoyed primacy among the advisers to kings and emperors, it is now the prerogative of the economist to stand at the executive elbow. Policy-making departments are top-heavy with economists; no politician's private staff is complete without one. No government contemplates any major initiative without first seeking the blessing of economists, no report is complete without first genuflecting to them.

But in Japan, and specifically in the Finance Ministry, economists rank second and remain suspect. The great bulk of men—yes, they are inevitably men—appointed to the top echelons of the Okurasho are graduates of Tokyo University's department of law, not economics. They are trained as lawyers and administrators, nationalists and politicians, but not as economists. While economists pull the levers of policy in most Western systems of government, in Japan the economists are themselves just another lever. The top officials of the Ministry of Finance keep the economists in a box in the corner, lift the lid to consult them when the mood strikes, then put the lid back on the box. Economics is a set of ideas and techniques to be used as one reference among many. It is not a dominant doctrine.

This is no accident. The Okurasho is proud of its defiance of U.S.-style capitalism. One noted American student of Japan, Chalmers Johnson, has said that the Cold War ended—and Japan won. At the end of its Cold War prosecution of political freedom and economic laissez-faire, the United States had a large Federal deficit, a burdensome trade deficit, and a host of social problems. Japan spent the Cold War sheltered under the American strategic umbrella, all the while running a successful interventionist economy. It emerged with a vast trade surplus, its national debt in check, minimal unemployment, and a relatively calm and untroubled society. The United States emerged from the Cold War as the world's biggest debtor, and Japan emerged as the world's biggest creditor. Indeed, one prominent ministry economist and thinker, Eisuke Sakakibara, argues that while the end of the Cold War may have ended one chapter of ideological competition between two extremes, it opened a new era of more subtle competition, a competition between the United States and Japan.[4]

According to Sakakibara, Japan is a market economy but not a capitalist one—it refers to itself as a "non-capitalistic market economy." Although its economy is based on market principles, it does not put the interests of the cigar-chewing capitalist at the center of the system. He claims that Japan's basic doctrine amounts to "anthropocentrism,"[5] by which he means that the Japanese people are at the center of the system.

Can the Okurasho be so bad, then? It resists undisciplined democracy and is cautious in its embrace of the free market. While a U.S. president might see this as antidemocratic and antimarket, couldn't it be argued that the ministry is in fact simply moderating the extremes of these imported doctrines in the defense of a pragmatic national interest? Wouldn't most countries profit by having such a strong, pragmatic, apolitical defender of the national interest?

Many observers, as well as the Japanese people themselves, might once have said yes, but increasingly this argument seems flawed. One reason is the simple question of competence. After pumping up Japan's economy to an unsustainable "bubble" in the late 1980s, the Okurasho then punctured it, plunging Japan into its first homegrown recession since World War II. The ministry's claims to extraconstitutional and supramarket privilege look tattier than at any other time since the war.

Another reason for doubt is the growing body of evidence that the Okurasho frequently acts not out of national interest but out of unenlightened self-interest. And this perception is winning increasing currency. Cabinet ministers accuse it of sacrificing the national good to its own lust for power. Other government agencies publicly criticize it for suppressing change, protecting its private-sector friends, and penalizing commercial initiative. Eminent foreign observers challenge its credibility. The serious Japanese media say the ministry has demonstrated that it is unfit to conduct its affairs. The popular Japanese media characterize it as a secretive, neofascist guerilla arm of the government.

Does the institution that has acted so long for the good of the nation now need to be purged for the good of the nation? If so, can Japan bring itself to overturn what is in many minds its most powerful institution? These are the questions I intend to explore and answer in this book.

THE CLUB

Japan's Ministry of Finance is headquartered in central Tokyo in a gray-tiled, six-story structure with all the architectural elegance of a prison block and the ambience of a Depression-era courthouse. Inside, the glare of fluorescent lights reflects off the uniformly white shirts worn by ministry officials, who scuffle across the floor from one pile of paper to another. Meanwhile, crowds of nervous petitioners shuffle on loose parquetry down long, chairless corridors. Blankets stacked in discreet piles testify to long nights at the office, and the occasional salacious poster of a barely clad woman points out at social attitudes as unreconstructed as the building itself. All the ministry's main bureaus are here, and their names largely advertise their functions: the Budget Bureau, the Banking Bureau, the International Finance Bureau. One exception is the small division on the second floor, responsible for the overall coordination of the ministry's many activities: the Minister's Secretariat.[1] This office is opaque to the Japanese public and unknown to the rest of the world. Yet it is a remarkable place, an obscure little office with the vast responsibility of setting economic policy for Japan. It is here that the thrum of the Japanese wealth generator is checked, its irregularities diagnosed, and remedies prescribed. And now that Japan produces one dollar in every six in the world economy, monitoring the fluctuations of its own economy has become a tremendous task. It is no exaggeration to say that the Minister's Secretariat in the

Okurasho is one of the most important centers of professional economic policy making in the modern world.[2]

Like the Okurasho itself, the Minister's Secretariat is suspicious of economists and employs relatively few. For every economics graduate hired into its executive stratum, three law graduates are hired. Often, the top officials responsible for economic policy have no formal qualifications in the subject. And in the postwar history of the secretariat, its uppermost officer has never held an economics degree. Perhaps the starkest proof of this dearth of expert economists is that the secretariat has traditionally been obliged to borrow a steady supply of economists from outside institutions such as commercial banks, life insurance firms, and even Japan's monopoly tobacco company, Japan Tobacco.[3]

Even those officials at the Okurasho and its secretariat who have earned economics degrees do not work as professional economists. They are instead encouraged to work as generalist administrators. Two of Japan's most eminent economics scholars—Ryutaro Komiya and Kozo Yamamoto—were able to write in 1979 that "there is not one professional economist employed by the Government of Japan."[4] In 1995, they said there was no need to review their earlier study—at least in the case of the Ministry of Finance and its secretariat, nothing had changed.[5]

The Minister's Secretariat is a particularly unusual office in that it operates as an employment agency and a matchmaking service as well as the coordinating administrative office of the Finance Ministry. These services are not offered only out of concern for staff welfare but reflect an important element of grander institutional strategy that sometimes involves the Okurasho's chief executive, the vice minister for administrative affairs. While the minister is the politician appointed to preside over the Okurasho, the vice minister for administrative affairs is the career bureaucrat who actually operates it.

Doing the work normally expected of an employment agency, a section within the Minister's Secretariat seeks out high-level positions outside the Okurasho for executives who are leaving. This does not happen randomly but in a meticulously organized manner that has helped the Okurasho to expand its network of influence far beyond its own gray walls. Through this practice—known as *amakudari*, or the descent from heaven—the Okurasho has established the exclusive right to fill top-level jobs throughout the public and private sectors. This practice has prompted accusations that it has "colonized" other government ministries, from defense to environment, and that it has subverted the proper priorities of a range of institutions, from Japan's central bank, the Bank of Japan, to its antitrust agency, the Fair Trade Commission.

In the role of matchmaker, the secretariat finds brides for single officials in the Ministry of Finance's executive career stream. By matching the ministry's elite officials with the daughters of politicians and industrialists, the secretariat has the ability to successfully forge feudal-style alliances between the aristocracy of the Okurasho and the political and industrial elites of Japan.

Based on the above facts alone, it is clear that Japan's Ministry of Finance is something more than just another government department.

■ How to join

Finance Ministry officials sometimes describe themselves as part of the Okurasho family. One told a foreign visitor that the ministry is more like "a rather splendid club."[6] And like any club, it sets its own rules for membership. This club has a strong preference for the graduates of a single institution, the University of Tokyo. For many years, the ministry accepted graduates from no other institution. There is a historical explanation. The university was founded in 1877 as the Imperial University of Tokyo during the early part of Japan's drive to modernize during the reign of the emperor Meiji, which began in 1868. Its law school was granted a very special status: supply source of bureaucrats for the new state. For graduates of the university, the usual laws of gravity were suspended, and they were allowed to enter directly into the national

> **One Finance Ministry official told a foreign visitor that the ministry is more like "a rather splendid club."**

bureaucracy without having to endure the rigors of the higher civil-service examination. Its critics said that the university was no longer a university but merely a school for bureaucrats. Nonetheless, within some thirty years its graduates came to dominate the national bureaucracy.[7] This system had a political purpose. In the words of a retired Tokyo University professor, "The Meiji ideal was to staff the [Finance] Ministry with the ablest graduates of the elite university so that they would be impervious to questioning from the public or the legislature."[8] The general disdain in which the Okurasho has long held politicians was captured by one Meiji-era bureaucrat who described the Diet as a collection of three hundred farmers.[9]

This was more than a century ago. The Allied occupation of Japan stripped the university of its imperial status and reorganized it as part of the country's democratization. In the latter part of the twentieth century, Tokyo University graduates no longer have an automatic entree into Japan's civil service. But the condescension with which elite bureaucrats regard politicians is unchanged. In the early 1990s, one senior Okurasho official accused the national politicians of practicing the "low politics" of building public works and soliciting budget appropriations. The civil servant Eisuke Sakakibara, demonstrating qualities neither civil nor servile, in 1990 summarized the role of the people's elected representatives as being "to request appropriations from the central bureaucracy. They serve, in effect, as executive treasury officers stationed in Tokyo for their various regional institutions."[10] While the bureaucrats and the private sector cooperated to create Japan's high-speed economic reconstruction after World War II, the politicians of the ruling party, the Liberal Democrats, "were," Sakakibara continued, "in a sense, bystanders left alienated from the machinery of high growth itself. Their function was to repair some broken parts of economic society which could not be repaired through the workings of the high-growth machinery." In the case of one particular Cabinet, Sakakibara was earlier reported to have gone so far as to suggest that the prime minister and his ministers—all political appointees—were "idiots," although this was denied strenuously by the Finance Ministry.[11]

One of the shrewdest postwar Japanese politicians, the corrupt but dynamic Kakuei Tanaka, who served as prime minister from 1972 to 1974, and as finance minister from 1962 to 1965, did not resent this tradition of elitism but actually exploited it. Mr. Tanaka, whose own education extended no further than his local elementary school, submitted himself to his mandarins at the Okurasho when he was first appointed finance minister with these words: "You are the true elite of the elite. Studying at the topmost university in this country, your brains are the highest quality in Japan. I will, therefore, leave the business of thinking to you, and I will, with your permission, take responsibility for the results."[12] Incidentally, as prime minister, Mr. Tanaka was more successful in extracting public funds from the Finance Ministry for his programs than any other postwar politician.

Disregarding the march of history, the graduates of Tokyo University have managed to bestow on themselves an effective stranglehold on posts in the Finance Ministry's executive track, what the Japanese refer to as the career stream. Career stream officials are the people for whom all senior positions are exclusively and permanently reserved, the elite, fast-tracked upper grade. They make up only 5 percent of the Finance Ministry's total staff but 100 percent of its directors-general and vice ministers. In the 1970s Tokyo University graduates routinely took about 70 percent of the entry-level positions in the career stream. By the 1980s they were typically taking more than 80 percent. Then, in its 1993 hiring, the ministry went too far. It recruited twenty-four staff members to enter its career stream, and twenty-two of them were from Tokyo University. At 92 percent, it was just too much.[13]

The prime minister in 1993 was the Liberal Democratic Party's Kiichi Miyazawa, a man who well understood the Okurasho club system and the importance of holding an entry ticket stamped by Tokyo University. This was because he had himself graduated from the university and gone on to become a senior official in the Okurasho before entering politics. But in spite of the natural sympathies he might have felt for the ministry and its traditions, Miyazawa decided that the situation had become unacceptable. Miyazawa said publicly that the proportion of Tokyo University types at the Okurasho had to be reduced. The following day, his chief cabinet secretary and the official spokesman for the government, Koichi Kato, elaborated. He said that the government had decided that the proportion of Tokyo University graduates was to be reduced to a maximum of 50 percent over the ensuing five years at key government agencies, including the Finance Ministry.

The next year, 1994, the Okurasho hired twenty-one career officials. This time, eighteen were from Tokyo University—still an unrepentantly high 86 percent. The recruitment from other universities was token. The Finance Ministry hired exactly one graduate from each of three other highly regarded universities (Keio, Kyoto, and Waseda).

Miyazawa was never able to take the Okurasho to task. In August 1993 he and his Liberal Democratic Party fell—marking the first time this dominant political party had lost control of the government since it came into power in 1955. But after nine months on the opposition benches, the party had reclaimed power, in a coalition government. When things settled down, Koichi Kato found himself in one of the party's three most powerful posts: chairman of the Policy Research Council. In February 1995, he called the Ministry of Finance to account. He summonsed the head of the Minister's Secretariat, Takeshi Komura, and asked him to explain the Finance Ministry's lack of progress in implementing the directive. The bureaucrat reportedly told the politician that the ministry had a problem with the new policy: "Graduates of other universities do not want to come to the Finance Ministry." A furious Kato put Komura under a so-called access ban in response to this preposterous claim, refusing to speak to him. Kato went on to become one of the more implacable enemies of the Okurasho.[14]

All the same, two months after his meeting with Komura, the ministry did exactly what Kato had feared—it hired twenty new recruits into its career stream, and eighteen—90 percent—were from Tokyo University. "It's a symptom of the stubbornness of the Ministry of Finance," said an official in the secretarial division of the Minister's Secretariat. The secretariat later set a target of 70 percent for Tokyo University new hires,[15] which was finally met in 1997, when they comprised 73 percent.

Tokyo University graduates typically make up 30–40 percent of those students who pass the exam given for entry into the career stream of the national ministries. More applicants are screened out during the initial interview process, with the result that 50 percent are Tokyo University graduates.[16] During the final round of interviews, the percentage reaches the extraordinarily high levels of 90 percent or more. The mechanism for skewing hiring is the interview process.

The gap between 50 percent and 90 percent or more indicates just how far the Finance Ministry is prepared to go to preserve its club. On this issue, the ministry's responsibilities as a public agency clash directly with the personal predilections of its officials. Personal predilections seem to have prevailed.

This is not the world's only example of a national bureaucracy dominated by elite universities. Britain's Oxford and Cambridge universities and France's Instituts d'Etudes Politiques hold similarly commanding positions. But a careful comparative study of five leading industrial democracies—the United States, Japan, Germany, France, and Britain— found that there is still no real match for the elitism in Japan's recruitment of career-stream bureaucrats. Japan's system is, in theory, the most open of all because it imposes no formal educational requirements on recruits. But in practice it is the least open of all, less flexible and less egalitarian than those of the other countries.[17]

■ The trouble with economists

If the Okurasho loves graduates of Tokyo University, there is one thing it loves even more—Tokyo University graduates equipped with law degrees. One reason for the 3 to 1 ratio of law school graduates to economists stems from the law school's 1877 mandate to turn out custom-built bureaucrats. Another reason is that the economics faculties at Tokyo and elsewhere were dominated by Marxists for several decades following World War II. It was not until the 1960s that non-Marxian economics was taught at Tokyo University.[18] Neither the ministry nor the Liberal Democratic Party it nominally served has ever been keen to promote Marxism. But these are historical explanations and not valid reasons; the Meiji era is long gone, and so is Marxism as a credible concern.

The real reason? It is not because the ministry rejects knowledge of economics. In fact, it has a tradition of offering its young officials intensive study of economic theory. For decades, a year-long in-house training program was conducted by a panel of highly qualified teachers, mainly academics from outside the ministry. Young bureaucrats in their third year at the ministry were given nine hundred hours of lectures and extensive tutorial and other work. Officials boasted that it was the equivalent of an undergraduate education in economics. A handful of each year's recruits was not processed through this system but instead sent to do postgraduate study abroad for two years—the favored subject being economics. In the 1990s, however, the in-house training program was abandoned and replaced with a new system. Now, all elite-stream officials are freed from their work at the Okurasho headquarters at 3-1-1 Kasumigaseki, Tokyo, and are sent overseas for postgraduate study for two full years. Just before they leave Japan, the Okurasho gives its future leaders a crash course in basic principles of economics and accounting. Thus primed, three-quarters of each year's recruits spend the next two years studying economic and monetary theory. Of the rest, most study business administration, while one in ten studies a miscellany of other subjects, including law. Their principal destination is the United States, but Germany, France, and Britain also feature.[19] This raises an interesting question: If a knowledge of economics is so highly valued, why does the Finance Ministry give clear and consistent priority to hiring staff who have *not* studied the subject?

Consider first that the screening process begins with the simple choice of Tokyo University as the preferred source of staff. Most students at the university came from relatively affluent backgrounds and have mastered a difficult and competitive system of exams. The nation views them as Japan's best and brightest. It is common sense that the graduates of this elite university—and particularly those who seek work in the civil service—are likely to be more conservative than the public they are supposed to serve. This assumption is supported by a 1983 survey indicating that 60 percent of bureaucrats in all national ministries who had graduated from Tokyo University were supporters of the conservative Liberal Democratic Party, compared with a support rate of 37 percent in the general population at the time. And while only 34 percent of the general population described themselves as conservative or somewhat conservative, 58 percent of the Tokyo University alumni in the bureaucracy did. Consequently, choosing a Tokyo University graduate is nearly the equivalent of choosing a conservative whose leanings in politics and policy will be fairly predictable.[20]

Second, consider the preference for those Tokyo University graduates holding law degrees. This, too, can be expected to yield a group of bureaucrats who can be expected to exert specific pressures on the ministry and its policies. And, according to a consensus of informed observers, it does. After a detailed study of Tokyo University law graduates, Byung Chul Koh of the University of Illinois suggested that "Tokyo University's law faculty may actually turn out narrow-minded technicians well versed in the fine points of legal theories and interpretation and supremely adept at taking examinations. As one writer put it, Tokyo University law graduates who become elite bureaucrats 'can see the trees but not the forest.'"[21]

The chief emphasis for economics students, on the other hand, is the pursuit of the most efficient allocation of resources in an economy—money and people—through a liberal play of market forces. This obliges economics students to consider the entire forest. Moreover, while the study of law naturally focuses on the significance of laws and ordinances, the study of economics tends to regard them as impediments to the invisible hand of market forces. It is an important difference; the economics graduate is far more likely to see regulation as a hindrance to be removed rather than an achievement to be preserved. Takahiro Miyao of Tsukuba University argues that the dominant reflex in Okurasho thinking is the "legal precepts-first"

The ministry has "no belief in what might be called economic principles."

approach, while the ministry has "no belief in what might be called economic principles."[22] This seems intimately connected to ministry officials' educational experience. "Most Okurasho people are from the law department, which maintains its prewar traditions—they have absolutely no understanding of the market," says Yoshiaki Miwa, a member of the economics department at Tokyo University.[23]

The ministry's hiring preferences get it the type of officials it wants—predominantly, generalist administrators. This is how these officials like to be seen, too. Within the ministry, it can be a career liability to be regarded as an economist.[24] The Okurasho wants its staff to understand economics but not to be possessed by it. It wants officials who see economics as one set of considerations within a larger framework of administrative and legal principles rather than those who see economics as paramount. It wants their mental framework to be that of the lawyer with a knowledge of economics rather than the other way around. For this reason, the Okurasho discourages qualified economists from working as professional economists in government and insists on rotating them into administrative jobs. Instead of letting economists pull the levers of power, it wants administrators who pull levers—including one lever marked "economics."[25]

The net effect seems to be that the lawyer's instinctive love of law predominates in the work of the Finance Ministry. An eminent economist who has taught many Okurasho officials is Ryutaro Komiya. He believes that the economic sophistication of the Okurasho is slowly improving, but thinks that overall these bureaucrats "don't have much faith in the market mechanism, and they like to intervene in the market."[26]

The lawyer's instinctive love of law predominates in the work of the Finance Ministry.

Kozo Yamamoto, a former elite official of the Okurasho and a respected economist, says "The Japanese public believes that the Okurasho understands the economy, but that's not true. When they make decisions, it is usually based on a common sense generalist approach, and not as economists. Many taxes are written without

any understanding of the economy, so they make many mistakes."
Mr. Yamamoto recalls that during the mid-1980s, when the Finance
Ministry was debating whether to yield to U.S. demands for the
opening of its financial markets, he mounted an economic case in
favor of the U.S. proposal. "Most people in the ministry could not
understand what I was saying, but they had no real choice because
the pressure from the U.S. was so great."[27]

Japan did indeed begin a slow but steady program of liberalization of its financial markets. But in general the Okurasho has been
reluctant to open any market or to deregulate any sector. Change
has been excruciatingly slow and grudging. Most liberalizations
have been a result of U.S. insistence and have not been self-initiated.
In part, this reluctance to change stems directly from the ministry's
hiring preferences. And, of course, it is convenient that this approach also preserves the ministry's power; officials who abolish
regulations are surrendering direct control. As we will see later in
the book, the Finance Ministry is one of the more important reasons that Japan's economy has been relatively slow to reform itself
in the latter part of the twentieth century, relatively slow to embrace
market forces, and therefore surprisingly ready to sacrifice new opportunities for growth. For this reason alone, the cost of preserving
the club Okurasho has been high.

However, there is a curious paradox in the ministry's approach to
economics. In its approach to regulating markets and industries, its
impulse is interventionist. Yet in its approach to the overarching
question of the size of government, it favors small government and
lower spending. So in *micro*economics it favors an expansive role for
the State, but in *macro*economics it wants a diminished State. The
first impulse is characteristic of a leftist approach to government,
the second a conservative approach. While this is indeed an ideological paradox, from a practical point of view it is entirely consistent. That is because both approaches resist change in Japan's status
quo and preserve the power of the Okurasho. They are conservative
in the literal sense of the word. Intervention in the affairs of the
marketplace preserves the ministry's powers of regulation in, say,
banking and the stock market. But cutting government spending in
the budget puts power into the hands of the ministry as the nation's
fiscal guardian, as we will see later. The vigilant keeper of the na-

tional treasury has immense leverage in dealing with politicians and other ministries.

■ Marriage and other intimacies

Being hired into the Okurasho career stream brings with it much more than a career. For many ministry officials, the Okurasho influences their choice of spouse and can take them deep into dynastic politics. This influence operates in two directions: from the ministry looking out, where ministry bureaucrats marry into the families of the rich and powerful, and from the ministry looking in, where officials marry the daughters of other ministry bureaucrats.

It is natural to expect some intermarriage between the different elements of what may be termed Japan's ruling class. This happens in most societies. It is also unsurprising that there should be some natural cross-fertilization within a large organization whose members often work together quite intensively.

But what distinguishes the practice of marriage at the Okurasho from what might naturally be expected is that matchmaking at the ministry is professionally organized—not just as a social activity or part of an extracurricular program but as a routine part of the ministry's professional work. The task of sorting candidates, filing dossiers, and suggesting prospective matches is done by full-time, career-stream officials working in the same section of the ministry responsible for high-level coordination of all personnel matters, including hiring, training, and promoting of staff—that is, the secretarial division of the Minister's Secretariat.[28] According to the division head, his subordinate bureaucratic Cupids succeed in arranging two ministerial marriages a year on average.[29] By one account, the photographs of young women being considered as prospective brides for ministry officials are stacked in a pile that commonly stands half a yard high. The daughters of politicians are the

> **What distinguishes the practice of marriage at the Okurasho is that matchmaking at the ministry is professionally organized.**

ministry's prospects of choice for its officials.[30] This not only improves the quality of the ministry's political relations but can be immensely valuable to the young official with political ambitions, and there are many of these. It has its attractions for the politicians, too—they are forever seeking leverage with the Okurasho in the hope of winning a bigger share of budget funds for pet projects.

It is hard to find official data on the subject, but there are at least forty-one known cases of Okurasho officials marrying into the families of politicians in the last forty years or so, or an average of about one per year. Most of these marriages have involved the families of politicians of considerable standing. Eight ministry officials have married into the families of prime ministers. At least 4 to 5 percent of Okurasho career-stream officials in recent decades have married into politicians' families.[31] It is not known how directly or deliberately the ministry was involved in these pairings, but we do know this: as a matter of unofficial Okurasho policy, the ministry favors the marriage of its officials into politicians' families, and it deploys public resources in the organized pursuit of this policy. This is not unique in Japan. Many large firms and public agencies also conduct matchmaking services for staff, an outgrowth of the twentieth-century Japanese principle of lifetime employment.[32] Nevertheless, in considering the performance and priorities of the Finance Ministry, it is useful to ask whether matchmaking is a legitimate task for a modern, professional agency of the civil service.

The bureaucratic elite are scornful of the dynastic nature of Japanese politics; more than a third of the politicians in the Lower House "inherited" their seats in the Diet from their fathers. This sort of feudalism, in contrast to the principle of merit that is at least supposed to govern admission to bureaucratic ranks, is ridiculed by the mandarins. Yet according to the Okurasho itself, 1 in 20 of its career-stream recruits, or an average of one a year, is the son of a former career-stream Okurasho official. Within the limits imposed by the examination system, the ministry, like the Diet, has a tendency to nepotism. Intermarriage between officials' families is another interesting phenomenon. Although comprehensive statistics are hard to find, some of the anecdotal evidence is intriguing. For example, the three officials appointed consecutively to lead the ministry in the first half of the 1990s all had sons-in-law among their subordinates. The chances of this happening by sheer coincidence are extremely small. From 1992 to 1993, the top Finance Ministry official, the vice minister for administrative affairs, was Mamoru Ozaki. One of his daughters married a young official who in 1994 was an assistant director in the Finance Ministry's Budget Bureau. Ozaki was succeeded in his post at the top of the ministry by the celebrated Jiro Saito, as tough as he was controversial. One of Saito's daughters, too, married a young official who could also be found working as an assistant director in the ministry's Budget Bureau in 1994. And the remarkable Mr. Saito was replaced by Kyosuke Shinozawa, who, again, was in the happy position of having one of his daughters wedded to a ministry official who, again, in 1994, was working as an assistant director in the Budget Bureau.[33] The Budget Bureau, incidentally, is the most prestigious in the Okurasho, and service here usually is a prerequisite for those aspiring to the top job in the ministry.

Consistent with all of this is the ministry's internal clubbiness. There are internal associations for all the career-stream staff who join the ministry in a particular year; other internal clubs for all past occupants of a particular post; still other clubs or "study groups" established around particular subjects, such as the Asia Club; internal groups arranged according to where officials went to high school; and a range of other criss-crossing associations defined according to common experience, attributes, and interests. And there is a range of other social, semisocial, and semiprofessional structures and events that are intended to engender solidarity and identification with the ministry. One such event occurs each year for each section or division, when it packs away its files for a few days and heads off for a weekend at a recreational resort for a lot of drinking, karaoke singing, and mah-jong. Another is the pairing up of a freshly recruited career-stream official with a colleague one year more advanced. The senior of the two (*senpai*) guides and advises the junior (*kohai*) and entertains him with food and drinks after hours and even buys him lunch daily for the one-month interregnum between his joining the government payroll and receiving his first paycheck.[34]

■ The price of membership

The Okurasho operates a bus service, with the first bus running around midnight, ferrying home staff who have outstayed the subway system. The buses run until 2 A.M. But that is too early for many staff to finish their work, and in the busier times of the year, hundreds miss the last bus. That's why the ministry also has a room full of beds, which the staff deprecatingly call the Hotel Okura, after the famous five-star establishment just a suburb away. But this room can accommodate only sixteen people, which explains the small stacks of blankets adorning most of the offices, up to and including the vice minister's. Most of those who are obliged to stay overnight are forced to sleep in their chairs or on sofas.

"Let's go home while it's still dark," is a catchphrase at the ministry. For while the Tokyo markets may close and companies shut down, the Ministry of Finance never sleeps. The late-night lights burning in the Okurasho building have become a symbol of the vigilance and tirelessness of Japan's public servants.

Officially, none of this happens. Officially, the Okurasho closes at 5:30 P.M. Officially, Japan's national government departments cut back to a strict five days a week in 1992. Officially, the ministry has endorsed a policy of cutting overtime hours. Government guidelines stipulate that public servants should not work more than 360 hours of overtime per year. The average at the Okurasho in 1992 was 1,428 hours. That's not only four times the stipulated limit, it represents 5.4 hours of overtime every working day. It's the equivalent of working an extra thirty-five regular working weeks a year.[35] Some of this overtime is paid at a premium above and beyond regular pay, ranging from 20 percent up to 50 percent for work done between 10 P.M. and 2 A.M., but officials at the rank of director and above are not paid for overtime. Instead they usually receive a manager's allowance, which can equate to about 25 percent of their regular salary. But these overtime figures do not convey

> **Government guidelines stipulate that public servants should not work more than 360 hours of overtime per year. The average at the Okurasho in 1992 was 1,428 hours.**

the full picture. Many career staffers work more than 2,400 hours of overtime a year, or more than nine hours a day, but do not record or report it.[36]

Why do they do it? A government survey of all the ministries asked this question in 1992 and got answers from 5,700 bureaucrats. One third blamed a heavy workload and a shortage of staff.[37] At the Okurasho, the work that most obviously falls into this category is the preparation of the national budget. From the time the examiners in the Budget Bureau begin their annual grillings of the suppliant agencies in September, through to December, many staff go home rarely and work eighteen-hour days, seven days a week. Their burden eases in January. It is said that this is the reason the babies of Budget Bureau staff are usually born in October or November.[38]

Another area demanding long hours is the defensive work done to prepare the finance minister when he appears before the Diet. Ministry staff stationed permanently in the Diet building talk informally to politicians and ask what issues they intend to raise in Diet questioning. With this information, plus the intelligence supplied by ministry staff working in the office of the finance minister and elsewhere in the political system, staff at the Okurasho compile a nightly list of questions their minister may encounter in the Diet session on the following day. Officials then sit up past midnight, drafting answers on the full range of potential questions.[39]

A notoriously onerous area of work is the National Taxation Agency, the Okurasho offshoot responsible for collecting taxes. Masaru Mizuno, a former chief of the Tokyo bureau of the agency who later became a senior Okurasho official, once claimed that an average of twenty-five people on his staff died of exhaustion caused by overwork—*karoshi*—every year.[40]

A senior Okurasho official claimed that an average of twenty-five people on his staff died of exhaustion caused by overwork—*karoshi*—every year.

The second most common explanation for overtime (after heavy workload coupled with staff shortage) was inefficient work habits, which were cited by 20 percent of the bureaucrats responding to the survey. Closely related to this was the answer given by another 7 percent of respondents—that they had to attend too many meetings. These answers suggest that much overtime is simply wasted time. But the third most common explanation for overtime was the "invisible pressure" from peers and superiors.[41] Evidently, going home at a reasonable hour was for wimps or, worse, those with questionable commitment to their section. Although none of the survey data applies *specifically* to the Okurasho, it is reasonable to assume that the same general conclusions would hold, both because of observed behavior in the ministry and because of the similarity in structure and practice across the national ministries.

All of this suggests that there is scope for a serious reappraisal of workload, staffing, and work habits to achieve a more methodical, balanced, and professional approach to the tasks of public service. The other big issue concerns whether unreasonably intense and unremitting workloads—in compiling the budget or in tax collection for example—can possibly produce optimum results if they are exhausting, perhaps even killing, staff. Whatever the reason, it is clear that the club Okurasho demands a heavy price for membership—not just hard work but absolute commitment.

■ Closing ranks

In most developed countries, the elected representatives of the people—the politicians—have considerable control over the appointment of the top government officials. In seeking the optimum balance between the principles of bureaucratic merit on the one hand and political control on the other, the United States offers an example of political excess. Japan is an example of the opposite, having denied politicians any role in choosing even the top official of its national ministries, the vice minister of administrative affairs. One of the Finance Ministry's greatest sources of power is its ability to appoint its own leader. This allows it to perpetuate its values and policies with a good deal of immunity from any outside force. It also severs a critical link in the transmission of political will; the people elect the politicians—in this case the finance minister—to govern, but the politicians cannot make even a limited choice in selecting the officials to carry out its policies. And if a finance minister en-

counters defiant officials, he has very limited leverage. He cannot remove them or choose their replacements except in extreme circumstances. (Officially, however, this is not so. Formally, the top bureaucrat in the ministry—the vice minister of administrative affairs—is appointed by the politician—the finance minister. But in truth it is only in the most unusual circumstances that the finance minister or any other politician has any real role in the appointment.)

Japan's system started to fray in the 1990s, most notably in the Ministry of International Trade and Industry. "The Okurasho's strength is its solidarity," says Kozo Yamamoto, a former official in the ministry's career stream who entered politics. "Other ministries—MITI, for example—have allowed political interference in appointments, but the Okurasho has not. If all the bureaucrats get together and say we don't like the minister and we will not work with him, then the minister can't do anything because he will not get any information and he won't be able to do his job. The most respected official among the Okurasho old boys is Teiichiro Morinaga. When he was vice minister, the finance minister directed him to appoint a particular official as director-general of a bureau. Morinaga refused and put himself at risk. But when a bureaucrat works to protect the ministry against a politician like that, all bureaucrats respect him."[42] This respect was no doubt one reason why the ministry successfully supported Mr. Morinaga's later nomination as governor of the central bank.

How then does the ministry choose its bureaucratic leader, the vice minister of administrative affairs, an event that normally occurs annually? The process begins with each year's intake of twenty to twenty-five junior career-stream officials who join the ministry together and then compete against each other for the next twenty years or so. By the time the escalator of progression through the hierarchy has taken this group close to the top echelon of executive jobs, the group itself has rated all of its members, and the ministry as a whole has carried out an informal evaluation of each member of that group. A natural sorting process has occurred. This process is largely opaque, and, importantly, it proceeds according to the criteria of the ministry itself, not any external standard. A senior serving official explains: "In each intake year, there is a strong sense of belonging and also a strong sense of competition. After you have spent ten years in the ministry together with the same group of colleagues, you know yourself how competitive you are, and it is already clear what you will be able to achieve ultimately, and the others know, too. It is judgment by peers, and it is an extremely harsh system."[43]

This system gleans the best from the rest—at least according to the ministry's internal standards—but it does not nominate the final successful candidate. The outgoing vice minister traditionally nominates his own replacement from among the top candidates in any particular "class year." Protocol and precedent dictate that he consult his predecessors—retired vice ministers—before making the final choice. There is usually a token consultation with the finance minister at the end of the process, but he is usually powerless to change the choice.[44] There have been exceptions. In 1974, for example, there were two equally strong candidates, and the Okurasho was divided in its choice. This presented an opportunity for politicians to play a decisive role. The prime minister happened to be the unusually strong-willed Kakuei Tanaka, who was intimate with the workings of the Okurasho as a result of his term as finance minister, and he took the opportunity to press his case. More recently, in 1994, a finance minister successfully insisted on his choice of candidate for a second-tier job in the ministry, director-general of a bureau. But this, too, was an exception to the rule. It occurred in unusual circumstances, when the ministry was under great duress.[45]

When the system works as it is intended to, it gives the ministry a thick wall of insulation against outside pressure. One administrative vice minister, Jiro Saito, took advantage of the system to unofficially nominate the next nine officials to occupy his job.[46] Perhaps the most remarkable aspect of this act was not its breathtaking degree of presumptuousness—even by Okurasho standards—but its plausibility. In fact, his chosen successors have been named as actual successors for at least two places down his list, a 100 percent success rate at the time of this writing.[47]

Mr. Saito himself was to become a fascinating test of the Okurasho's control over its destiny in the face of a political confrontation. As we will see in more detail later in the book, he cut an important deal with Prime Minister Morihiro Hosokawa in 1994.

As mentioned earlier in the chapter, Mr. Hosokawa was the first Japanese leader in thirty-eight years to unseat Japan's party of vested interests, the Liberal Democrats, who spent an angry nine months in opposition before sweeping back into vengeful victory in a new coalition government. When they did, they decided to punish Mr. Saito for having accommodated Mr. Hosokawa.

The lines of the contest were clearly drawn, pitting the highest-ranking bureaucrat of the Okurasho against some of the most powerful individuals in the country's dominant political party. Both institutions had recently been damaged. The Okurasho was hurt by its own succession of failures to fulfill its core responsibilities—resulting in a protracted recession and a deteriorating banking system—and by its attempt to strong-arm Japan into accepting a major new tax increase. The Liberal Democratic Party had lost a thirty-eight-year old monopoly of power.

What happened? On March 14, 1995, during an informal meeting of the national Cabinet, one minister pointed out to his colleagues a fact that all literate Japanese over the age of twelve already knew: the Okurasho had been responsible for a series of policy failures as well as several scandals of note. In the latest front-page exposé, two top Okurasho officials had been revealed to have a suspiciously close relationship with the modern villain of Japan's financial system, Harunori Takahashi. An entrepreneur of considerable profligacy, Mr. Takahashi had effectively bankrupted two credit unions he controlled. The Okurasho had then stepped in to rescue depositors with the use of taxpayers' funds, generating national outrage. Finance Minister Masayoshi Takemura had, one day earlier, timidly issued nothing more substantial than a reprimand to the two officials. He also admonished their superiors, including Mr. Saito, for failures of supervision.

The outspoken minister for Home Affairs, Hiromu Nonaka, told the Cabinet that this was not good enough. He reminded his colleagues of other Okurasho failings, including its responsibility for the what came to be known as the "bubble economy" of the late 1980s and the hangover of recession that followed it. Mr. Nonaka added that Mr. Saito bore responsibility for the 1991 stock investment compensation scandal in which brokerage firms made secret deals to refund any losses big clients might suffer. And, he said, he

held Mr. Saito personally responsible for a political fiasco in which
the vice minister had persuaded an earlier administration to introduce a new consumption tax in the guise of a "welfare tax." The
penalty he demanded was the immediate removal of Mr. Saito.
Other Cabinet ministers voiced support. After the meeting, Mr.
Nonaka repeated his demand to reporters, along with his views on
the Okurasho's many failures. Finance Minister Takemura, who was
not drawn from the Liberal Democrats but from a tiny splinter
party in the ruling coalition, initially defended the mild reprimands
he had handed out the day before. The official spokesman for the
government, the chief cabinet secretary, told reporters that the
finance minister was responsible for his ministry and that no further
action was to be taken. The matter was closed.

But it was not. Together with Liberal Democrat colleagues—including the man who had been so infuriated with the Okurasho's
inflexibility over its intake of Tokyo University graduates, Koichi
Kato—Mr. Nonaka continued to agitate. A press campaign against
Mr. Saito and the Okurasho was one manifestation. Eventually, the
finance minister joined in. To protect the Okurasho from paying a
larger institutional penalty later, Mr. Saito decided to make a personal sacrifice. He began negotiating with the politicians over his
early departure.

The outcome was that a little more than two months after the
Cabinet meeting, the finance minister announced that Mr. Saito was
to be replaced not at the usual time—when his term expired in late
June—but one month earlier. And that was it. So the Okurasho
stood charged with a series of policy failures and scandals. Its public
standing was probably at its lowest since World War II. It had
received direct and public demands for the resignation of its chief
bureaucrat. It ultimately came under pressure from the finance minister as well. And yet the most that all this could achieve was to
bring forward a normal retirement by one month. The ministry
even denied the politicians the satisfaction of being able to show
that Saito had been sacked—the entire institution's personnel rotation was brought forward by one month so that Mr. Saito's retirement appeared to be nothing out of the ordinary. Not only this, but
Mr. Saito's preferred candidate as his successor, Kyosuke Shinozawa, was duly endorsed. Mr. Saito offered no apology and made

no statement of regret or remorse as he departed office to take up a new position as a special adviser to the Okurasho, on an undiminished salary, just down the corridor from his former office. Indeed, he took the opportunity to do exactly the opposite. Mr. Saito's memorable parting words were: "It was not my intention to have my name in the media so many times. But even with the new vice minister, the way the Okurasho does things will never change."[48]

Within four months, other outrages emerged, prompting politicians to attempt an attack on the ministry once more. In late 1995 a senior ministry official's relationship with the tainted entrepreneur Harunori Takahashi was shown to be not just suspicious but positively corrupt. The official, Yoshio Nakajima, was asked to resign from the ministry. The media luxuriated in the institution's embarrassment. The new vice minister at the Okurasho, Mr. Shinozawa, agreed to suffer a 20 percent pay cut for two months in ritual remorse. But the ministry's humiliation worsened with the revelation of yet another outrage: the Okurasho had decided to use 685 billion yen (the equivalent of $6.85 billion) of taxpayers' money to rescue a disastrously mismanaged collection of mortgage lending firms known as *jusen*. The media and the politicians were scandalized. The Finance Ministry had been partly responsible for the difficulties and the supervision of the jusen. It was now defenseless and friendless in the face of first-order national outrage. Again, attempting to minimize institutional damage, the vice minister offered to resign. Mr. Shinozawa served only seven months in the post.

His sacrifice was a recognition of deep and cumulative anger at the ministry, but it served the institutional interest. Once again, his replacement was the choice of the bureaucrats themselves (or, more particularly, of Mr. Saito, as indicated on his ten-man list of preferred successors). The convulsions of scandal and outrage and early retirements proved powerless to disturb the orderly succession of office or the tight system of bureaucratic self-determination. In fact, in conceding to resign, Mr. Shinozawa strengthened the position of his successor. The new vice minister, Tadashi Ogawa, took office in combative style, dismissing the ministry's corruption scandals as the problems of individuals, advancing the case for the public funding of the jusen rescue, and rejecting any notion of change in the way the ministry conducted itself.[49]

It is not unusual for the civil service in an industrial democracy to resist its politicians. But the Japanese Bureaucracy's impermeability has given it an unusually high degree of success. As a result of its impenetrability, "the Japanese system does resemble an exclusive club more closely than any of its counterparts in the Western democracies," concluded Professor Koh in his study.[50] Nor is Japan's bureaucratic willfulness necessarily a part of any broader East Asian system of mandarin supremacism. In Japan's neighbor and former colony, South Korea, where the bureaucratic system is largely modeled on Japan's, top ministry officials serve at the convenience of politicians. The country's first civilian president, Kim Young Sam, not only replaced the country's military leadership but also dismissed the heads of seven national ministries in a single stroke on May 23, 1994—including the official at the head of the Finance Ministry. He chose their replacements, all career bureaucrats, from a range of levels of seniority without regard for strict hierarchy. His aim was reportedly "to break up the current bureaucratic inertia."[51] In short, Japan's bureaucracy has a great deal of control over its affairs by any standard. And within Japan, the Okurasho is the most robustly and successfully impenetrable of the ministries. This is not based on law, which gives the power of appointment to the minister, but on the culture of the ministry.

REWARDS AND PUNISHMENTS

In the president's office at the headquarters of the fourth biggest tobacco company in the world, a grim and silent sacrifice is being offered up. Masaru Mizuno is smoking a cigarette. For the first sixty-one years of his life, he did not smoke. But now Mr. Mizuno is forcing himself to work through a quota of five a day. "Smoking isn't painful," he suggests, "it's just that I've never had time for it." But when he was appointed president of Japan Tobacco, with a staff of 23,000 and revenues of 2.7 trillion yen ($27 billion) a year, he decided that it was time to assume the habit.[1]

Mizuno's experience in running a company is as comprehensive as his experience in smoking: his arrival at Japan Tobacco in 1994 marked his first day of work as a corporate manger; indeed, his first day of work in a company in any capacity. If you are beginning to wonder precisely what qualifies this nonsmoking, noncorporate, nonmanager for his current position, you need to know only one thing about him: he once worked as a public servant in the Okurasho. The Finance Ministry believes that this is the only qualification Mizuno needs to do the job. The shareholders who have invested 567 billion yen ($5.67 billion) to buy shares in the company might not agree, but they were never consulted. Mizuno was installed shortly before the Okurasho offered one-third of the state-owned company's stock to the public.

Mr. Mizuno spent most of his thirty-four years at the Okurasho in the Tax Bureau, where, as an career-stream official, his mission was to craft new and better ways to extract tax money from the economy. His work in revenue raising produced his only other significant encounter with the tobacco industry. In 1986, he successfully prosecuted a campaign to raise the level of special tax, or excise, on sales of tobacco. It was one of his finest moments. He was credited with increasing the effective excise on tobacco from 57 percent to 60 percent, yielding the Okurasho about a trillion yen ($10 billion) in extra revenues annually.[2]

Mizuno and his ministry were the chief winners in this event, and Japan Tobacco—Japan's monopoly cigarette maker—was the chief loser. Indeed, it is Japan's most heavily taxed company by a wide margin. Apart from the 40 billion yen ($400 million) in income taxes it paid in the year to March 1994, it paid another 1,685 billion yen ($16.85 billion) in tobacco excise. Altogether, the company hands over to the Okurasho 63.6 percent of every yen it generates, or almost two-thirds of total revenues. Even in the tax-tired tobacco industry, this is particularly onerous. The American company Philip Morris, for instance, paid only 30 percent of its U.S. revenues as tobacco tax.[3]

But even if it was a wicked sense of humor that moved the men at the ministry to appoint as Japan Tobacco's president this very man, who had made his name imposing burdens on the company, this should not have mattered. Because on taking his seat behind the chief executive's desk at Japan Tobacco, Mizuno assumes a new set of responsibilities. He is no longer a tax collector but a wealth generator, appointed to maximize the value of shareholders' investments in the company by the shrewd expansion of income and the judicious cutting of costs. Or so the theory goes. But in practice, Mizuno shows a remarkable reluctance to challenge the single greatest imposition on his company. He even goes so far as to defend the high level of tobacco tax: "This is unavoidable. Cigarettes are a luxury, and the level of excise is bearable."[4]

The shadow empire

Welcome to the world of the *amakudari*, literally translated as the descent from heaven. When a career-stream official in a national ministry reaches the point where he must leave his ministry—

usually between the ages of fifty and fifty-five—he enters the realm of mere mortals. But his heavenly brethren at the ministry will continue to watch over and protect him, arranging for a senior position and a substantial remuneration, such as Mr. Mizuno now enjoys. The Finance Ministry offers an unwritten contract to its executive stream: faithful service at the Okurasho for the first twenty-five years of an official's working life is repaid with comfort and ease in his remaining years. It is his reward—and the looser definition of amakudari.

Other countries have a heavy traffic in officials leaving government service for the wider world. This is not only common but inevitable. The Japanese system, however, is more organized, more carefully structured, and more centrally controlled than that of any other country.

The legal retirement age is sixty, yet no official is ever left on any ministry payroll by then. Why do officials leave at such a relatively young age? It is not because they are anxious to leave. There is very little natural attrition in the career stream at the Okurasho. In 1995, for instance, only one official among almost 800 employed in the career stream left prematurely, and that was to enter politics.[5] The reason for relatively early retirement is the strict observance of the seniority rule. That is, officials from an intake group move together in uniform progression through the ranks until they approach the narrowing peak of the hierarchial pyramid, where there is no longer a job for everyone. By custom, those who are not promoted must leave. Members of most intake groups reach this point when they become fifty. Within three years, half of the group will have left, and by age fifty-six or fifty-seven, only one survivor remains: the administrative vice minister. He will also be the oldest official in the Finance Ministry. This gives him absolute seniority in both rank and age.

But the high value placed on rank and age is not the substantive reason for the strict policing of the seniority rule. It is used to churn all the career-stream officials through the system at a sufficiently rapid clip so that the prospect of promotion to the top remains open for every year's intake group, keeping the fires of ambition alive. This is also why the administrative vice minister usually stays in the post for only one year.[6] Although members of the ministry leave before they reach the legal retirement age, they qualify for a lifetime pension. Moreover, the size of their lump-sum payout is increased by the obligatory nature of their departure. For an official with twenty years of service, a forced departure increases the size of his lump sum by 37.5 percent.[7] So by leaving the ministry before retirement age and at the ministry's convenience, an official will have not only the satisfaction of knowing that he is making way for the younger generation, he will also receive a pension, an increased lump sum, and an appointment to a new position.

The rewards for faithful service

Because the potential for abuse of the retirement system is clear, a legal safeguard has been built in to prevent flagrant favor trading between regulators and the regulated; an official may not move directly from a position as a regulator of a company with which he has "a close relationship" to a job with that company but must wait two years. However, there are ways around this sensible structure. Exemptions are granted by the National Personnel Authority on the advice of the ministry the official is leaving, and many are granted every year.[8] There is also the fact that State-owned and semigovernment institutions are not covered by the law.[9] So to help the official wait out his two years in the most comfortable manner possible, his ministry will arrange for him a position in just such an institution.

The public sector supports a vast and variegated structure of government institutions, commissions, boards, banks, corporations, funds, and agencies. These bodies are captive clients of their master ministries. Officials can appoint each other to jobs in these organs at will. There are ninety-two major bodies, so-called special corporations. They employed a total of 569,203 people in 1994 and absorbed cumulative government capital of 24.5 trillion yen ($245 billion).[10] Of their directors, 52 percent were amakudari officials.[11]

As a group, these special corporations lose money and are continually subsidized by the taxpayer. The size of this subsidy in the fiscal year of 1994 was 4.9 trillion yen ($49 billion). This is roughly equivalent to one-tenth of all taxes raised by the national government that year, or the size of the total annual output of the economy of Singapore.[12]

Among the special corporations within the domain of the Okurasho—as 100 percent government-owned entities—are two of the world's top one hundred banks. The Okurasho's Japan Development Bank, with assets of $111 billion in 1993, was ranked as the fifty-eighth largest in the world—bigger than Chase Manhattan in the United States, the Canadian Imperial Bank of Commerce, China's People's Construction Bank, or the National Australia Bank. And the Okurasho's other big bank, the Export-Import Bank of Japan, is not far behind; with assets of $76 billion, it is ranked eighty-third in the world. Of the other major special corporations controlled by the Finance Ministry, another half-dozen would be on the list of the top one hundred if they were constituted as banks. They include the Housing Loan Corporation; the Agriculture, Forestry, and Fishery Finance Corporation; the People's Finance Corporation; the Finance Corporation of Local Public Enterprise; the Small Business Finance Corporation; and the Environmental Sanitation Business Financing Corporation.[13]

These institutions are top-heavy with Okurasho amakudari. The proportion of their directors who are former officials ranges from a low of 40 percent at the Japan Development Bank to 100 percent at the Finance Corporation of Local Public Enterprise. On average, 58 percent of the directors at these Okurasho client organizations are retired officials.[14] Some are there for as long as they can possibly manage, occupying senior but usually undemanding jobs in major institutions on attractive salaries. Others are just filling in the obligatory two years before moving on. This system of special corporations serves the dual purpose of providing remunerative havens for former officials and of extending ministry influence.

What it means for many ministry officials is more than one reward. Each time an official leaves an amakudari position, he receives a substantial lump-sum retirement payout. Consequently, a sensible safeguard designed to restrain abuse of position has simply been turned into abuse of position in a different form— officials use their ministry positions as entitlements to jobs in captive,

Officials use their ministry positions as entitlements to jobs in captive, semigovernment institutions.

semigovernment institutions, and then as a bonus extract a second retirement payout in addition to the one they received on departure from the ministry. The average lump sum paid to an amakudari on leaving a semigovernment institution after an average service of about three-and-a-half years was 17 million yen ($170,000) in 1995. Among the amakudari officials from all of Japan's national ministries, 25 percent move on to two or more postministry positions. Among those from the Okurasho, forty percent enjoy such multiple positions and the payouts that accompany them. Virtually all upper officials of the Finance Ministry are in this fortunate category.[15]

For example, Mitsuhide Yamaguchi relinquished his post as administrative vice minister in 1986 with a lump-sum payment of 59 million yen to become president of an Okurasho client corporation, the Japan Center for International Finance, where he was paid a monthly salary of 1.2 million yen ($12,000), commensurate with his ministry salary. He then collected a second lump sum after four years of service and moved on to an Okurasho-controlled, State-owned bank, the Export-Import Bank. As its governor, he was paid 1.6 million yen ($16,000) a month. After four years here, he collected his third lump sum and went on to a longstanding Okurasho sinecure, the presidency of the Tokyo Stock Exchange, in 1994. The cumulative total of lump-sum payments and salaries he received after leaving the ministry and before arriving at the stock exchange was estimated at 260 million yen ($2.6 million). At the stock exchange, he was looking forward to a fourth lump sum. In a nice turn of phrase, such people are known as *wataridori*—migratory birds.[16]

The Okurasho has even made arrangements for the occasional hiatus and the odd quiet moment in an official's progress through the amakudari system. For instance, reserved for the top-most Okurasho mandarins—retired administrative vice ministers—is a suite of four private offices in the prestigious Toranomon business district of Tokyo. The offices and the two secretaries who serve them are permanently available for the use of former vice ministers. Since the offices were set up in 1973, only two vice ministers have not at some time availed themselves of the services. The time they spend in these offices has varied from two months to two years, depending on the circumstances and convenience of the amakudari themselves. The suite is discreetly located on the fifth floor of the Mori Building, no. 37, where a small nameplate announces it as the Kasumi Economic Research Group.

The situation is in fact so discreet that it is not a registered organization and makes no financial disclosures to the public or even to its members. But the banks, insurance companies, and stockbrokerages of Japan know a little about the finances of the Kasumi Economic Research Group. That's because senior serving Okurasho officials asked them to fund the office. The result is that a group of fifty companies and banks that operate under the direct regulatory aegis of the Ministry of Finance pays annual fees of 1–3 million yen ($10,000–$30,000) to provide former ministry officials with this facility, paying the annual rent of 15.6 million yen ($156,000) plus the cost of staffing and maintaining the offices.[17] This arrangement allows amakudari officials to observe the letter of the law—that is, they are not hired by a company in the industries they have been regulating for at least two years after leaving government service. But there is obviously plenty of room in such arrangements to allow for the trade in favors that the law was intended to prevent. Implicit in the very existence of the Kasumi Economic Research Group is the fact that the Okurasho will confer favor on those companies which fund it. The former officials do not take salaries from the Kasumi Economic Research Group but instead depend on government pensions, consultancy fees, and other sources of income during their time there.

All of Japan's national ministries practice amakudari. The Okurasho, however, has relocated more officials into Japan's economic architecture—in the public and private sectors—than any other ministry. As we will see, they are installed in a greater concentration of core institutions of power than are those marshalled by any other group in Japan.[18]

"Helping" the private sector

Officially, this reassignment of ministry officials is merely the random movement of retiring public servants who, after developing much-prized skills in the service of the State, find appreciative employers in the private sector. Actually, the Okurasho carefully plans and coordinates the deployment of its officials after they move from the headquarters building to the outside world. A former vice minister for international affairs at the Okurasho, Tomomitsu Oba, confirms the ministry's top-level involvement in the system: "The director-general of the Minister's Secretariat and the vice minister for administrative affairs have to organize posts for the old boys." At the upper level of the system—finding positions for the heads of the seven main bureaus and other top officials—Oba explains, "they have to find three to six vacancies a year—the vice minister is the one who asks them to move to semigovernment institutions. . . . If there are insufficient jobs, then the director-generals keep their current positions."[19] If such placements continue to be held up, the orderly clockwork progression of ambition, recruitment, dedication, promotion, seniority, power, and amakudari would be thrown into disorder.

An official in the Minister's Secretariat describes the levels of difficulty in arranging amakudari positions for Okurasho staff. He says that when officials are moved into public-sector institutions, there is "no difficulty."[20] Experience or relevant knowledge is no barrier. When Mr. Yamaguchi took up his new post as president of the world's second-richest stock market, he readily conceded that he had no experience whatsoever of the market—not even as its regulator. He spent his career in the ministry in other bureaus. "I am an amateur in the securities business, but I will do my best," he assured reporters at his inaugural press conference.

But finding jobs in the private sector is harder. The official in the Minister's Secretariat dispenses with the well-worn argument that amakudari officials are generally received gratefully by appreciative new employers: "In 1985 to 1990, we had very good conditions in the private sector and many people came to us to get good people for their boards or staffs. But now there is a lot of restructuring and it's very hard to get positions. For an official with specific knowledge or qualifications, it's very easy to find placement. But for people in the Budget Bureau or the Finance Bureau, it's hard to place them."[21]

In this task of arranging amakudari posts, the Minister's Secretariat not only has the assistance of the Okurasho's top official but also an informal club of some forty senior ministry old boys. This club, named the Fourth Wednesday Group (*yon sui kai*) after the day on which its monthly meeting occurs, helps to allocate, manage, and negotiate amakudari placement for its members and for their younger colleagues still at the Ministry.[22] Amakudari arrangements are a matter that receives the closest attention of the ministry's most senior former and serving officials.

The main value of an amakudari official to a corporation is his access to the information and decision-making processes of the major ministries. But overrelying on an amakudari can be costly, as Japan Air Lines (JAL), the nation's flagship carrier airline, knows well. It bet billions of dollars on the strength of inside information supplied by an in-house amakudari.

JAL buys its aircraft from Boeing in United States and so has to pay for them in U.S. dollars. The problem is that it does not sell enough airline tickets in the United States to satisfy its hunger for dollars. So JAL, like many other companies, sometimes needs to go into the foreign exchange market to buy extra supplies of green-backs. When it was considering how to do this in 1985, the company officials considered themselves fortunate to have the perfect adviser on their payroll—a former Okurasho official who had reached the lofty height of director-general for international finance at the ministry before descending to the private sector. Japan Air Lines had hired Toshio Nagaoka as managing director for finance, and it turned to him expectantly for help.

Mr. Nagaoka advised the airline that in the ever-shifting sands of the global foreign exchange market, one truth would stand like stone: the value of the dollar would not fall in value below 180 yen—the Okurasho would not allow it. Company executives decided to exploit this valuable insight. They took the risky step of contracting to buy $3.6 billion over the coming ten years at an average price of 185 yen per dollar. It looked like a bargain. When Japan Air Lines took out the contracts a dollar cost about 240 yen, and it knew from Mr. Nagaoka that the dollar would never get cheaper than 180 yen, so it was buying dollars at a rock-bottom price.

The company's internal auditor was alarmed. It was extremely irregular to risk long-term exposure to such a volatile commodity as a currency, and the auditor pointed out that it was a very risky deal. The company weighed the benefits—buying dollars discounted by 23 percent compared with the then-prevailing exchange rate— against the risks. Well, the company concluded that there was no real risk. It took out the contracts on August 8, 1985.

It was one of the most quixotic foreign exchange deals since the advent of the system of floating exchange rates. Just forty-five days later, the finance ministers of the world's seven biggest economies, including Japan, gathered at the Plaza Hotel in New York and decided that the dollar was over-priced and the yen too cheap. They agreed to correct the problem with one of the landmarks of modern financial history, the Plaza Accord, pitching the dollar into instant and precipitous decline. By the time JAL finally disclosed the details in 1994 because of an accounting requirement, its accumulated losses were 176 billion yen and its anticipated losses another 44 billion yen, combining for a total loss of 220 billion yen ($2.2 billion). Its blunder was obliging it to pay some 80 percent more than the market price for every dollar it was buying in 1994. The company established a world record for a foreign exchange loss of this type. There have been bigger losses on investments, but Japan Air Lines is the titleholder for losses suffered through financial dealings in corporate operations. This was not Mr. Nagaoka's fault. It was the airline's willful abandonment of normal practice, its excessive faith in the value of privileged information and official power, its naïve disregard for market forces. So it is perhaps fitting that Mr. Nagaoka's career did not suffer. He was appointed company auditor.[23]

JAL's blunder was obliging it to pay some 80 percent more than the market price for every dollar it was buying.

Some companies ferociously resist the prospect of any amakudari intrusions. The companies that have refused to accept amakudari are generally the stronger ones. The Mitsubishi Bank, for example, counts it as a point of honor that it has always had power enough to keep amakudari at bay and thereby maximize its independence. The bank's resolve was sorely tested, however, when it decided to explore a merger with another of Japan's major commercial banks, the Bank of Tokyo. It was to be a very large deal, creating the world's biggest bank. But Mitsubishi Bank's strong anti-amakudari policy clashed directly with the culture at the Bank of Tokyo, formerly a State-owned bank known as the Yokohama Specie Bank. Although it had long been a purely private-sector affair, amakudari officials occupied very senior positions at the Bank of Tokyo, including that of chairman. Toyoo Ghyoten was formerly a vice minister for international finance at the Okurasho, as had been the chairman before him.

During exploratory talks, the robustly independent Mitsubishi Bank stipulated the exclusion of amakudari officials from any executive role in the new bank. The Bank of Tokyo refused, and Mitsubishi walked away from the discussions rather than yield.[24] It is interesting that Mr. Ghyoten was prepared to push the point this far; he later said that the Bank of Tokyo had decided to merge because it was ultimately a matter of survival for the bank.[25] The negotiations later resumed and a compromise was reached: Mr. Ghyoten would relinquish his claim to a position in the executive structure, but he was allowed to remain in the bank as a special adviser.[26] Mitsubishi Bank is a colossus of world finance. Resisting the Okurasho's amakudari is not so easy for smaller, weaker banks. Indeed, the weaker the bank, the more likely it is to be run by an amakudari rather than a professional banker.

Among all of Japan's private-sector banks, those run by professional bankers have been consistently more profitable than those managed by amakudari officials. In the seventeen years to 1992, the independent banks were on average 4.6 percent more profitable than those run by former officials of the central bank, and they were 7.4 percent more profitable than those headed by former officials of the Okurasho.[27] This does not necessarily mean that the amakudari were responsible for the poorer

The independent banks were on average 4.6 percent more profitable than those run by former officials of the central bank, and 7.4 percent more profitable than those headed by former officials of the Okurasho.

profits. In general, it works the other way around; only the weaker banks feel obliged to appoint amakudari officials. Often, they do so in the expectation that this will improve the level of official support they will receive in the event of trouble or that it will stave off disaster.[28] As we shall see, this expectation has proved to be seriously misplaced.

Entitlement

As the Mitsubishi Bank discovered, once the Okurasho has secured a beachhead for its kind, it does not easily relinquish it. Once it has installed one of its relocated officials in a position, it regards the position not as a job for one amakudari bureaucrat but as a permanent entitlement to be passed on to succeeding generations of retired officials. In effect, the ministry takes the view that the offer of an amakudari position is not made to an individual but to the ministry itself. It is perhaps analogous to the guest invited to dinner who decides to bring his family, move in permanently, and then bequeath a share in his host's house to his children and grandchildren.

The ministry takes the view that the offer of an *amakudari* position is not made to an individual but to the ministry itself.

As we have seen, the Okurasho amakudari make themselves at home in captive public corporations, the institutions under the ministry's direct control, occupying 58 percent of the top jobs there. Among the government agencies outside the direct control of the Okurasho where the ministry has established a permanent but wholly unofficial and extralegal entitlement to the very top bureaucratic post are the Defense Agency, the Economic Planning Agency, the National Land Agency, the Board of Audit, and the Fair Trade Commission. It alternates in appointing the head of the Bank of Japan and the Environment Agency. At the very least, this keeps the Okurasho extremely well informed. But in some cases it has cost these agencies of government their independence. A former minister of State for the Economic Planning Agency, Yoshio Terasawa, says that the agency, though formally independent, "is totally, completely controlled by the Okurasho."[29] There is not one known case in which the Okurasho has willingly surrendered its grip on any senior amakudari or transfer post in any institution.

The same pattern emerges in amakudari employment in the private sector. After a close study of the positioning of amakudari officials at the top levels of Japan's private banks, Adrian van Rixtel observed "a very consistent pattern at specific banks." He sorted the banks into four categories: one that employed amakudari only from the Okurasho, another that employed them only from the central bank, one that hired them from both these official organs, and a fourth that never employed amakudari officials from either organization.

> It is important to note that this distribution is extremely persistent: during the period from 1975 until 1993, at the specific banks belonging to these four different categories of banks, the fundamental characterization of the presence of former Ministry of Finance and Bank of Japan officials never changed. . . . Even more striking is the fact that the . . . Ministry of Finance and Bank of Japan dominated banks are characterized by high succession rates. . . . That is to say, both the Ministry of Finance and the Bank of Japan seem to have "secured" a number of postretirement positions for their staff members as the final prizes.[30]

And this does not involve a handful of banks. Of Japan's 150 privately owned banks, 36, or 24 percent, had Okurasho amakudari in top positions in 1995.[30]

The same pattern persists in core institutions of Japan's economic and financial and government landscape. At the Tokyo Stock Exchange, the first three postwar chiefs were the heads of substantial stockbrokerage firms. The fourth was an amakudari from the Bank of Japan. Then, in 1967, the Okurasho decided to take hold of the prestigious post. Its most senior amakudari—officials retiring from the pinnacle post of administrative vice minister—monopolized the job. Since 1967, the Okurasho has never moved out.[31] The fifth ministry man to be cycled through the job was Mitsuhide Yamaguchi, who, as we have already seen, was ready to admit his total lack of experience relevant to the job. But he resisted reporters' criticism that his only qualification for the post was the fact that he was an amakudari from the stock market's ultimate supervisor (the Finance Ministry), and instead offered the pretext that invading armies have used for centuries: he was invited. "The securities industry chose me," Mr. Yamaguchi said, "and I accepted the choice." His predecessor in the post, Minoru Nagaoka, also from the Okurasho, elaborated a little. He said that the industry had asked him to nominate his successor from among the old boys of the ministry, and he chose Mr. Yamaguchi.[32]

Another strategic institution headed by an Okurasho amakudari is Japan's trust-buster, the Fair Trade Commission. The commission is responsible for making and enforcing competition policy in all industries. It has the power to tolerate or terminate cartels in any and all sectors, a formidable force in any economy but particularly so in Japan's cartel-crowded system. The Okurasho first maneuvered one of its amakudari into the chairman's job at the Fair Trade Commission in 1958, but it was obliged to struggle for the permanent right to the job and did not monopolize it until 1977. Since then, an unbroken succession of four Finance Ministry amakudari has chaired the commission.[33] Has this affected Japan's approach to preventing collusion between firms and promoting competition? We will explore this in a later chapter.

The Okurasho campaign to establish an entitlement in another crucial institution, the central bank, met very determined resistance and was not as unambiguous a success as these other examples. The Bank of Japan—which is responsible for setting interest rates in the world's major creditor nation and for policing banks in the country that is home to the world's largest—is denied independence in law but has fought hard to try to establish it de facto. Its first three postwar governors were all internal appointments, men who had spent their careers at the Bank of Japan. The Finance Ministry positioned one of its amakudari into the five-year governorship for the first time in 1956. The rivalry between the two institutions for the right to replace him was so intense that the government of the day stepped in to appoint someone from the private sector. After this experience, in which both parties lost, the ministry and the bank agreed to a settlement.

They contrived a deal to rotate the governorship, taking turns in the occupancy of one of the world's most important monetary jobs. Ever since, the governorship has alternated between a career central banker and an amakudari from the Okurasho—always a former vice minister for administrative affairs. And there is a second element of the deal: during the years when a career central banker has his turn as governor, the Okurasho is entitled to appoint one of the two deputy governors. This brings with it the automatic right to sit on the bank's crucial policy-making committee, where decisions on setting interest rates are made. So although in this one case the Finance Ministry did not win an outright monopoly on the key job, it did win direct occupancy of it half the time, plus permanent representation on the bank's main executive body.[34] Does it make any difference to monetary policy? The Okurasho has considerable power over the central bank in any case. Has its alternating right to nominate the governor made any difference? Research in 1994 by a specialist at the Swiss-owned UBS Securities in Tokyo suggests there has been "a higher degree of monetary accommodation under the stewardship of career MoF versus BoJ officials."[35] In other words, amakudari from the Finance Ministry are more likely to keep rates low and monetary policy loose.

Why? The reason is that when interest rates are low, they tend to support the economy. And this means that the Okurasho is less likely to come under pressure to boost the economy by spending more government money. Defending the budget is one of the ministry's greatest institutional priorities. Consequently, through its power over the governorship of the central bank, the ministry transfers the burden of stimulating the economy onto monetary policy to protect its own aims.

The ministry even managed to establish an amakudari beachhead in a foreign country with the 1994 appointment of one of its "family" to the board of the Singapore International Monetary Exchange, or SIMEX, one of the main world markets for trading futures contracts.[36]

Critics of the practice of amakudari argue that it is a form of structural corruption. But there is no need to ask the critics. The respected newspaper *Asahi Shimbun* asked the bureaucrats themselves. In a 1994 survey, it asked division chiefs at all national ministries whether civil servants were "using their power and government regulations to conduct amakudari?" Of the 267 who answered, 37 percent said no and 44 percent said yes. But there was not much argument over whether they *accepted* the practice; 92 percent endorsed it.[37]

One reason for the widespread acceptance of amakudari is undoubtedly the bureaucrats' belief that they need to secure their postministry livelihood. As one former Okurasho vice minister asked pugnaciously: "Well, just what do you suggest we do? Eat mist?"[38] Another reason is their sense of entitlement. In a syndrome common to bureaucracies everywhere, Japanese government workers complain that they could earn far more in the private sector, and in many cases this is probably quite true. Thus they expect and demand that the amakudari process help recompense them for some of the income they have forgone.[39]

■ A head start in politics

One of the most important rewards the Okurasho offers its members is a platform from which to launch a political career. Indeed, the Finance Ministry has incubated more of Japan's national politicians than any other institution. In the more important of the two chambers of Japan's Diet, the Lower House, twenty-eight were former Okurasho members, or about 5 percent of the total, in 1992.[40] These representatives are not technically amakudari, but they fall into the same general category. And some of them occupy strategic political positions with critical bearing on Okurasho policy.

For instance, the chairman of the committee that decides tax policy for Japan's Liberal Democrats is a former Okurasho bureaucrat, Tatsuo Murayama. He played a pivotal role in one of the ministry's greatest victories—which was also its most unpopular with the public—the introduction of the consumption tax in 1989. He remains so close to his former employer that he bears the unofficial honorific of "consultant to the Okurasho."[41] The pool of former Okurasho officials in the political system is such that the Finance Ministry sometimes operates under an appointed minister who is, as some put it, part of the Okurasho family. This has not always worked to the advantage of the ministry. Kiichi Miyazawa, for instance, was a member of the "family," yet as finance minister he frequently disagreed with the Okurasho. He did not succeed in confronting it on major or minor issues during his term, but he had the seniority, power, and wit to keep his independence. And he did manage to win some concessions. In the main, though, the Okurasho prefers to work with ministers who share the family background in the expectation that they will also share the same values and priorities. One recent example is finance minister Hirohisa Fujii, who was considered so subordinate to the Okurasho that the bureaucrats gave him the unofficial title of *kakaricho*, or section chief. He was an ardent advocate of the ministry's unpopular campaign for a higher consumption tax.[42]

Incubation as a would-be politician is one of the greatest rewards the Okurasho offers its members. It gives them an intimacy with politics and public finance that puts them far ahead of other novice politicians. One former finance official who had newly entered the Diet, Kozo Yamamoto, put a specific value on the advantage conferred by his Okurasho background: "I wonder about freshmen elected to parliament. They probably don't know what to do. But I know. I am doing the job as a fourth-term or fifth-term politician."[43] With elections held every two to three years, this means he believes that his sixteen years in the ministry were the equivalent of somewhere between eight to fifteen years in the Diet. In his case, his time at the ministry gave him the customary in-house training plus two opportunities to study abroad—at Cornell Business School and at Harvard University. His assignments at the ministry included high-ranked postings to two regional tax offices, economic policy making in the Minister's Secretariat, and attachment to the prime minister's personal office as an official secretary—enough political connection to launch him into politics—and all by the age of forty-seven. In effect, he was simultaneously pursuing

> **Incubation as a would-be politician is one of the greatest rewards the Okurasho offers its members.**

three careers—bureaucrat, academic, and politician. Incidentally, he is married to a daughter of another ministry official turned politician—the same Tatsuo Murayama just mentioned.

Specifically, how did Mr. Yamamoto's bureaucratic background help him in his work as a politician?

> My basic priority now is to build roads and sewage systems in my district. These matters are discussed between the Ministry of Finance and the Ministry of Construction. For example, local mayors ask me for help. I call the ministries and ask them about it. Then I call my colleagues in the Finance Ministry—specifically, the budget examiner [in charge of the relevant budget allocation]. And I usually get the information I want; not always, but they usually cooperate. And if they have room to negotiate, then they pay attention to my request. A freshman politician doesn't know anyone—he's in trouble. . . . The best thing is that I get the answers [to budget requests] earlier than others, and I pass the information to my local district.[44]

But Mr. Yamamoto is not working on a one-way street. The Okurasho expects some loyalty, even from those family members who have moved away from home. Says Mr. Yamamoto: "The Okurasho expects me to support ministry policy. Basically, I do now. But there were many cases where I had a different opinion. The ministry says that in such times you can do anything you like and say anything you like—but please, don't do it officially. So I raise my opinions in party meetings, but I don't try to raise issues and criticism directly."

■ Did anybody check with the taxpayers?

After the bubble economy burst in 1991, after its full and disastrous consequences became entirely clear, Japan's bureaucratic structures sank to one of their lowest points ever in the estimation of the Japanese people. So did practice of amakudari. A 1994 poll by *Asahi Shimbun* found that only 13 percent of people polled endorsed the practice of amakudari. That is about the same proportion of the population that either works in the public sector or is married to a public servant. Seventy-eight percent of those polled criticized amakudari.

Around the same time there was a chorus of condemnation from the academic community and the media. Among the serious members of the press, the staid and formal *Nihon Keizai Shimbun* attacked amakudari for having created a system that ensured the "double or triple echo" of the Okurasho voice in all quarters of the Japanese system. In effect, the paper was arguing that the legitimate voices of different parts of the system were strangled or muffled by official opinion.[45] Moreover, official opinion had been demonstrated to have failed—witness the bubble economy and its aftermath. The newspaper noted that in early 1994 the Okurasho appointed amakudari to the top jobs at the Tokyo Stock Exchange, the Bank of Yokohama, the Export-Import Bank of Japan, and the People's Finance Corporation. Then, in an unusually tough critique, the newspaper articulated a widespread sentiment: "What is strange about this is that such senseless exclusive personnel appointments were decided solely on the convenience of Okurasho officials, as if this is a matter of course. If Okurasho officials think such personnel appointments are in accordance with custom, there is a wide discrepancy with what society sees as common sense. If they are not aware of this discrepancy, we cannot entrust important administration to them."[46]

It was a few months later that the government announced the appointment of a new governor of the central bank: Yasuo Matsushita, a former top official of the Okurasho. The bubble economy had come and gone, public and media opinion had turned decisively against the Ministry of Finance and the practice of amakudari, but at the Okurasho it was business as usual.

■ Innocent, even when proven guilty

Japan's national civil servants have generally been free of the taint of corruption. It is one of the sources of the bureaucracy's moral authority, one of the reasons it has received more respect than the politicians it serves. In 1994, a senior Okurasho official, Eisuke Sakakibara, accurately summarized a widespread perception when he said, "There are vested interests to be attended to. But the basic integrity of Japanese bureaucracy has been maintained. I don't think we have anything to be ashamed of. There is some corruption—for example, in the Construction Ministry—but our system is relatively clean. Maybe it doesn't get an A plus, but perhaps a B plus or a B minus, certainly not an E [equivalent to an F in the United States]."[47]

By the end of 1995, this perception still hold true for most of Japan's national ministries. But Dr. Sakakibara could no longer say that the Okurasho had nothing to be ashamed of.

Early that year, Japan was agonizing over whether to support a Finance Ministry proposal to use taxpayers' money to recompense depositors in two scandalously mismanaged credit unions. The two small institutions had been ruined by the bubble-era profligacy of the young entrepreneur who controlled them, Harunori Takahashi. A magazine summarized the scandal, not with total accuracy but neatly, on its cover: "How a shady financier ran his own bank, lent a fortune to himself, defaulted, then got the government to bail him out."[48] The politicians demanded Mr. Takahashi's appearance in the Diet, where he was publicly interrogated. Needless to say, he was an intensely controversial figure; the taxpayers had not been prevailed on to cover for any such financial failure in the postwar era.[49] In the course of the questioning, it became known that he had developed a close relationship with some civil servants. Mr. Takahashi admitted that he had flown an elite Okurasho official to Hong Kong on his private jet for a recreational trip and that the official had not paid for the trip. The official was the chief of the Tokyo Customs House, Hiroaki Taya. Four days later, Finance Minister Masayoshi Takemura called a press conference to announce that Mr. Taya had been removed from his post and reprimanded for improper behavior. He remained on the ministry's payroll, however, and suffered no loss of salary or any other benefit. Although he received the maximum penalty under the Okurasho's internal rules, it was relatively mild because the ministry ruled that Mr. Taya had been acting in a private capacity rather than an official one. In monetary terms, the finance minister actually suffered more than the guilty bureaucrat. As mentioned previously, Mr. Takemura cut his own salary by 20 percent for a month as an act of contrition. Wisely, he said that while he thought there would be no other such cases, he could not guarantee it.[50]

A little less than six months later, Takemura told reporters that he was outraged at the behavior of another finance official, this time Yoshio Nakajima, a high flier who had been the deputy head of the Budget Bureau, official secretary to two prime ministers, and candidate for the ministry's top job of administrative vice minister. He had been revealed to have developed a close relationship with the beleaguered Mr. Takahashi. Apart from his acceptance of expensive entertainment and golf games as gifts, Mr. Nakajima was under investigation for insider trading involving stocks of Takahashi companies.

It grew worse. Mr. Nakajima had gone into a private business venture with a Takahashi associate, importing Chinese herbal drinks, and handled sums of cash in his ministry office. He had introduced some of his dubious acquaintances to other Okurasho officials. He had been given some 120 million yen ($1.2 million) by "donors" in the private sector and failed to report the income to the tax authorities. Officials quoted Mr. Nakajima as telling them during an internal investigation, "It is shameful, but I don't have much basic knowledge about taxes. I thought I did not have to declare the money that donors gave me."[51] He had earlier served as the head of a regional tax office and as deputy chief of tax intelligence in the national tax agency. Mr. Nakajima resigned from the ministry, forestalling any disciplinary action. "How can the Finance Ministry talk of the obligation of citizens to pay their taxes after revelations of Nakajima's action?[52] the *Asahi Shimbun* asked in an editorial typical of the national mood at the time. A similar thought occurred to the ministry's officials: "How can we cut the budgetary requests of other ministries or ask banking organizations to pursue severe financial reform plans in the face of this?"[53] one lamented. It was a serious blow to the authority and credibility of the Okurasho.

The *Asahi Shimbun* again captured widespread sentiment: "Their sense of decency is simply appalling. . . . The problem is that the Finance Ministry is all too indulgent. The ministry took no disciplinary action at all and let [Nakajima] retire with impunity. The ministry says it must pay his retirement allowance unless he is charged with a crime. No way."[54]

The ministry's culture has indeed tolerated dubious practices among its elite officials, although this does not seem to be because it has any problem grasping the principles or practice of discipline; there are suggestions that it has been much more rigorous with its noncareer officials.[55] But in recent years the ministry has done little that would encourage its career-stream bureaucrats to show any restraint.

To begin, there was nothing unusual in the extravagant entertainment Mr. Takahashi lavished on Mr. Nakajima and other ministry officials. In a 1979 scandal, several officials were reprimanded for similar behavior—accepting expensive entertainment from bureaucrats from another ministry who were lobbying for favorable budget treatment for their institution. Among those reprimanded were two top officials, but the affair had absolutely no appreciable affect on their careers. After leaving the ministry, one, Minoru Nagaoka, was appointed president of the Tokyo Stock Exchange, while the other, Yasuo Matsushita, is now the governor of the Bank of Japan.[56]

It also seems that other aspects of Mr. Nakajima's scandalous behavior were not a complete surprise to the Okurasho. Its own investigators discovered that he had been accepting large sums from "donors" for ten years or so, and other officials in the ministry had noticed and urged him to be more prudent.[57] Again, nobody seems to have taken the matter seriously until it broke into public view. In addition, there were suggestions that Mr. Nakajima had been exempted from routine tax investigations simply because of his Okurasho membership. And when the ministry did launch a formal investigation into his affairs, it gave credence to his own defense; in its interim report, the ministry said that Mr. Nakakjima regarded the payments from "donors" to be the equivalent of *tanimachi*, the gifts sumo wrestlers receive from their patrons. These sporting sponsorships were supposed to be obligation-free. This feeble excuse only invited more criticism of the Okurasho's handling of the matter.[58]

When it came to punishing Nakajima, the ministry found itself unable to act credibly against one of its own. Again, this was not a new phenomenon. The Okurasho has long been deeply reluctant to take serious disciplinary action against its elite members, even in the face of extreme public outrage. For example, public anger spread in the midst of the stock market collapse of 1991 when it was revealed that the big brokerage firms had been secretly refunding the investment losses of big clients. Less privileged clients, naturally, were obliged to accept their losses. As the story unfolded, it emerged that Okurasho officials responsible for the brokerage industry had officially banned the practice by administrative order in 1989 but tolerated it after that nonetheless. The whole episode was plainly outrageous. After initially refusing to punish its officials, the Okurasho ultimately agreed to modest temporary pay cuts for the administrative vice minister, Hiroshi Yasuda, and the head of the Securities Bureau as a token of remorse. The finance minister made a similar salary sacrifice. Two years later, however, Mr. Yasuda showed every sign of regretting having agreed to any punishment: "The reason was probably because I was weak. Even at present, I am still troubled over whether it was really correct."[59] This suggests that, contrary to the common understanding, the ministry might see discipline as a weakness rather than a strength.

No Okurasho official has been arrested since the early postoccupation years. The last one who did suffer this indignity, Takeo Fukada, on suspicion of taking bribes in a shipbuilding scandal in 1954, not only beat the charges but went on to become prime minister of Japan.[60] Some informed observers speculate that the Okurasho enjoys special protection from the law because Japan's prosecution apparatus depends on the ministry's cooperation for access to tax records, an important resource in many investigations.[61] Whether there is any truth in this or not, the weight of history certainly is on the ministry's side. Even a particularly notorious case, such as that of Mr. Nakajima, has not succeeded in provoking the prosecutors into taking any action against the ministry elite, past or present.[62] In this light, its standard defense—that its officials should not be punished because they have not committed a crime— looks distinctly thin.

Unfortunately for the ministry, the Nakajima case was not the last scandal of 1995. A newspaper reported that the deputy commissioner of taxation had been living in a government-supplied apartment for public servants at concessional rent while at the same time owning two luxury apartments that he rented out. Again, the instinct of the Okurasho and the tax office, against all common sense, was to defend him as blameless. It emerged, however, that the Finance Ministry was the only one among Japan's national agencies to condone this practice, and eventually the ministry was obliged to open an investigation to assuage public indignation.[63] The mounting number of cases makes it harder for the ministry to sustain its claim that each is simply an isolated case with no bearing on the ministry as a whole.

■ Rewards for allies

The Okurasho likes not only to reward and shelter its membership but to assist its allies. For this purpose, control of the National Tax Administration Agency has proved very useful. The agency is under the direct legal supervision of the ministry, and its head, plus about eighty other senior officials, are assigned there from the Okurasho. It has been regular practice for the tax office to do favors for political allies of the ministry, even if this has meant the perversion of due process.

For instance, one of the ministry's key allies in the 1980s and 1990s has been Noboru Takeshita, a former finance minister, former prime minister, and the real power in the main faction of Japan's dominant political party, the Liberal Democrats. Among other things, Mr. Takeshita was the prime minister who forced the unpopular new consumption tax through the Diet, a long-standing policy priority for the Okurasho. While he was in a number of ministerial portfolios and afterward, Mr. Takeshita's office reportedly sent more than ten requests to the tax agency to extend "special consideration" to companies it was investigating. According to the *Asahi Shimbun*, a former senior official of the agency said it had received many petitions from Mr. Takeshita's staff. People at the agency were "very perplexed," according to the official, "and came under pressure."[64] No fuller report was made on whether the agency complied in these cases.

In another case, another former finance minister and an important politician who was considered sympathetic to the Okurasho, Michio Watanabe, phoned the head of the tax office to ask that "special attention" be paid to an industrialist under investigation for tax evasion. The result was that the industrialist—who had already been convicted on one charge of evading 34 million yen ($340,000) in taxes—was permitted to file a revised tax statement and the tax office dropped its plan for a compulsory investigation. The prosecutor's office later asked the tax agency to reopen the investigation after newspaper reports of the man's alleged tax evasion. Mr. Watanabe later agreed that he had given the industrialist some tax advice, but said he could not remember phoning the tax office.[65]

An investigator at the tax agency who is also an official in one of the labor unions covering tax office staff, Toshiaki Okada, says that it is common practice for the Okurasho to apply political pressure to the agency.

> Officially the Okurasho has no control over the daily operation of the tax agency. But if something happens—for example, if the Okurasho wants to sweep away evidence of a crime—then it happens. If the Okurasho wants to change the tax agency's organization structure, it can do this very easily. Officially, it can't control investigations. And they don't directly say "stop that" or "go and look here," but they can intervene. For example, they can make an investigation into a company quite harmless by indirect means, such as asking for good relations. In most cases, the Okurasho will call a tax agency official, who will call a lower official. Or sometimes, a higher Okurasho official will call a tax agency official and just say, "What's going on?" And he has made his point.[66]

The tax agency response to such pressure?

> Usually, when there's such intervention, the official just drops the case. Sometimes, it's on the suggestion of his *senpai* [senior colleague], who says, "In consideration of your future, you'd better not go any further with that case."

Mr. Okada relates a personal example of Okurasho intervention in a tax investigation:

> The target of the investigation was a celebrity. The originator of the intervention was a politician who asked a high official of the Okurasho to intervene, and he called me directly. He asked me to make a detailed

written report on the case and send it to my boss. They need the report so that they can report back to the politician or high official. It puts pressure on you, and they can use it to find some weakness in your report. The outcome was that the celebrity filed a revised declaration and that was the end of the matter. Without the intervention, the case would have been much more serious.

■ Punishment for troublemakers

A Japanese bureaucrat draws much of his power from a legal gray zone in administrative procedure known as *gyosei shido*, or adminis-trative guidance. It is a way of bending people or companies to the bureaucrats' will, not by means of any formal law or regulation but by means of persuasion, negotiation, or coercion. It is usually opaque to anyone who is not directly involved. Although such prac-tice is alien to the notion of democratic control of the State appara-tus, it is at "the very core of postwar Japanese public administra-tion," according to Muneyuki Shindo of Tokyo's Rikkyo University. He continues:

> In Japanese administration, utterly extralegal administrative guidance is a source of authority on par with—indeed, superior to—discretionary application of the law to specific cases. And the commonality of interests between administrators and the private sector . . . makes possible the bureaucrats' expectations of a comfortable second career after they leave public service and gives rise to official corruption. It has been argued that administrative guidance has contributed a major element of stability to administration, economic growth, and society in Japan. In a time of increasing economic friction between Japan and its trading partners, however, administrative guidance is seen as a nontarrif trade barrier and, as a type of government-business collusion, is severely criticized by foreign countries.[67]

The Okurasho, like all of Japan's national ministries, has routinely used this mechanism. The depth and breadth of this gray zone is so great that the ministry's client industries consider it vital to be on intimate terms with the Okurasho so that no subtlety of official thinking goes unnoticed. Every national bank, for instance, appoints one of its elite executives to the full-time task of monitoring the ministry, a post known as *moftan*—*MoF* being the English acronym for Ministry of Finance, and *tan* meaning responsibility in Japanese. The moftan, who calls on the ministry daily and entertains its officials nightly, is considered an important person in the bank. One moftan related how the Okurasho's Bank Bureau had treated him coolly at first, ignoring an application for a new banking product for so long that it died. But when the officials needed a favor, he had used the opportunity to earn a warmer reception. The ministry's request was this: Politicians had lobbied the ministry to deliver support to some distressed companies that were in danger of bankruptcy, and the Bank Bureau wanted the moftan to oblige. Accordingly, he visited the companies in question. Although it was not clear precisely how this affected the bank's lending decisions, the ministry responded to his efforts by inviting him into the policy-making process. He was asked his opinion on policy matters and was given the opportunity to help draft documents for the chief of the bureau and for the finance minister. Another moftan recalled how the ministry had tipped off his bank about a forthcoming audit inspection of the bank's books.[68]

The Okurasho has not hesitated to use administrative guidance to take action against people it considers to be troublemakers. Take, for example, the occasion in 1977 when a Hong Kong investment company, Newpis Hongkong, bought a 13 percent stockholding in a big Japanese paper company traded on the Tokyo Stock Exchange, Oji Paper Company. It was an entirely legal investment, but when the Finance Ministry decided it did not like the foreign firm's apparent intent to win control of Oji Paper, it effectively shut the firm out of the market by notifying Japan's stockbrokers that they were not to accept any further orders from Newpis. The brokers did what they were told, and the foreign investor found itself unable to buy any more stock and, worse yet, unable to sell any. Newpis watched helplessly as New Oji's stock price fell, and it lost 5 billion yen ($50 million) on its investment.

Newpis took the brokers to court. It was rewarded with a ruling from the Tokyo District Court that the brokers had no right to refuse to accept clients' orders. The court judged that administrative guidance from the Okurasho did not constitute a legal direction. This case confirmed three important points: first, that administrative guidance can be very powerful; second, that it has no basis in law; and third, that even the bold should hesitate before confronting the Okurasho. Although Newpis won the case, it took sixteen years to do so, and it was awarded no compensation for its losses.[69]

The problems of administrative guidance are well known in Japan. A panel of scholars, under the sponsorship of the Finance Ministry's Institute for Fiscal and Monetary Policy, called for a review of the practice in 1993 because "it has become the source of international friction and appears to the Japanese as collusion between the Government and the private sector. . . . Because of administrative guidance, to protect and foster industries, the great principle of fair competition under fair rules has not been thoroughly observed." The group nominated the stock-loss compensation scandal as a direct product of this sort of collusion.[70] The government legislated in 1994 to improve the transparency of the process. This changed the form of the system, not its substance.[71]

■ Summary

One of the ministry's high institutional priorities is to reward its elite members through rapid promotion in the ministry and then guaranteed and lucrative employment afterward. This occurs even where it may involve expense to reluctant taxpayers, the coercion of other institutions, the loss of independence of other organs of government, the imposition of inexperienced executives on private or semiprivate firms, a compromise of the legitimate interests and goals of those firms. The ministry protects its elite members from scrutiny, censure, and discipline even in cases where they have acted improperly. It allows the abuse of its powers for the gratification of its political allies and the intimidation of potential enemies, and it has used extralegal powers to punish private-sector institutions that happen to offend its views about how they should behave. In short, the club Okurasho seems to have a culture in which self-interest overrides all other considerations. An institution that is by law a servant of the people has become, in fact, their master.

A SUPERPOWER IN MIRAGE

An American investment banker, Ted Rall, received a privileged look inside the phenomenon known as the bubble economy while it was still in its early stages. Although he was part of the machinery of modern international capitalism in his job as an investment banker— a deal-maker—in the new York office of the Industrial Bank of Japan, the experience shook his faith in the free-market economic system. "In early 1986, my boss and I were invited by the honchos at Mitsui Real Estate Co. to discuss buying the Exxon building in Manhattan," he recalls. Mitsui Real Estate, part of the mighty industrial conglomerate of the same name, is one of Japan's premier property companies. It was strong and rich and looking to buy an American landmark to prove it.

> We were asked to contact Exxon and find out how much they wanted. Exxon's asking price of $375 million for its 1970s-style stack of glass and plastic seemed high. . . . We relayed this information to the greasy guys from Mitsui. A few weeks passed, and I had almost forgotten about it when they called us to say they wanted us to broker a deal. Mitsui wanted to offer $610 million.
>
> This was not a mistake. After we prodded our rep at Mitsui for more information, he finally confessed their motivation for deliberately overpaying by $235 million: "Our president read that the current record price paid for a single building, as listed in the Guinness Book of World Records, is $600 million. He wants to beat the record."

. . . Neither my boss nor I could believe it. Although we played with millions every day, a quarter-billion bucks was still a vast, unknowable sum, the purchase price of a decent-sized company or a used jumbo jet, for instance. No one would just piss it away for a listing in a book read exclusively by twelve-year-old boys. No one except Mitsui Real Estate. Exxon's lawyers were perplexed. "Look, just pay us the asking price and everything'll be fine. We can't accept more than the asking price—the regulators'll think you're bribing us."

Mitsui overpaid for the Exxon building by $235 million. The president wanted to beat the record for the *most* ever paid for a building.

. . . Exxon almost turned down the money, but in the end, greed conquers all. Finally the lawyers came through: "If Mitsui can get us an opinion stating that it is legal to overpay to this extreme extent, we will consent to accepting the offer."

. . . The signing ceremony took place amid a dozen reams of contracts in a drab conference room in the newly acquired Exxon building, with nineteenth-century American quilts mounted behind Plexiglass on the walls. My boss and I sat down with Mitsui's president a half-hour before the signing to argue with him. We presented our research: "It isn't necessary to go through with this. If it's publicity you're looking for, there are better ways. We could put Mitsui's name on every billboard in America for a year. . . . We called the New York City Board of Education. That money would bring every public school in all five boroughs up to current standards. The press would be huge. Isn't that better than some listing in the Guinness Book of Records?" This clearly wasn't registering.

The City says they can build apartment units for homeless people at $10,000 a pop. That's 25,000 people off the streets. . . . Think about it—"Mitsui Virtually Eliminates Homelessness in New York City!" . . . He listened politely as we pleaded for his quarter-bil. Then he got up, went off to sign the papers, and left. We went back to our offices. I'd never felt so soiled.[1]

In the years 1986 to 1991, Japan generated a wave of hyperliquidity. This extraordinary surge of money created one of the great collective madnesses of world financial experience, a speculative excess that created what came to be known as the bubble economy, an event that *Forbes* magazine in 1987 identified as comparable with the notorious Dutch tulip bulb craze of the seventeenth century or the South Sea bubble of the eighteenth.[2] In all three cases the price of assets rose high above their true, or fundamental, worth. When drawn on a graph, the increase resembled a blip or bubble. Hence the term "bubble economy," which proved to be just as fragile as its name suggests. If the tulip bulb symbolized the Dutch bubble and the stock certificate of the South Sea Company of London represented the bubble in British stock prices, the Japanese bubble of the twentieth century may be best expressed if not by the purchase of the Exxon building by Mitsui, then perhaps by the image of the golf course. Membership rights to golf course clubs in Japan became a big professional market, traded by brokers and more valuable than the stock markets of some medium-sized countries. Prices were measured by Japan's other Nikkei index—the average price of membership in one of Japan's 500 major golf courses, published daily by the same newspaper group that lent its name to the famous Nikkei stock market index. In the course of the 1980s the Nikkei golf index multiplied eightfold, in close tandem with the national price of land. By the end of 1989, the price of membership in any of the top twenty golf courses was more than 100 million yen ($1 million) in a country where the average annual income was only around 4 percent of this amount.[3]

By the end of 1989, membership in one of Japan's top twenty golf course clubs was more than $1 million.

Since World War II, Japan has witnessed three periods of spiraling land prices and four of booming stock prices. All of these price surges had only one circumstance in common: they coincided with an easing in official interest rates.[4] The bubble and its prelude were no exception. In the early 1980s, well before the bubble actually developed, the authorities—the Bank of Japan and the Ministry of Finance—eased official interest rates modestly in a series of moves that ended in October 1983. It was around this time that a sustained but moderate upswing in the price of land and stocks actually began, several years before the beginning of the time recognized as the bubble.

The process began to spiral out of control only in 1986, when the authorities unleashed the supply of money with a second round of easings in monetary policy. They halved the official discount rate from 5 percent to an all-time low of 2.5 percent in February 1987. It was only after this second round of cuts in official interest rates that asset prices punched violently upward through all the restraints of reason and the lessons of history. Why did Japan's authorities do this? Did they realize the likely consequences of their action? Did they have a choice? What was the Okurasho's role?

■ A decoy at the Plaza Hotel

Two major pressures converged to push Japan's policy makers toward stimulating the economy from 1985. One came from abroad. In 1985, U.S. concern over its trade deficit with Japan reached a crescendo. In four short years this imbalance had almost tripled to a record $43.5 billion. Congress responded by turning toward protectionism, raising the possibility that Japanese companies might find access to their largest market obstructed by new tariffs. The Reagan Administration was almost as worried as the Government of Japan. Major disruptions in the world's second-greatest traffic in goods and services might have disastrous effects for both countries and for the entire global trading system. The two powers looked for an alternative solution to their mutual problem and struck a historic deal that became known as the Plaza Accord. Rather than close the stadium of world trade and ruin the game, as the protectionists threatened to do, the Plaza Accord was designed to move the goalposts and hence even the score by adjusting the values of the world's main currencies. The two countries persuaded their fellow members in the Group of Five (G-5) major industrial democracies—Germany, the United Kingdom, and France—to join them in piecing together the pact.

The Plaza Accord, named after New York's Plaza Hotel—where the deal was consummated on September 22, 1985—pledged its five signatories to do two things. First, they were to intervene in the world foreign exchange markets to push the dollar down; second, they were to adjust their economic policies to try and hold it there. Secretly, the group aimed to cut the value of the dollar by 10–12 percent.[5] The theory was that a cheaper dollar would lower the price of U.S. products enough to increase their penetration of the markets of other countries, including Japan, so American exports would grow. The yen, which would become more expensive when translated into U.S. currency, would put Japanese exports at a price disadvantage, so they would shrink. The net result would be a smaller U.S. trade deficit with Japan. The protectionists would lose their platform.

The first part of the scenario—intervention in the foreign exchange market—was more potent than expected. Between the signing of the Plaza Accord in September 1985 and the end of that year, the dollar fell by some 18 percent against the yen.[6] Soon afterward, in January 1986, the G-5 met again. Now it was time to deliver the second part of the deal—adjusting economic growth rates to lock in the new currency values. The United States and the other members of the G-5 wanted Japan to stimulate its economy. This was supposed to help cement the yen into its new, stronger position. In addition, a faster-growing Japanese economy would have the effect of sucking in more imports from all countries and assisting the growth of the global economy. Other countries were to improve their economic performances, too. All G-5 members, including Japan, concurred in this strategy.

In understanding the emergence of Japan's bubble economy, the key point is this: Japan was to stimulate its economy, but it had full and free choice in deciding how to do it. There was absolutely no requirement for it to do so by easing monetary policy—or, in other words, cutting official interest rates. Indeed, at the outset the United States told Japan that it would prefer instead the use of an alternative fiscal policy—either a cut in taxes or an increase in government spending—to get the job done.[7] Japan also had a third avenue open to it: to use a prudent balance of both approaches, monetary and fiscal. But from the beginning, Japan was determined to avoid any recourse to fiscal policy. So the burden of stimulating the Japanese economy fell solely to monetary policy. And rather than the G-5 forcing this approach on Japan, it was in fact the other way around. Among the members of the G-5, Japan was the country most determined that members pursue the monetary option.[8]

■ A fateful obsession

How did Japan arrive at the decision to stimulate the economy with the use of monetary policy alone? Three groups ultimately agreed—Japan's politicians, the central bank, and the Okurasho—but the plan was designed according to the policy of the Okurasho. Indeed, Japan's original enthusiasm for the entire Plaza Accord was rooted in the Okurasho's hope that it could use the accord's emphasis on realigning currencies to deflect pressure from fiscal policy.[9] The top Okurasho official at the time of the Plaza Accord was Mitsuhide Yamaguchi, the same official who later was awarded the amakudari position as president of the Tokyo Stock Exchange. During the Plaza discussions, Mr. Yamaguchi repeatedly told his representative at the negotiations "that Japanese strategy at the Plaza should be first to realign the currencies, and second, to reduce interest rates jointly, stressing the need to leave the 'main castle [fiscal policy] free from attack.'"[10] The ministry forced its view onto the central bank, revealing the stark fact that the Bank of Japan, struggle as it might to assert some independence in its control of monetary policy, was unable to resist a determined Finance Ministry. At the time, the Okurasho was fortunate in having like-minded politicians to work with—Prime Minister Yasuhiro Nakasone and Finance Minister Noboru Takeshita.

A top Finance Ministry priority was to leave the "main castle"—fiscal policy—free from attack.

One interesting lesson of the Plaza experience is that it highlighted not just the dominant role of the Okurasho but also that of its Budget Bureau. The Budget Bureau's preoccupation with minimizing government spending shaped the ministry's overall approach to fiscal policy—this much might have been expected. But the bureau also appears to have had the power to veto the foreign exchange intervention. After Japan negotiated the Plaza Accord and endorsed it at the G-5 meeting, Finance Minister Takeshita, while

passing through New York's Kennedy Airport, moved to implement it immediately. He told accompanying finance officials to convey to the Okurasho's top official in Tokyo, Mr. Yamaguchi, an
instruction to step into the foreign exchange market "as decisively as
possible" to bring down the dollar. It is hard to imagine that Mr.
Yamaguchi could need any additional authority. He had received a
specific instruction from the finance minister to implement an international agreement of the Okurasho's own making. Yet before he
issued the orders to his subordinates, he sought permission from the
director-general of the Budget Bureau, Yoshihiko Yoshino, on the
ground that the intervention could involve a loss of several tens of
billions of yen, or hundreds of millions of dollars. Mr. Yoshino
approved.[11]

So the first major force that pushed Japan to stimulate its economy was comprised of its chronic trade imbalance with the United
States and the congressional protectionism this provoked. The
Plaza strategy was the chosen response to these twin problems. Still,
it should be emphasized again that it was Japan, in its fateful obsession with a conservative fiscal policy, that decided to use monetary
policy alone. And the decision was made according to Okurasho
policy. It was a fateful choice at a fateful juncture. Japan launched its
second round of interest rate cuts on January 30, 1996, lowering
official rates from 5 percent to 4.5 percent, and the rest of the
Group of Five followed.

The second major force pressing Japan to stimulate its economy
stemmed from the Plaza Accord itself. The accord was too successful for Japan's comfort. The yen appreciated steeply and continually, and within a year it had
strengthened by 60 percent
against the dollar. Japan's exporters were suddenly at a disadvantage, their products potentially
priced out of competitive range
on stock shelves around America.
This was, of course, one of the primary aims of the Plaza Accord.
However, the G-5 had intended to achieve only a mild realignment
of 10–12 percent, not such a brutally large and abrupt one. The
Japanese economy, which had already started to slow from its 1985

**Within a year, the yen had
strengthened by 60 percent
against the dollar.**

peak, looked to be headed toward recession. Obviously, the government needed to add some stimulus to counter the effects of the rising value of the yen. The Ministry of Finance remained resolute, however, refusing to make any significant contribution from the national budget.

By the time of the first anniversary of the Plaza Accord, September 1986, Japan's official discount rate had been cut three times, from 5 percent to 3.5 percent. In contrast, in Germany, another Plaza Accord partner under pressures similar to those in Japan, the official discount rate was cut just once—from 4 percent to 3.5 percent. It was plain that in Japan the work of stimulating the economy was falling lopsidedly onto monetary policy. The national budget for 1987, compiled by the Okurasho in 1986, was a case study in fiscal rectitude. The ministry allowed zero growth in spending from the general budget account, making it the most restrictive budget in thirty-two years.

The new finance minister, Kiichi Miyazawa, an Okurasho old boy, was worried about this skewing of policy. Mr. Miyazawa wanted to correct the imbalance and did manage to win one concession from his ministry in late 1986—a 3.6 trillion yen ($36 billion) supplementary budget to increase government spending and stimulate the economy. The pressure to spend intensified. The yen continued to appreciate, a growing chorus of demand at home and abroad favored more government fiscal stimulus, a group of the more powerful politicians in Japan's party endorsed Miyazawa's campaign, and the other four members of the G-5 also demanded fiscal action. The Okurasho, with utmost reluctance, complied and put together a 6 trillion yen ($60 billion) supplementary budget in late 1987. The vice minister of administrative affairs, then Yoshihiko Yoshino, accused Mr. Miyazawa of being a "traitor" to the Okurasho for undermining its campaign for fiscal rectitude.[12] The next year's budget was more expansionary, too, with spending from the general account growing at a rate of nearly 5 percent. Apparently, the main castle was under attack, and the enemy was winning.

In fact, these concessions by the Okurasho to the needs of the economy were token. And the impression they created—that there was some fiscal relaxation—was illusory. The ministry executed one of its greatest victories in fiscal reconstruction during the bubble years. It successfully contained spending and increased its tax intake. It actually managed to reduce the outstanding total of government debt during the years of the bubble economy.

The ministry executed one of its greatest victories in fiscal reconstruction during the bubble years. It actually managed to reduce the outstanding total of government debt.

The Okurasho held down spending from the budget's general account so that it was consistently lower than the rate of projected economic growth.[13] Consequently, in proportion to the total economy, the general account shrank slightly during the latter half of the 1980s. It was held to 17.7 percent of the size of the national economy in 1980 and 16.3 percent in 1985. By 1990 it contracted to 16 percent and by 1991 to 15.5 percent.[14] Within the general account, the ministry clamped down particularly hard on public works spending; in all the initial budgets from 1982 through 1988, allocations for public works were smaller than in the year before.[15]

On the other side of the ledger—government tax revenues—the Okurasho drew a fat dividend from the bubbling cauldron of price and trading activities in Japan's markets. Each time a company took a profit from trading stock or land, it paid part of it as tax. Whenever its rental income rose to reflect rising land prices, this increase was passed on to higher tax payments. In 1987, corporate tax payments to the Finance Ministry shot up by 21 percent, and the next year they rose by another 12 percent. In 1987, only about a quarter of the increase was generated by normal economic activity. In 1988, less than half the increase was due to regular activity. The bubble economy was unequivocally good for government finances. Taxes and stamp duties increased as a proportion of the national economy from 14.5 percent in 1985 to 17.5 percent in 1990.[16]

Put the two trends together—restrained spending on the one hand and surging income on the other—and the outcome was not just fiscal consolidation but, for the Okurasho, a sublime alchemy of determined policy and sheer luck, making it possible for the ministry to indulge one of its fundamental desires. The government sector as a whole had been in deficit until 1986, but from 1987 until

1989 it went into serious surplus. In 1990, the Okurasho achieved a goal it first set for itself in 1980: stop issuing new bonds to finance the deficit. The balance of government debt had been a record 42.9 percent of the size of the total economy in 1986, but by 1990 the ratio had fallen to 38.5 percent. It was the first time since 1965 that government debt had shrunk in proportion to the size of the economy.[17]

The main castle had not only been defended, it had been rebuilt and fortified. And in the meantime, the Bank of Japan kept cutting official interest rates. Whenever it hesitated, the Finance Ministry simply bullied it into submission.[18] And ultimately, it did not matter that the new finance minister, Mr. Miyazawa, and the Liberal Democrats wanted the ministry to change policy. They won tokens of change, but they could not seriously affect the course of policy. Did the ministry realize the dangers involved in this monotheistic approach to operating the economy? As early as September 1986, Mr. Miyazawa, in the company of senior Okurasho officials, told his U.S. counterpart, James Baker III, the U.S. Secretary of the Treasury, that he was reluctant to cut official interest rates any further. The reason? Miyazawa said that Japan was experiencing extraordinary growth in its money supply and spiraling real estate prices in the Tokyo area.[19] But official interest rates were nonetheless cut twice more, while the rebuilding of the fiscal fortress continued. It was with on this macroeconomic stage—loose money and tight budgets—that the tragicomic drama of the bubble years was played out.[20]

The main castle had not only been defended, it had been rebuilt and fortified.

■ Frenzy

At the beginning of the 1980s, the value of all the real estate in Japan was about equal to that of all the real estate in the United States. By the end of the decade, it had become almost four times as valuable, although Japan's population was only half as big and its economy only 60 percent the size of America's. The official estimate of its value, at its peak in 1990 was 2,389 trillion yen ($23.89 trillion).[21] At that point, Japanese real estate accounted for about 50 percent of the value of all the land on the face of the earth, while representing less than 3 percent of its total area. Theoretically, the people of Japan could have sold their small group of islands and bought the rest of the world with the proceeds. Japanese real estate prices

Midway through the bubble era, 1 Tokyo family in 10 could call itself a millionaire based solely on the value of the land beneath its home.

loomed so large in the makeup of world wealth that one U.S. analyst suggested that the world had moved onto a Japanese real estate standard.[22] Midway through the bubble era, 1 Tokyo family in 10 could call itself a millionaire—worth 100 million yen, or $1 million—based solely on the value of the land beneath it home.[23] This opened many opportunities. Vast sums were made in short spans. Anyone who bought residential land in Tokyo in early 1986 might have sold it late the next year for three times the price.[24]

The Tokyo stock market caught the fever. In the course of the 1980s, the value of Japanese stocks increased eightfold. By 1987, Japanese stocks were worth 42 percent of all stocks on issue worldwide, even though Japan's economy accounted for only about 15 percent of the global economy.[25] The Tokyo Stock Exchange displaced Wall Street to become the world's biggest by value. The market valued one Japanese company—the dominant telephone firm, NTT—at a higher price than the combined value of five giants of U.S. industry: IBM, AT&T, Exxon, General Electric, and General Motors. A journalist recorded the story of a U.S. executive who arrived in Tokyo to take up a post as president of the local operation of an American stockbrokerage firm. One of his analysts came up with a recommendation that clients buy stock in a major Japanese airline, ANA. The problem, however, was that the price of buying one share in the company was 305 times the value of the corporate income that it represented (its price to earnings, or PE, ratio). This standard gauge of stock valuation indicated that at its current rate of earnings, the airline would take 305 years to generate enough profit to match the price of its stock. The newly arrived

American decided that his staff had lost touch with reality and summoned them to his office: "ANA might be the greatest company in the world, but how can we recommend a Japanese airline stock with a multiple of 305 to American investors, when the whole U.S. airline industry is trading at a multiple of 15?"[26]

Amidst this glut of money, major companies found they could raise funds on the stock market at an interest rate approaching zero, while their traditional supply of money, bank loans, cost 5 percent.[27] They exploited this opportunity, abandoning traditional relationships with their banks and raising money directly from the capital markets. The amount that corporate Japan raised this way soared from 5 trillion yen ($50 billion) a year in 1985 to four times this sum in 1989.

An important source of discipline—the prudential oversight traditionally exercised by banks over their client firms—was lost. Many companies were quite carried away and raised funds not because they needed them but simply because the money was so cheap. It was common bubble-economy practice for big corporations to raise large sums from the stock market at a cost of less than half a percent and then simply put the money into bank deposits, where it earned 6 percent.

In 1985, Japanese companies put about $130 billion on deposit at banks—roughly the equivalent to the operating profits of all companies listed on the Tokyo Stock Exchange for that year.

In 1985, Japanese companies put about 13 trillion yen ($130 billion) on deposit at banks. To put that sum into perspective, it was roughly equivalent to the operating profits of all companies listed on the Tokyo Stock Exchange for that year. In 1988, with the bubble in full bloat, Japanese companies put 23 trillion yen ($230 billion) on deposit, more than double total profits of all listed companies for the year.[28]

The major stockbrokerage firms encouraged corporations to raise cash from the stock market at a very low cost and to channel the money back into stock investment through special trading accounts named specifically for this practice, called *tokkin* accounts—a name synonymous with speculation by the end of the bubble years. It was an attractive proposition because stock prices were booming and yet there was no risk—the brokers guaranteed their big corporate clients a minimum annual return of 8 percent.[29] It is difficult to know exactly how much money major companies put into stock market speculation in this way, but in the five years to 1989 it is estimated that they directed about 23 trillion yen ($230 billion) into speculative stock trading accounts.[30]

Japanese companies set new records for buying French impressionist paintings at auction. And they bought overseas assets with a determination and with a disregard for price that alarmed the people of many countries. For example, during the bubble years, Japanese institutions reportedly bought one-third of all commercial real estate in Los Angeles.[31] But they were not only making investments, they were collecting trophies. Mitsui's purchase of the Exxon building was only one example of many. Its rival, Mitsubishi Real Estate, bought the Rockefeller Center for $850 million, Sony acquired the Columbia Pictures movie studio for $3.4 billion, and Matsushita bought MCA for $6.59 billion. Four elements were common to the major purchases of the time: (1) they were mainly American trophies—a prize from any smaller market would not be as rich; (2) name value was important—an obscure trophy is no trophy at all; (3) the buyers paid too much, as U.S. observers noted at the time—this is consistent with making big ego statements but not big investment returns; and (4) naturally, all were disastrous investments.

> **During the bubble years, Japanese institutions reportedly bought one-third of all commercial real estate in Los Angeles. They were collecting trophies.**

Ego simply displaced evaluation. Yoichiro Suzuki was sent to the United States to represent a joint venture between Japan's major life insurance company, Nippon Life, and the Bank of Tokyo. He remembers touring major U.S. cities with executives of other major Japanese investors: "Each of us would point out a major building and boast, 'That's one of ours.' There was a lot of pointing going on."[32]

What did stockholders think of this orgy of extravagance? Did they really want their funds put on deposit in a bank? Couldn't the stockholders do that themselves? Weren't they investing in companies as an alternative to bank deposits? Did Mitsui Real Estate's stockholders really want to waste $235 million? Did Yasuda Fire & Marine Insurance stockholders truly want to spend $53 million on a painting? One of the problems with this period is that nobody asked the stockholders what they thought, and nobody cared. During these years banks lost their traditional oversight function because large firms no longer needed them. Yet the system of accountability to stockholders that operates in the United States and other markets had not been developed. Most major Japanese corporations are largely immune to the influence of stockholders because two-thirds of their stock is typically held by other firms with shared interests. So during the bubble era, corporate Japan was operating largely in a void of oversight or accountability, freed of traditional bank discipline and not yet subject to stock market discipline.

Although Japanese companies were then commonly seen as invincible, given their unimaginably large cash resources, they were revealed to be extremely vulnerable. Corporations' unchecked extravagance and lack of rigor brought returns on capital to a low point. The return on capital employed in the biggest 245 manufacturing companies in the second half of the 1980s was its lowest since the end of the U.S. occupation following World War II. Consider the deterioration between 1981 and 1991, when their return on total assets fell from 8.9 percent to 5.6 percent. "It's not that the planning people of major Japanese companies don't understand about rates of return on capital employed or discounted cash flows," said a specialist in corporate governance at the Nomura Research Institute, "they knew all about them—but they had cash and so they just had to spend it. They just didn't care about their returns."[33]

"Each of us would point out a major building and boast, 'That's one of ours.' There was a lot of pointing going on."

Judging from what we have already seen, it may seem like corporate Japan should have had enough cash to get it through the 1980s. But there would be more to contend with, much more. As the yen rose in value, it increased the purchasing power of the Japanese currency. For example, in the two-and-a-half years after the Plaza Accord, the yen doubled in value against the dollar. So it now cost anyone paying with yen only half as much to buy U.S. products. This put a vast, unexpected, and wholly unearned windfall into the hands of Japanese importers. Its value was a cumulative total of 35 trillion yen ($350 billion) in 1985–88. The beneficiaries should have been Japanese consumers, but by the time these cheaper imports reached the shelves, only one-seventh of the savings remained. The balance was captured all the way along the Japanese distribution chain by importers, wholesalers, distributors, and retailers. Because of rigidities and cozy arrangements in the distribution system, companies were under no pressure to pass these gains along to the Japanese people. The net effect was that an unexpected 30 trillion yen ($300 billion) was pumped into corporate coffers, and that extra injection of liquidity contributed to the cash surpluses available for investment in land and stocks.[34]

Japanese consumers only saw one-seventh of the savings from cheaper imports—the balance went to the Japanese importers, wholesalers, distributors, and retailers.

The banks were in a dilemma. Their best customers—big corporations—were not only walking away from them to raise money on the stock market, they were also paying back earlier borrowings. The big firms would then turn around and, loaded with cash from their stock market dealings, put large amounts of it into bank accounts. The banks very soon discovered that they were facing an embarrassment of riches on the deposit side of the ledger but a shortage of borrowers to loan the money to on the other. Instead of paying interest to their bankers, Japan's manufacturing companies became net recipients of interest payments during the bubble years.[35] The banks started to cast about in search of new borrowers. It was then that a dashing young entrepreneur named Harunori Takahashi first caught the attention of the banks. It was in 1985, just as the bubble was beginning to form and the old verities of Japanese finance dissolve. Mr. Takahashi had just closed an innovative deal to buy the Hyatt Regency Hotel in the U.S. Pacific protectorate of

Saipan, financed by the Hong Kong and Shanghai Banking Corporation, when he captured the attention of the Long-Term Credit Bank (LTCB) of Japan. One of the world's top twenty banks and in search of big new borrowers, the LTCB approached Mr. Takahashi and his small company, EIE International, in its unimposing office on a back street in Ginza, Tokyo's famous high-rent, low-brow entertainment and shopping district. Next time you need money, the bank suggested, come and talk to us.

As it happened, Mr. Takahashi did need more money, a great deal of it. He conceived a plan to build a tourism empire around the Pacific Ocean, and the LTCB was grateful for the opportunity to finance it. It was unorthodox for a powerful bank to lend billions of dollars to an entrepreneur with untested acumen and little collateral. Mr. Takahashi's only other corporate experience had been as a junior employee at Japan Air Lines, a job he got through a relative who was the minister for transport. Similarly, nepotism had brought him to control the stripling EIE International—he took over from his father and a friend in 1983. But it was a new era, and the LTCB decided that orthodoxies were for the past. Mr. Takahashi seemed to represent the future. He had already foreseen the opportunities in golf and was involved in developing new courses.

Mr. Takahashi's plan for a Pacific tourism network was multinational in scope and promised to capitalize on the globalization of the world economy. It was based on a booming service industry, tourism and its subindustries of hotels, resorts, and airlines. He planned to buy assets that bankers could understand—primarily real estate. His approach already appeared to have won the endorsement of a major international bank. And he was not entirely unknown. One of his antecedents had been prime minister of Japan. Another of his relatives had once been president of the Long-Term Credit Bank itself. His father-in-law was a wealthy industrialist (although after the collapse of a stock market speculation syndicate with which he had been involved, he was untraceable for some years). And Mr. Takahashi was obviously well connected—two of the big men of Japanese politics had been guests at his wedding. The main consideration, however, was that he was a borrower with a large appetite for money. Mr. Takahashi, whose company had only fifty employees, bought his first corporate Boeing jet.[36]

Once the trends triggered by the Plaza Accord were in place, they started to reinforce each other. As stock prices rose, they generated profits for investors. They also encouraged companies to issue new stock to raise money. The companies then used some of that money to invest speculatively in the stock market. This in turn pushed stock prices still higher and began the cycle afresh. This was one loop of self-reinforcing behavior.

Another self-perpetuating cycle began when the big companies found they were sitting on enlarged stock market profits—even though they were mainly paper profits, or so-called hidden assets. This increased their sense of security and emboldened them to invest more aggressively. And they did, putting more money into stocks and land in Japan and also investing more in assets overseas. This, in turn, drove up the price of these assets, increased the paper profits of the companies, and started the cycle anew.

Rising land prices helped support rising stock prices, too. As the price of Japanese stocks grew increasingly out of proportion to the income they generated—as we saw in the case of ANA—brokers and investors justified the high prices by pointing to the value of the hidden assets they represented. Chief among these was the value of companies' landholdings. One commonly quoted example was that of Mitsubishi Real Estate. The company acquired a large slab of prime land bordering the Imperial Palace in Tokyo in 1892

Promoters of Nippon Steel argued that for every thousand shares of stock an investor bought, he was actually buying about two square yards of land in central Tokyo.

and valued the land in its accounts at 193 billion yen ($1.93 billion). Its market value in 1989 was estimated at 8.96 trillion yen ($896 billion). Similarly, promoters of Nippon Steel argued that for every thousand shares of stock an investor bought, he was actually buying about two square yards of land in central Tokyo, where the firm has its headquarters.[37] This argument won some support from foreign investors, too. "In terms of real asset value as opposed to simply conventional valuation, some of the cheapest stocks in the entire world are in Japan," reported a manager for the big U.S. mutual fund company Fidelity as he plunged into Japanese equities in 1986.

The approach underlying this method of valuation was elevated by the fact that it had a name—it was based on the Q ratio.[38]

These increasingly valuable "hidden assets," both land and equities, also gave Japan's banks an extra cushion of comfort in their capital bases and so contributed to aggressive, and other imprudent, lending practices. The banks, laden with new corporate deposits yet losing their best corporate customers, started to pour loans into the real estate sector. While the banks' total lending grew at an annual average rate of 9.2 percent in 1985–89, lending to the real estate sector grew at twice this pace, at an average 19.9 percent. The speculative real estate excesses of the bubble years depended heavily on this bank backing; three-quarters of all financing for the real estate sector, a very substantial 62.3 trillion yen ($623 billion), was provided by the banks.[39]

And the more money the banks gave to the real estate companies, the more land they bought and the higher land prices climbed. This trend then reinforced many other aspects of bubble behavior; it increased the value of hidden assets, which justified rising stock prices and encouraged companies and banks to commit yet more money to investment in stocks and real estate. This in turn drove stock and land prices higher still, and the cycle began once more.

Amplifying the misjudgments was the pack mentality of Japan's institutions. For example, immediately after Mitsui Real Estate bought the Exxon building, New York investment banks received calls from two of Mitsui's major competitors, Sumitomo Real Estate and Mitsubishi Real Estate. "Look, we need something," they said. "And we need something slightly above Mitsui."[40] The banks and the big, private-sector institutional investors, the life insurance firms, are particularly notorious for traveling in packs. When one major bank moved, the others tended to follow. Likewise, when one big life insurance company moved, all the others followed. Because of the sheer size of these institutions and the stampeding rush in which they traveled, their arrival in a market usually generated its own price surge in the assets they were all pursuing. As the price of, say, Canadian bonds appreciated as a result, the life insurance companies would congratulate themselves and find apparent confirmation of the wisdom of their investment. However, as they were to learn later, the same effect also worked in reverse; when they quit an investment, their collective withdrawal drove prices down. And they were notoriously bad judges of investment opportunities. As one life [insurance] company investment manager wryly remarked: "When you see the Japanese life insurance companies buying something, it is a signal to sell."[41] The reason for this pack mentality? The root cause was their traditional dependence on bureaucratic control and administrative guidance; independent thinking and self-accountability were discouraged, while safety was to be found in numbers.[42]

In the meantime, the yen kept appreciating, pumping more cash into the liquidity trap formed by the rigid distribution system. And official interest rates continued falling, guaranteeing an ever-cheapening flow of money into the swirling vortex of liquidity. These self-reinforcing cycles continued unchecked for three-and-a-half years. Official post-mortems of the bubble economy found that the expectation of ever-rising asset prices was an important cause of the madness. Without action by the authorities, this madness fed on itself and continued unchecked.[43]

"When you see the Japanese life [insurance] companies buying something, it is a signal to sell."

Harunori Takahashi was being chauffeured through the streets of Sydney, Australia, in 1987 when he first spotted the Regent Hotel, its tower rising above the city to gaze across the harbor. It was in the same instant, without even getting out of his car, that he decided to buy it. He had no idea whether it was for sale or what the price might be, but these matters did not concern him. He dispatched an aide to buy the property for what turned out to be 14 billion yen ($140 million). By now Mr. Takahashi had bought his second Boeing jet. His vision of a Pacific tourism empire was well on its way toward realization, and he was its emperor. He had assembled a major portfolio of properties in half-a-dozen countries and enjoyed all the access and influence that comes from close association with vast wealth, even if it was the Long-Term Credit Bank's rather than his own. On one occasion, he took half of the Cabinet of the small South Pacific nation of Fiji for a pleasure trip in one of his jets. On another, he ferried one of the powerbrokers of Japan's Liberal

Democratic Party, Ichiro Ozawa, together with eight of his secretaries and a bodyguard, to Australia for a vacation at one of his company's resorts.[44]

As Mr. Takahashi's accumulation of assets continued apace for its fourth year and EIE International's debts approached a trillion yen ($10 billion), he was asked by a reporter for the newspaper *The Australian* whether he might not be overextending himself financially. "I can borrow at least $20 billion more if we need it," he replied. As if this were not adequate, he also claimed that there was "no limit" to the credit at his disposal.[45] And there was certainly no evidence that the LTCB might consider contradicting him. As his assistant and chief deal maker, Bungo Ishizaki, said years later: "It got to the point where it was an embarrassment even for us. We did these bullshit feasibility studies with flowery words and some glorified numbers." They would then hand the document to the LTCB. "They wouldn't even scrutinize it, but rip the cover off, put their own cover on it, and syndicate the damned thing," bringing other banks in on the deal and backing yet another triumph for Mr. Takahashi.

The visitor to Mr. Takahashi's humble backstreet office during this period might have noticed an array of French Impressionist paintings on the walls. The LTCB helped finance the purchase of these, too. Dr. Ishizaki explained that Mr. Takahashi and he would pick a painting, pick a price, and then call on the services of a female French friend, a retired prostitute:

The bankers didn't know a Cezanne from a Monet, but they'd nod and say, "Yes, this is worth $10 million, and we'll lend you $8 million against it."

> She had grown too old to be a hooker—a few too many wrinkles—so she decided to become a freelance art dealer. I'd ask her to draw up a valuation certificate for, say $10 million, and then the bankers would come and look at this painting. The bankers didn't know a Cezanne from a Monet, but they'd nod and say, "Yes, this is worth $10 million, and we'll lend you $8 million against it." Then my French friend would sell us the painting, probably under a different name, and take a commission on the deal.

Dr. Ishizaki's summary of EIE International's experience with the LTCB was this: "They were just looking for an excuse to shovel their money out the door and we provided that excuse."[46]

But the LTCB's relationship with Mr. Takahashi went deeper. In 1985 the smart young entrepreneur had happened across a distressed credit cooperative. Formed by a group of Chinese businessmen to finance each other's Chinese restaurants, it ran into difficulty and the owners offered it for sale. Mr. Takahashi bought the Tokyo Kyowa credit cooperative, appointed himself executive director, and started authorizing loans to himself and his companies. The LTCB realized that this presented another opportunity to invest. It paid half of Tokyo Kyowa's capital and put large sums on deposit—up to 37.6 billion yen ($376 million)—at the credit co-op to earn interest, making it the biggest depositor.[47] This obscure credit co-op would later become Japan's most notorious financial institution.

■ Rich country, poor man

The juxtaposition of world-renowned multimillion-dollar French Impressionist paintings with the cramped, low-grade EIE office that housed them symbolizes one of the ironies of the bubble period—that is that its vast wealth was directed not to improving living standards but largely to the trading of assets. Indeed, the bubble probably retarded progress in the improvement of living conditions.

The price explosion made life difficult for those who did not already own property. For many Japanese workers, any prospect of being able to buy a home vanished.[48] On average, an ordinary dwelling cost the equivalent of seven years' salary and as much as ten years' salary in some areas in 1988, when in comparable countries the ratio was three to four years' salary.[49] One-room apartments in the Tokyo suburbs sold for 50 million yen, or half-a-million dollars.[50] The exorbitant price of land discouraged new businesses from starting up.[51] It thwarted government efforts to begin new public works and to improve the quality of city life for its citizens—the cost of buying the land for road and right-of-way projects consumed 80 percent of all the money allocated to them.[52]

It bears note that in very basic areas the Japanese do not enjoy the same access to public facilities as the people of other major industrialized nations. Less than half Japan's population is served by a sewage system; in the other countries of the Group of Five major economies, at least 68 percent of the population has access to this facility. Five percent of the Japanese people do not enjoy running water; in the other G-5 nations, this figure is much smaller at 1 or 2 percent. Only 72 percent of Japan's roads are paved, compared with 90–100 percent in the rest of the G-5 countries. It is a little ironic that the country that has led the world in manufacturing and exporting cars should be inadequately equipped for using them.[53]

Historically, the Japanese have generally placed little value on the comforts of their people; consequently, it's no surprise that they sunk none of their vast earnings during the bubble era into infrastructure. In the words of one Japanese scholar: "[D]omestic savings were directed not into improvement of domestic infrastructure but into the acquisition of assets abroad. The Japanese, with their low levels of social capital, may be compared to a family living in a dilapidated house who have worked hard and scrimped to save money and have then used it not to improve their own home but to lend to others."[54] During the latter half of the 1980s, more than a third of personal savings was channeled overseas.[55]

Further, the speculative excesses and unearned profits of the period have been blamed for corrupting the ethical fabric of the nation and for eroding the work ethic of the people.[56]

■ Failing to see the obvious

Did the Okurasho see the madness that was going on in the marketplace? One senior official, Makoto Utsumi, director-general of the International Finance Bureau, described Tokyo land prices in January 1989 as "really crazy." He told of a ministry discussion of a Japanese investor's application to buy a small local bank in the United States. "I asked the cost involved in this deal. My staff said it was $2.3 million, less than 300 million yen. I said, 'Hey,

". . . An apartment in Tokyo costs the same as a bank in the U.S."

that's the cost of buying a mansion!' This does not mean a mansion in English, it's just an upgraded apartment in Japan. An apartment in Tokyo costs the same as a bank in the U.S." Rather than convey any concern or promise any action, he instead sought to explain why this situation was actually positive for the economy.

Mr. Utsumi gave three reasons. First, the high price of land forced businesses and families to extract the maximum possible efficiency from their landholdings, prodding them to rebuild more frequently than in any other country and so helping to support domestic demand in the economy. Second, he cited an Okurasho poll of Tokyo entrepreneurs that listed the increased value of assets as one of the four main factors contributing to the strength of domestic demand. And third, he said that as people abandoned any hope of buying a home in Tokyo because of exorbitant prices, they worried less about saving and turned instead to consume more: "My friends decided to give up hope of a house and buy an expensive car." He said that the same ministry poll had rated this phenomenon as the sixth most important contributor to domestic demand. In sum, said Mr. Utsumi, "For two years domestic demand has developed very strongly and steadily and now I have begun to realize that the crazy land prices in Tokyo are functioning as one of the supportive factors for the expansion of domestic demand." He found no economic fault with the boom in asset prices.[57] This was not just a calm face put on for the public but an expression of a general ministry complacency with the state of asset prices.

Isao Kubota, an official in the Minister's Secretariat involved in the overall analysis of the economy toward the final phase of the bubble, and who later wrote about the period, explains how the ministry saw the economy:

The rate of economic growth was around 4 percent, and that was broadly consistent with our view of the economy's potential growth rate, and prices were extremely stable so there was no fear of an outbreak of inflation. Where we saw the risks was on the downside. We were worried that the rate of economic growth would slow. We wanted Japan to have higher growth, and so did foreigners at that time. We did not consider that there was any danger of a bubble economy. There were only two indicators which could have told us; growth in the money supply and the level of fixed investment. If we had studied these indicators we should have realized what was happening in the financial world, that the cost of money was extremely cheap, that corporations were taking money almost for free and investing in land and fixed investment. We didn't see it at the time and there were very few opinions along that line. . . .

But even if we had known the answers at the time, there would have been a great deal of difficulty in explaining the need for slowing down the economy. Inflation was low, and there were no external constraints. People prefer high growth to low growth. How could you persuade people that there was a need? The general mood at the time was that people were afraid of slower growth, and the Finance Ministry was no exception. Nobody was thinking about slowing down the rate of growth. Were there any indicators that would have allowed us to find a better course? I think there were two."[58]

Mr. Kubota elaborates on the signals the ministry missed:

It seems that the analysis of two indicators could have led to proper assessment, and hence to proper policies. One is money supply . . . [It] had increased by around 8 percent in the previous four years up to 1986 . . . [It] increased by 10.4 percent in 1987, the year the economy started expanding too rapidly, and continued increasing sharply up to 1990. It grew 11.2 percent in 1988, 9.9 percent in 1989, and 11.7 percent in 1990. . . . Had economists paid more attention to these now abnormal increases in money supply and tried to search for the cause, they could have found extremely lax lending policies of banks, which not only contributed to a rapid growth of the economy but also weakened financial institutions in the end. While it may be too simplistic to conclude that money supply dictates economic activities unless you are monetarists, these figures should have drawn more attention.

Another economic indicator that [we] should have studied more carefully was private fixed investment. In 1988 it suddenly increased by 14.8 percent. The following year saw a big increase of 16.6 percent. In 1990, it recorded an 11.4 percent rise. . . . The indicator's continuous increase at such rapid rates for three consecutive years should have been more critically examined. Though economists were quick to judge that these investments would not lead to overcapacity because the majority of the investments was directed to nonproductive facilities for employees, they were slow to notice that a part of the robust investment was merely a by-product of too much liquidity [in] the firms concerned.[59]

Did the Okurasho discuss these developments in the two indicators at the time? "We had a discussion, but we didn't go far enough," said Mr. Kubota. "Central bankers should be in a better position to look at the money supply."[60]

■ No checks and balances

If the Okurasho could not see the immense problem building beneath its feet, credible figures elsewhere in Japan did. In the private sector, for example, Masaru Takagi, the chief economist at the Fuji Bank, began making speeches and TV appearances in 1987 calling for a reversal of monetary policy and a sharp increase in the official discount rate of 1 percentage point to control land and stock prices.[61] Less publicly, a respected figure in the monetary world, Yoshihiko Yoshino, senior adviser to Yamaichi Securities Research Institute and former executive director of the Bank of Japan, privately warned the members of the central bank's policy-making board that a bubble was forming in asset prices.[62] And among the official organs of government, the Economic Planning Agency used its 1988 Economic White Paper to point out that land prices were way out of line with the fundamentals.

Most significantly, the checks and balances on Okurasho policy proved ineffective. One of these checks is political supervision. One finance minister, Kiichi Miyazawa, foresaw the possibility of the bubble. In 1986 he pointed out that the money supply was growing too quickly—nearly a decade before the rueful Mr. Kubota drew the same conclusion. Mr. Miyazawa was Finance Minister, the leader of a major political faction and acted in concert with pressure from the ruling party and the opinions of leading commentators. Yet as we have seen, he had little power to affect the course of ministry policy. The ministry evidently has developed a high degree of immunity to the system of political oversight.

Another potential check on the Okurasho in the realm of monetary policy is the central bank, for this is where official interest rates are actually set. Unlike its splendidly autonomous German counterpart, the Bundesbank, the Bank of Japan is not an independent institution; it is subject to supervision by the Okurasho. That supervision includes the right to issue general directives, to dismiss central bank officials, and whether to permit almost all activities of the central bank.[63]

On the crucial issue of interest rates, the two institutions, the foreman and the laborer of Japan's monetary system, are in close although unofficial contact week by week, by phone and in visits to each other's offices.[64] The closeness of this contact is intensified by the Finance Ministry's alternating amakudari assignments in the bank's most senior positions. As we have seen, the Bank of Japan operated largely according to the will of the Okurasho during the inflating of the bubble. Yet it did have a different view of the economy, and, if it had been permitted to operate independently, it might have chosen a different course. A member of the central bank's executive board at the time and an eminent monetary economist, Yoshio Suzuki, explains that in the earlier years of the bubble era the central bank essentially shared the Okurasho's view. It later came to develop reservations about the easy money policy:

> In 1987 the Japanese economy already started to recover, so we thought our low monetary policy should be raised. We led call rates [short-term money market interest rates] up, and we thought about raising the official discount rate toward the end of 1987. But then Black Monday [the stockmarket crash of October 1987] occurred. Then the Ministry of Finance people said, again and again, "A Bank of Japan decision to raise the official discount rate in late 1987 should be accused of ignoring international circumstances." That was the pressure on us—it originated with U.S. authorities, but the Ministry of Finance was the messenger.[65]

The Black Monday stock market crash, which began on Wall Street but led to a staccato echo of crashes in markets around the world, persuaded the United States, Japan, and others that easy money was the best policy. This created a cushion of liquidity to absorb financial shock and to prevent the trauma from being transmitted to other parts of the economy. The policy was largely successful. But in the United States and Germany, this was a only short-term response. Within five months the United States raised official interest rates, and Germany followed four months after that. Japan's central bank waited much longer under the combined pressure of the Okurasho and the Americans—until May 1989, allowing the bubble to inflate still further.

Dr. Suzuki continues:

> So we kept our low interest-rate policy through the essential period of October 1987 to May 1989. During that time of about one and a half years, the economy was rising vigorously, so there was no reason we had to keep the low interest-rate policy and we should have raised the official discount rate. . . . But the judgment we made at the time was incorrect. Though [consumer] prices were stable, asset prices rose too quickly, and [this] would create much trouble later. The German Bundesbank was clever enough to know that. They raised official rates four times before us and eliminated the bubble.[66]

Once again, the Finance Ministry worked to reinforce its policy agenda. In this case, it did so by helping to deflect the Bank of Japan from forming its own independent judgment. It is difficult to believe that the ministry was simply the handmaiden of the United States because, as we have seen, it happily resisted the Americans when this was convenient. It selectively worked with, or against, the United States according to its own convenience; it fought the United States on fiscal policy yet formed an alliance with it on monetary policy. Whatever mechanism it used, the point is this: the Okurasho successfully used its power to deflect or defeat the checks and balances that, in theory, are supposed to operate to ensure prudent policy. The result was imprudent policy on a momentous scale.

The Okurasho successfully used its power to deflect or defeat the checks and balances that, in theory, are supposed to operate to ensure prudent policy. The result was imprudent policy on a momentous scale.

This is not to argue that the ministry was acting maliciously or malevolently. Its basic approach during the latter half of the 1980s—loose money, tight budget—was designed above all to serve the ministry's primary self-assigned task of minimizing the national debt and building strong public finances. The problem was that the ministry was preoccupied with this single aim. And the institutions that might have checked or balanced its preoccupation were instead so influenced by it that they, too, came to serve the same monotheistic doctrine.

■ (Mis)managing the bubble

While the Finance Ministry clearly provided the macroeconomic preconditions for the bubble economy, there was still much it might have done to mitigate the damage wrought on the microeconomy. We have already seen that the bubble was pumped up by self-reinforcing cycles of behavior. Did the ministry do anything to try to short-circuit this process and break the cycles?

One unfortunate side effect of the Okurasho's retrenchment of government debt was the reduction of government bonds on issue for investors to buy. In fact, the contraction of government led Japan to lower its issue of bonds by about 20 trillion yen ($200 billion).[67] This meant that a ready and regular absorber of liquidity was withdrawn from the marketplace just as the supply of liquidity swelled. This had the effect of concentrating the tremendous flow of corporate money into the other classes of assets available for investment—chiefly stocks and land.

In the stock market, the ministry gave three major classes of investors better access to equity investment as the bubble was pumping itself up. First, the ministry progressively freed big institutional investors and fund managers to make more aggressive stock market investment, but it failed to introduce any corresponding measures to improve their accountability or risk management. For example, in 1984, the biggest of the institutions, the life insurers, were permitted some access to the highly speculative tokkin accounts. In early 1988, after the market had suffered a temporary setback, the ministry lifted remaining restraints on these accounts for the life insurance companies, and the mere announcement so excited the market that the Nikkei index of 225 stock issues soared by 1,215 points, its second biggest one-day gain on record. By 1990 the life insurers admitted to having 4 percent of their assets in them, worth a very substantial 5.2 trillion yen ($52 billion).[68]

Second, access to stock market investment for the Japanese public was improved by the ministry, but corresponding policies to improve the transparency of the market were not taken. For example, restrictions on sales of investment trusts were abolished in 1986, and these trusts tripled their holdings of equities in the bubble years as their stockholdings soared by 24 trillion yen ($240 billion).[69] In the face of blatant and well-publicized cases of insider trading, the Finance Ministry tightened the relevant laws in 1988, but enforcement remained little more than token.[70] It was during this period that the big brokerage companies offered secret investment guarantees to big clients but nothing to smaller ones. The ministry tacitly endorsed the practice, as we have seen. The investing public only learned about this years later.

Third, the Okurasho was a party to the decision to add the weight of public money to the hyperliquidity that was gushing through the stock market. In the first six months of 1987 it allowed, for the first time, the immense repositories of public-sector savings to begin investing in equities; this meant freeing up funds in the national pension program, the national welfare insurance program, the postal life insurance system, and the world's biggest single accumulation of money, the postal savings system.[71] Behind this move was the idea that the public funds needed to be competitive with private-sector competitors. The effect was that the funds bought expensive stock and helped drive stock prices yet higher.

The Okurasho took advantage of the strength of stock prices to sell a little of its own stock. By selling part of its holdings of stock in the dominant phone company, Nippon Telegraph and Telephone (NTT), from 1986 through 1988, the ministry reaped some 10 trillion yen ($100 billion). This privatization received tremendous media and market attention and, since NTT is a household name and its sale was a novelty, it brought many ordinary Japanese into the stock

The number of ordinary Japanese invested in the stock market skyrocketed from 16 million in 1985 to about 24 million in 1989.

market for the first time. The first time NTT stock was made available to individuals, 10 million people applied to buy. Partly because of the fever of bubble-era expectations and partly because of the unique circumstances of the NTT stock market float, the number of ordinary Japanese invested in the stock market sky rocketed from 16 million in 1985 to about 24 million in 1989.[72] Of course, most of these people were bound to be disappointed, including those who bought into NTT. The Okurasho, however, was not.

As the forest fire of land prices burned out of control, the ministry came under popular and political pressure to do something. It got involved in three responses: one was to throw a smothering blanket of direct controls onto prices and sales, another was to reduce the heat by changing the tax system, and a third was to squeeze the hose pouring gasoline on the fire—that is, to choke off bank lending for real estate. In the first two courses it acted jointly with other national and local agencies. It was only in discouraging bank lending that it was essentially alone.

The first measure—a selective surveillance system that gave local governments the power to "correct" prices of deals on large lots of real estate that were thought too expensive according to an arbitrary standard—was generally perceived as a success. However, its success was ambiguous. It has been pointed out that in most cases the system was introduced after land prices had peaked. And in one region of Japan prices kept rising anyway, regardless of the system.

The second measure—a review of land taxes—was generally a case of too little, too late. After U.S. complaints that the high price of land was an impediment to foreign firms doing business in Japan—as indeed it was to new Japanese businesses—the government launched a major inquiry and then legislated to put its main recommendations into effect. However, the changes were implemented in 1991 and 1992, six and seven years after the bubble had started to develop and, actually, at the time it was beginning to deflate. And the change that was most squarely designed to punish speculators—increases in the landholding tax—was gutted by the Liberal Democratic Party to the point where the real estate industry considered it tax relief rather than reform.[73]

The tax on nonresidential land in Tokyo was found to be the lowest among nine major international commercial capitals when considered in proportion to the rent that land produces. This arrangement provided little inducement to use the land efficiently and dealt out minimal penalties to speculators who held land in anticipation of a price upturn. For instance, Mitsui Real Estate was estimated to be paying 4 percent property tax on the Exxon building and 0.3 percent tax on comparable real estate in Tokyo.[74] This will not change under the new land tax laws. As the Economic Planning Agency has observed, "Generally speaking, the efficient use of land had not developed in Japan." The changes introduced in response to the bubble economy will do very little to alter the situation.[75]

In pursuing the third measure—discouraging bank financing of real estate investment—the Okurasho reached instinctively for a familiar tool, administrative guidance. In the bubble years to 1988, the ministry asked the banks five times to cut back on loans that were to be used for speculative purchases of real estate.[76] Later, the ministry extended this guidance to other financial institutions as well, notably, life insurers. This informal and extralegal pressure seemed to work. Market prices of commercial land in Tokyo were down by 4 percent in 1988, and residential land prices fell by 8 percent.[77] But while the fire had been contained in Tokyo, the administrative guidance merely spread the flames to the rest of Japan. In 1988 commercial land prices in Osaka, Kyoto, and Kobe shot up by 21 percent, and residential prices went up 13 percent. Throughout the period of the bubble, at no point did the banks ever stop the flow of new lending to the real estate sector. They merely switched locations, moving out of Tokyo, where Okurasho attention was focused, to where it was not—the rest of Japan. The more channels the ministry shut down, the more the banks opened. Banks increasingly used affiliates, leasing companies, and small nonbank institutions, such as the Tokyo Kyowa Credit Co-op.

In 1988, the liabilities of bankrupted real estate companies multiplied by 133 percent.

The 1988 pause in Tokyo prices sent tremors through the ranks of speculators, whose whole approach was premised on ever-increasing prices. The liabilities of bankrupted real estate companies that year multiplied by 133 percent—from 196 billion yen

($1.96 billion) to 456 billion yen ($4.56 billion)—and virtually all of this amount was attributable to companies described as speculators. Such companies accounted for Japan's two biggest corporate bankruptcies that year.[78] Did this sober the banks and tame the recklessness of their lending? Not at all. Rather than reduce their exposure to speculators in difficulty, many banks increased it by lending the speculators more money so they could meet the interest payments due to the banks. Tokyo's weak prices in 1988 turned out to be just a pause. In 1990 they zoomed to new highs, powered by yet more bank lending. The banks had learned nothing. Real estate prices broke new records.

The Okurasho's reflex response to the problem was to impose direct controls and bureaucratic directives. If the ministry had greater faith in the market mechanism, it might have considered quite a different course. The Ministry could have supplemented this approach with stricter prudential requirements on the banks, obliging them to improve their risk management, their reserves, and their accountability. Such changes would have left the banks free to make their own lending decisions, but it would also have forced them to assume the responsibility that must accompany such freedom. These are precisely the banking reforms that were advocated by the governor of the Bank of Japan, Yasushi Mieno, years later.[79]

The Finance Ministry was actually presented with an opportunity to revise its approach to bank supervision in 1988. The high liquidity and loose lending practices of Japan's banks sent them into the world market with such force during the bubble years that by 1988 they had captured 12 percent of the U.S. banking market, 23 percent of the U.K. market, and 38 percent of all international lending. American and British banks were distressed at the competitive strength of the Japanese, while American and British bank regulators were troubled by the flimsiness of the prudential requirements under which the Japanese banks operated. The United States and United Kingdom opened negotiations with Japan over ways to strengthen the capital bases of Japan's banks to bring them more into line with the Anglo-American norm. But rather than see this as an opportunity to improve the quality of Japan's banks and to rein in reckless real estate lending, the Okurasho saw it instead as a foreign threat to Japan's international financial ambitions. Japan's banks were required to improve their levels of capital reserves—from 4 percent of all assets to 8 percent—but in tough negotiating the ministry won a special concession specifically designed to ease the burden of compliance for Japan's banks. As a result, the new global banking standard set at the Swiss-based Bank for International Settlements[80] allows banks to count as capital reserves up to 45 percent of their "hidden assets"—specifically, their unrealized paper profits on stock market investments. Rather than short-circuit the self-reinforcing nature of the bubble, this deal assisted it. The higher stock prices climbed, the greater the banks' capital reserves would be, and the more they would be able to lend.[81]

■ Dining with the devil

In these boom years, while all financial institutions grew and prospered, there was a steady stream of Finance Ministry officials retiring in amakudari fashion into all the usual industries supervised by the Okurasho: banking, stock, insurance. A new development, however, was the unusually large number moving into the least respectable parts of the system—the parts inhabited by speculative, smaller firms that were mushrooming in this darker area of the financial forest—the personal finance companies, credit cooperatives, and home-loan companies, where lending rules were relaxed and collateral requirements low. The number of notified amakudari moving from the ministry into this sector is more than doubled in the 1987–89 boom. There were ten such appointments in those three years, compared with four in the previous three. This is significant. It was more than the number who were appointed to amakudari jobs in the banking industry in the same years. Before the boom, only 2 percent of notified Finance Ministry amakudari hirings were in this speculative end of the spectrum, but during the boom this proportion tripled to 6 percent. The ministry family became significantly more reliant on these companies for retirement jobs.

Harunori Takahashi earned effortless profits every day during the bubble years, and he celebrated every night. He hosted business acquaintances, friends, and contacts at his favorite restaurant, an establishment named Sato located in the expensive nightlife district of Akasaka and modeled in the traditional Japanese style. He presided nightly at dinner with ten or twenty guests at a cost of some 30,000 yen ($300) each. After a while, Mr. Takahashi's accountant remarked that he spent so much money at the restaurant that he might as well buy the place, which, of course, he did.[82]

Neither Mr. Takahashi nor anyone at his companies hired any amakudari officials, but he did strike up some close personal relationships with Finance Ministry bureaucrats. At least eight senior ministry officials are known to have become regular guests at his restaurant. Others played golf with him at his courses regularly and traveled with him on his jets.[83] His chief strategist and deal maker, Dr. Ishizaki, describes how this arriviste entrepreneur established close relationships with the aristocracy of Japanese officialdom:

> It's very hard for most people to establish a relationship with these guys at the Ministry of Finance. If you just ring them up cold and ask to talk to them, forget it. But once you have an introduction, once the ice is broken, they grab you like a long-lost friend. It's like finding that one orgy that you are assured is safe. You always wanted to do it but you were afraid of the consequences. Well, this was their big chance; they felt completely safe and they let it all hang out.

For Mr. Takahashi and his friends, the icebreaker was a onetime consultant and lobbyist for IBM Japan, Kunio Kubota, who arranged some of the initial introductions to senior Okurasho officials. "The secret of Kubota's success was that he looked so completely harmless," recalls Dr. Ishizaki.

> He would invite the bureaucrats to a karaoke bar. They would never go with someone they were unsure of. And because they knew there would be pretty young things around, they would accept. . . . Maybe it's in exchange for all their training and their grooming, but the guys at the Finance Ministry have no common sense. The career guys have no

friends outside the ministry, and they have zero street sense. Once you broke the ice with them, they'd go out with you, they'd go drinking with you, they'd go fucking with you, they'd do anything with you. . . . There's a sugar daddy around who picks up the tab—no quid pro quo. Do this for a year, build up their confidence. Then it starts, dropping hints that you want a favor. These guys would consider small favors harmless, and so it begins.[84]

As the Japanese bubble of the late twentieth century approached its bursting point, Mr. Takahashi, now able to choose between any of three corporate jets and any of at least eight Okurasho officials, was observed presiding over his usual evening gathering at his restaurant, Sato. An executive of one of Japan's major banks arrived. The banker fell to his knees. He shuffled all the way from the doorway to Mr. Takahashi's side, still on his knees, and then, bowing very low, he offered his name card. He stayed on his knees and kept his eyes on the floor. All Japan, it seems, including the mighty Okurasho, worshipped at the restaurant Sato, at the shrine Takahashi, and did homage to the deity named greed.

THE MIRAGE DISSOLVES

The bubble economy was in its final fizz of effervescence, yet to the end Tokyo stock prices gave no sign of flagging, leaping from one giddy peak to the next. The Nikkei index of 225 stock prices bounded effortlessly from a record high of 30,000 points at the opening of 1989 to yet another of nearly 39,000 at year-end, rewarding investors with their fourth year of profits of 30 percent or better. The question then in the markets was whether the benchmark would hit 40,000 points. Opinion polls of brokers and big investors showed confidence that it would.[1] Over drinks one evening, I asked a senior salesman at Nomura Securities, the world's largest brokerage firm, for his opinion. I was expecting optimism, but I'm still taken aback at his answer: "The question is not whether it will reach 40,000, it's whether it will reach 60,000."

The Tokyo stock market boom generated extraordinary wealth and corresponding arrogance. As the undisputed monarch of that market, Nomura developed wealth and arrogance of imperial proportions. The chairman of the company's U.S. subsidiary, Masaaki Kurokawa, conceived a grand plan to establish California as a joint Japanese-U.S. economic zone with a single currency. The American state would get guaranteed access to Japanese capital in return for guaranteed access to Californian territory and U.S. markets.[2] The Nikkei, alas, was not destined to go beyond 38,915, and Mr. Kurokawa still needs to pay his Californian taxi fares in dollars.

The Okurasho and its monetary agent, the Bank of Japan, finally set in motion the machinery for bursting the bubble economy by deciding to increase the official discount rate in May 1989. It was the first time the rate had been raised in nine years. At first the increase had little effect. The self-reinforcing circular swirl of money had become so powerful, and expectations of its durability so strong, that the markets failed to see its significance as the expression of official determination. It was the first of three hikes that year that took the discount rate from 2.5 percent in May to 4.25 percent on Christmas Day. Just as loose money had been a precondition for the bubble to form, so tighter money was necessary to its collapse. Land prices nationally began to suffer, and as 1990 opened on the Tokyo stock market, equity prices began to ease. Few had yet recognized it, but the bubble economy was finished.

What finally persuaded the ministry to move? As we have seen, Japan's interest rates—or monetary policy—had been set to suit the convenience of the Budget Bureau. The Budget Bureau wanted low interest rates because they stimulate the economy. If the economy was growing strongly, there would be no pressure on the Budget Bureau to spend more government money to stimulate it. The bureau would be free to concentrate on its campaign to cut government spending and reduce the national debt. And as long as the Budget Bureau wanted interest rates to stay low, they stayed low. Policy was changed in 1989 not because the Budget Bureau had been overpowered but because it had changed its mind. "The proposal came from the Budget Bureau," recounts a senior official in the Banking Bureau, Sei Nakai. "They said to us, 'The economy may go into a slump, and we will need to cut rates then.' They wanted to make some room for loosening monetary policy so that they wouldn't have to relax fiscal policy."[3]

In other words, the priority in setting interest rates was not the smooth management of the national economy but the protection of the "main castle"—fiscal policy. Foreseeing the inevitability of an economic downturn, the Budget Bureau was once again attempting to protect fiscal policy at the expense of monetary policy. The Bank of Japan, timid and ineffec-

The priority in setting interest rates was not the smooth management of the national economy but the protection of the "main castle"—fiscal policy.

tual, sat waiting until the Okurasho's Budget Bureau was ready to move—the monetary agent awaiting the pleasure of the fiscal authority. This mismatch of institutional power translated directly into a mismatch of policy. Because there was no one to challenge the Okurasho, and its Budget Bureau in particular, its policy went un-challenged.

■ Bursting the bubble

At the Long-Term Credit Bank of Japan, a sense of disquiet finally took hold. The bank had among its top ten borrowers a small com-pany whose cash flow had never been enough to service its interest payments—EIE International and its principal, Harunori Taka-hashi. Whenever the firm needed to make a payment, it always just sold a property, crystallized its capital gains, and used part of the profit. With the change of climate, the bank decided that it might be a good idea to place one of its senior executives at EIE, and from 1989 he shadowed Mr. Takahashi, even traveling with him on one of his three jets.[4]

The market had begun to pay attention to the message from Japan's authorities, but the official who was taken most seriously was the chairman of the U.S. Federal Reserve Board, Alan Greenspan. When he indicated on February 20, 1990, the need to bring U.S. inflation in check, any remaining hope of easy money in Japan was finally abandoned.[5] The next day was the dawning of the great collapse: the Nikkei fell by 1,161 points. But still the Okurasho and the Bank of Japan were not content, and what happened next would be the subject of recriminations years later.

Once the authorities finally took steps to deflate the bubble, they acted with the zeal of a penitent. Even after the stock market had pitched into steep decline, the authorities kept pushing up official rates. In March, the discount rate was raised by an unusually large increment of 1 percentage point, taking it to 5.25 percent. In six weeks, the market lost a quarter of its value. The Bank of Japan announced its conclusion that loose money had helped cause the bubble in land prices. And now it plainly stated that its reason for raising official rates in 1989 had been to achieve "stability of the financial market"—that is, an end to the bubble. The markets had now experienced four successive increases in official interest rates and had even received an explicit written explanation of official intentions.[6] At this moment—in the midst of this rout of stock speculators and the fierce tightening of monetary policy—the Okurasho fired the administrative equivalent of a nuclear weapon into the midst of the real estate market. In April 1990, through the vehicle of administrative guidance, it ordered the banks, life insurers, nonlife insurers, and credit co-ops to introduce a limit on the total volume of lending to the real estate sector. They were directed to hold the increase in lending to the sector to a rate lower than the increase in overall lending. It was the first time in seventeen years that the ministry had taken such direct action to restrain lending.[7]

After a purgative exploration of the 28,000-point range, the stock market seemed to steady around the 30,000 level in mid-1990. The Gulf War in August and jumpy global oil prices wrought further uncertainty, and the Nikkei resumed its fall. Tighter money and the restraint on bank lending for real estate seemed to be putting the squeeze on land prices. Official surveys showed that the finances of real estate companies were being sharply reduced.[8] At this moment, on August 30, and for the fifth and final time, the authorities once more raised official interest rates, from 5.25 percent to 6 percent. On this occasion, the reason was to prevent inflation rather than to deflate the bubble, but by then the bubble had already been flattened.

■ Damage reports

The destruction of wealth that followed the government's "corrective" actions was so savage that it far outstripped the cost of the physical damage inflicted on Japan in World War II. The official estimate of the total cost of wartime damage to Japan, adjusted for inflation and including lost military hardware, is 19.5 trillion yen ($195 billion) in today's (1995) prices.[9] In the three years after the bursting of the bubble economy, the lost value of land and stocks totaled around 800 trillion yen ($8 trillion). Proportionately, too, the bubble was a more costly event for Japan. The cost of war damage was the equivalent of about one year's national economic output.[10] The losses following the bursting of the bubble were equal to almost two years' national economic output.

The nature of the damage in the two events was, of course, vastly different. The wartime damage spelled the physical ruin of the nation's productive capacity, while the cost of the bubble was chiefly translated into an attack on private paper assets—that is, on balance sheets and unrealized profits. And the gains made during the bubble economy were themselves so outlandish that their loss was really just a return to reality. Still, the comparison puts into some perspective the enormity of the losses brought about in the aftermath of the bubble.

And those losses were not just an abstract notion. They were a reality that affected real-world behavior for many years. For while the profits soon disappeared, the borrowings that had been undertaken on the basis of those profits did not. Hidden profits and latent gains dwindled and, in most cases, vanished with the receding memory of the era, as ephemeral as a dream. But debts remained, contractual and binding, as lasting as the law and as hard as cash flow. At the beginning of the bubble, corporate Japan's debt

The destruction of wealth that followed the government's "corrective" actions was so savage that it far outstripped the cost of the physical damage inflicted on Japan in World War II.

was twice its annual profits, already double the average for the other members of the Group of Five major economies. By 1990, corporate Japan's debts were three times its annual profits, while the ratio in the other G-5 nations stayed the same. Similarly, although this time in step with the trend in other countries, the debt owed by Japanese households grew from the equivalent of eleven months' income to around fourteen months' income.[11] This debt legacy, particularly in the corporate sector, proved to be a drag on the economy for years to come. Money borrowed on the fantasy of spiraling asset prices had to be repaid in the reality of an economy with vast idle capacity and in prolonged stagnation. Three years after the bubble, Japan's factories were running at just 70 percent of their capacity, the lowest since the first oil shock of the early 1970s.[12]

The governor of the central bank in 1994 suggested that some of the corporate facilities bought with this debt during the late 1980s would never be used.[13]

Growth of technical know-how in Japan's most competitive sector—manufacturing—fell to its lowest on record as spending on research and development was restrained and companies hesitated to introduce new technologies.[14] Companies were instead preoccupied with rationalizing and reorganizing, fitting their bubble-inflated expectations to the rediscovered economic realities. Japan's competitiveness in the world economy, which had been unmatched for eight consecutive years, fell out of first place in 1994 and into third, yielding to the United States and tiny Singapore. The next year, it slipped one place further, displaced by the deregulation drive in New Zealand.[15]

The total market value of land in Japan fell from 2,389 trillion yen to 1,823 trillion yen in 1994, a loss of 24 percent.

Exactly where did the losses lie? From its 1990 pinnacle, the total market value of land in Japan fell from 2,389 trillion yen to 1,823 trillion yen in 1994, a loss of 24 percent, or 566 trillion yen ($5.66 trillion). In 1985 the total value of land had been 3.1 times as great as annual economic output as measured by gross national product (GNP); at its 1990 peak, it stood at 5.6 times GNP; and by 1994 it was down to 3.8 times GNP and still falling.

In the stock market, prices fell from their 1989 peak of 38,915 on the Nikkei index to a low of 14,309 in August 1992 for a loss of 24,606 points, or 63 percent of the market's value. The value of all listed stocks in 1985 had been 0.6 times the size of the total economy as measured by GNP; this swelled to 1.6 times GNP in 1989, then fell sharply, so that by 1994 it was about back to where it had started, at 0.8 times GNP. The loss in value amounted to 261 trillion yen ($2.61 trillion).[16]

The Okurasho accused the Bank of Japan of excessive zeal in bringing the bubble to an end, in wringing monetary policy too tight to squeeze out speculators. A senior official claimed: "The breaking of the bubble should have been more controlled. The Bank of Japan was overenthusiastic. It seemed quite pleased to see the sudden decline in stock and land prices." A member of the central bank's executive board at the time and a career man at the bank, Yoshio Suzuki, says that this accusation is an ex post facto fabrication designed to shift blame: "The Finance Ministry did not raise any objections at the time. There was no argument with them when these decisions were being made."[17]

■ Nothing was what it seemed

With the bursting of the bubble and a return to fundamentals, many myths were laid to rest, many ambitions laid to waste, much foolishness laid bare. The rise and fall of the bubble quickly laid to rest an economic argument that movements in asset prices—stocks and land—had no bearing on the so-called real economy with its factories and workers, stores and shoppers. The bubble's buildup in fact contributed to the economic boom of the late 1980s, and its collapse helped pulled the real economy down with it.[18] It was an expensive lesson. The postbubble downturn was Japan's first self-induced postwar recession.

The bursting of the bubble also exploded one of Japan's greatest postwar myths. This was the land myth—that the price of land never fell but could only rise. From the end of World War II until 1991, there had been only one year in which land prices had generally fallen in Japan, and that was in the oil-shock year of 1973, when the skyrocketing price of oil gave rise to the direst forecasts for Japan's economy. The myth was now seen to be exactly that.[19]

Stock market prices on the Nikkei index fell from their 1989 peak of 38,915 to a low of 14,309 in August 1992—a loss of 24,606 points, or 63 percent of the market's value.

The strikingly dishonest basis of the entire Japanese stockbrokerage system was suddenly clear, too. Throughout the development of the industry, Japan's stockbrokers had issued only one investment recommendation to their clients: "Buy." The familiar Western stock adviser's vocabulary of buy, sell, and hold was unknown. The industry treated its clients on the premise that equity prices would only rise; it was never time to sell, time to reconsider, time to realize a profit. "We misled investors," was the simple confession of the chairman of Nomura Securities, Yukio Aida.[20] The presumption of ever-increasing values put the stock industry on a footing similar to that of the real estate business. Interestingly, Nomura had long issued comprehensive and more scientific stock recommendations to its clients abroad; they were required to do so by the norms of international practice. But its Japanese clients had to wait until January 1994 for Nomura to issue its very first "sell" recommendation on a stock—116 years after the founding of the industry. The other major Japanese brokers followed suit three months later. "It wasn't just our clients who lost confidence in the system, but even our own salespeople," said the manager of corporate research at the Nomura Research Institute, Yadahiro Yamamoto.[21] The outbreak of the stock-loss compensation scandal only emphasized the dishonesty and opacity of the system and the extent of collusion with the Okurasho.

When the bubble deflated, so did "the myth of able and trustworthy bureaucrats."

Viewed through the distorting prism of the economic bubble, the skills of Japan's bureaucrats seemed to be great indeed and their popular image of superior intellect and ability safe. When the bubble deflated, so did "the myth of able and trustworthy bureaucrats," according to a former career-stream bureaucrat at the Ministry of International Trade and Industry, Taichi Sakaiya. It had been thought "that even if the political system becomes paralyzed, the country's superlative bureaucrats will see to it that nothing major goes amiss." He argued that this belief was in part based on the successful growth of the economy, but the end of the bubble demonstrated that economic success was in fact due to "nothing more than . . . the global Cold War setup and the Japanese economy's growth structure." Japan's military and foreign policy dependence on the United States had allowed Japan to concentrate on economics while operating with very minimal defense budgets. The second basis for the myth of trustworthy bureaucracy was its incorruptibility; the bubble and its aftermath had blown much of this belief away, too.[22] By 1994 an opinion poll showed some 80 percent of the Japanese public calling for reform of the bureaucracy. Collusion and elitism were images the people most closely associated with their public servants.[23]

■ The ministry versus the market

Yet it seemed that destruction of wealth and economic stagnation might be only a precursor of things to come. As the stockmarket's precipitous decline continued unchecked through 1992, the hidden profits of the bubble years shrivelled and seemed on the verge of disappearing altogether. This directly attacked the hidden profits that had been accumulated on company and bank balance sheets. These hidden profits formed a part of the capital base of the banking system and the big institutional investors; they were part of the bedrock of Japan's financial and economic systems. The aggregate hidden stock profits of the life insurance companies peaked in 1988 at 45 trillion yen ($450 billion) and slid to 10 trillion yen ($100 billion) by March 1992.[24] At Japan's twenty-one major banks, hidden profits on equities slipped from 46 trillion yen ($460 billion) in 1990 to 17 trillion yen ($170 billion) during the same period. And these totals conceal the unequal distribution of the comfort cushions—the weaker institutions were coming uncomfortably close to losing all their hidden profits and instead becoming holders of hidden losses.

But the stock market collapse showed no sign of stopping, and in the course of 1992 prices just continued falling. By August, when the market reached its postbubble low point of 14,309 points, the hidden profits of some major institutions in all sectors of the financial system had been completely wiped out. If stock prices had remained at this level on the next accounting date just a few weeks later—the end of the financial half-year on Septem-

When the market reached its postbubble low point of 14,309 points in August 1992, the hidden profits of some major institutions in all sectors of the financial system had been completely wiped out.

ber 30—four of Japan's twenty-one major banks would have been obliged to record the total evaporation of their hidden profits: the Bank of Tokyo, the Yasuda Trust Bank, the Nippon Trust Bank, and the Chuo Trust Bank.[25] The banks—together with some major life insurance companies, general insurers, and other institutions—would have been technically insolvent and yet, in the climate of the time, incapable of recapitalization on normal commercial terms. A major, urgent, and extremely smooth government intervention would have been required to reorganize the industry.

Three of these four banks were among the world's sixty biggest at the time.[26] And by now Japan had become the world's major creditor nation. A financial crisis of global proportions was a likely prospect. If the authorities had been skilled and lucky, they might have been able to forestall disaster. The Okurasho was not prepared for any such emergency. And even if it were, there was still no guarantee that this would be the end of the great fall. So rather than allowing market forces to have full play and to then reshape the banking system in their wake, the ministry decided to challenge the forces of the free market head-on.

The Okurasho decided that Tokyo stock prices could be allowed to fall no further. In a breathtaking demonstration of its determination, it stepped directly into the marketplace and pitted its power and resources against the world's investors in the second-biggest stock market on earth in the full cry of collapse.

It took three approaches to this awesome task. First, it changed the rules of the market. New equity issues were already banned unofficially, eliminating any possible source of new stock.[27] Second, it used the coercive extralegal pressure of administrative guidance to discourage investors from selling any of their stockholdings and, where possible, to start buying instead.[28] This squeezed the flow of existing stock into the market. With these first two measures acting to amplify any increase in stock prices, the ministry took the third and most unorthodox step—it opened the great dams of public liquidity, channeling trillions of yen worth of savings into the stock market in search of stocks to buy.

The Finance Ministry did not use language as direct as this. It merely announced in August 1992, as part of a new spending package to stimulate the now-flagging economy, that it was liberalizing the stock investment activities of the big public-sector repositories of savings: the postal life insurance system (*kanpo*), the national pension funds, and the postal savings establishment (*yucho*). The new setup would allow a minimum new allocation of 2.82 trillion yen ($28.2 billion) from these funds to flow into stock investment in the remaining half of the financial year.[29]

The ministry did not officially declare its campaign against the stock market collapse, but it did not need to. The market made the announcement itself, wittily declaring the Okurasho's new stock market strategy to be a "price-keeping operation," or PKO—a pun on a United Nations peace-keeping operation that was then the subject of political controversy. The military overtones suited the combative mood of the ministry's operation. And the success of both PKOs—as with any government intervention in a war, marketplace, or other scene of chaos—was to be an open question. The stock market PKO was, however, a covert operation. The announcement of the liberalization of stock investment by the big public funds was the first and only official evidence of the ministry's will. There was never any open declaration of official intent to support stock prices.

The de facto announcement of the PKO, in combination with the economic stimulus package—valued at a record 10.7 trillion yen—was persuasive. In concert with the announcement of a cut in official interest rates, the total effect was compelling. The plunge in stock prices was arrested, and then reversed. The banks, the life insurance companies, the entire financial community closed its accounts for the half-year to September 30 supported by hidden profits. Systemic crisis was averted. This triple punch of official action—fiscal policy, monetary policy, and direct stock market intervention—was coordinated to produce the maximum effect. One of the coordinators later spoke about it. An Okurasho official who went on to become a legislator in the ruling Liberal Democratic Party, Yuji Tsushima, said, "We [had] to do whatever [was] necessary to stop stock prices from falling freely . . . I sat in the headquarters of the ruling party, keeping in close contact with people in the capital markets and the Ministry of Finance so we could more or less combine our efforts to maintain stability." He was also involved in arrangements for the coordinated easing in official interest rates:

"I would say I had a direct contact with the [Bank of Japan] governor [on this issue]—I know him from my school days."[30]

Mr. Tsushima describes the market as being held aloft by two pillars: one is the pillar of routine daily investment activity, and the other is the pillar of official support "to keep the market behaving in an appropriate manner." He continues: "If there is a justifiable reason for avoiding a free fall, then we must do that. What we can do is encourage the administration [bureaucracy] and institutions to guide their investment policy according to this second pillar."[31] The powers that be in other economies of the industrialized world have only one pillar. Governments ordinarily see themselves as setting the investment climate for their stock markets—through economic policy and market regulation. But they do not see a role for themselves in deciding actual investments or, indeed, in setting any targets for market prices. The second pillar—the pillar of direct official intervention—is what sets Japan's authorities apart.

How does the Finance Ministry justify its support of the market? According to Eisuke Sakakibara, a senior Okurasho member and its sharpest intellectual, "It's a question of relative social costs, a question of preserving order in the markets." Speaking in general terms, he contrasted what he described as the Anglo-Saxon approach of allowing markets to fall and institutions to fail with the Finance Ministry's attempts to keep all participating players in operation:

> The key issue is the relative cost-effectiveness of the two systems. And it's our experience that the social costs of our approach are smaller. It's a sort of consensus by participants in the structure that those social costs should be borne by all participants in the system. There's a consensus to socialize the costs . . . not to let selected individuals or institutions bear the cost of the system. This is not the time to change our system, it's a very hard time and it's difficult to share the costs.[32]

Do the other countries of the industrialized world have the intellectual infrastructure to conduct such an operation? Intellectually, most of the other major countries are too deeply conditioned to accept the essential correctness of market forces, too long accustomed to regarding the stock market as an intervention-free zone. Stock markets are regarded as places where companies surrender some of their privacy and autonomy in return for the right to solicit funds from the public. And it is where investors surrender the security of their money in exchange for the possibility of earning extraordinary returns. When they enter a stock market, both companies and investors willingly yield up some of their security in return for the prospect of increasing their gains. It is not considered legitimate for governments to interfere in the risk and reward calculus that occurs as an accepted part of the market's operations. The government is not expected to butt directly into other normal commercial transactions; why should it interfere in normal commercial transactions in a stock market?

But these doctrinal objections could well prove surmountable in extremis. Governments everywhere commonly intervene in currency markets. This can be justified because a country's exchange rate is a fundamentally important economic variable that deeply influences imports, exports, capital flows, debt, inflation, and the rate of economic growth. Normally, stock markets do not fall into this category—they are pits of private interest and only in the most extreme cases do they influence the larger economy. However, in the face of the crisis confronting Japan, the market's illness was about to infect the solvency of the banking system and the country's major institutional investors—an impending financial and economic crisis of considerable proportions. It had ceased to be a matter of purely private interests and had become a threat to the public good and national welfare.

■ What if . . .?

What if the ministry had not intervened? The answer is, of course, unknowable, but it is interesting to speculate, nonetheless. Nomura Securities, as the world's biggest stockbroker, was not only deeply interested in the outcome but was also consulted by the Finance Ministry on its PKO plan. A top market strategist for Nomura Securities' research institute, Chisato Haganuma, later estimated that the Nikkei might have fallen as far as 10,000 or 11,000 points in the absence of the August 1992 announcement, although he noted that it was not possible to separate the effects of the individual components of that announcement, which included 10.7 trillion yen in economic stimulus spending.[33] His estimate suggests that without intervention, Tokyo stock prices would have fallen another 23–30 percent. At 11,000 points, thirteen of Japan's major banks would have had their hidden profits obliterated. At 10,000 points, there would have been no banks at all with any hidden profits.[34] A fall of such proportions is entirely plausible. In pro-

If the Nikkei had been allowed to fall to 11,000 points, thirteen of Japan's major banks might have had their profits obliterated. At 10,000, *no* bank would have kept hidden profits.

portion to the economy, it would have valued all Japan's listed stocks at around half the size of annual GDP. This is well within normal historical ranges and is, in fact, considerably higher than the 1980 ratio of about 30 percent of GDP.

The "other" Nikkei index—the one that measures the value of membership in Japan's 530 leading golf courses—was not subject to any official manipulation or PKO. The golf index may be the closest thing Japan has to a free market. How far did it fall? By March 1995 it had fallen 74 percent from its bubble-economy peak. If the stock market Nikkei index had paralleled the movement of its golfing namesake, it would have finished at about 10,100 points, squarely within the range suggested by Mr. Haganuma.[35] The two indices measure entirely different things, and so the parallel might be nothing more than an interesting coincidence. However, there is some overlap; the movement in both indices was at least in part a reflection of Japan's liquidity, of the levels of speculative activity, and of expectations of asset price increases. The chief underlying commodity tracked by the golf index was land, and, as we have seen, land prices were intimately related to stock price valuations during the expansion of the bubble. One observer, Neil Rogers, a strategist at the Swiss brokerage of UBS Securities in Tokyo, said that in the broadest-sense, the two indices were moved by the same phenomenon: "The deflation that's taking place in the economy."[36]

The inevitability of further stock market declines in the absence of official intervention is not universally accepted. The market analyst voted as the most respected by major Japanese investors in the mid-1990s, Peter Tasker of Kleinwort Benson Securities in Tokyo, for example, argues that the market had probably reached a natural point of recovery: "The stock market had gone down 63 percent when it reached the bottom — markets don't like to go down much more than that." Neither does he credit the official intervention with halting the collapse: "The thing that is new [in the months following the intervention] is President Clinton's deficit reduction plan." This changed the anticipated return from bond investment in U.S. Treasury bills and so prompted large amounts of investment capital to go in search of stock investment instead, including stock investment in Japan. "These are things that are happening in the world which have nothing to do with Japanese bureaucrats."[37]

By March 1995, the "Nikkei golf index" had fallen 74 percent from its peak.

The ministry saw its campaign as a success. "At the first stage of propping up the market in 1992, the worst was avoided, so we think it was a success," explains an official in the Securities Bureau.[38] Whatever the reason, by the end of 1992, the Okurasho had won a reprieve from what certainly appeared to be a very serious crisis. However, it did not use this opportunity to make fundamental changes in any of the policies or sectors over which it presides. Decades of worldwide experience with government interventions in foreign exchange markets has shown that they generally fail to change the market's direction; unless they are supported by changes in economic policy or other fundamental factors, interventions can only smooth out some of the more violent fluctuations or perhaps buy time.

The Okurasho gave every sign that it wanted only to buy time. It resisted structural change in the Japanese economy, as we will see in later chapters. It impeded a rejuvenation of the industrial structure. It refused to cooperate in attempts to recast the major public-sector corporations. It proposed no changes in the structure or practices of the banking industry, the insurance industry, or the stockbrokerage industry. Rather than introduce reforms, it did the opposite. The ministry gave life insurers a special exemption from declaring losses on foreign exchange; it pardoned regional banks from disclosing

bad debts; trust banks were allowed flexibility in reporting default-
ing borrowers. The ministry's approach was, in short, to maintain
the status quo. It not only resisted structural change, it assisted the
financial sector in resisting the forces of gravity. Although it had
been a close witness to the inher-
ent vulnerability of the capital

**The ministry's approach was to
maintain the status quo. It not
only resisted structural change,
it assisted the financial sector in
resisting the forces of gravity.**

markets and had been forced to
contemplate imminent disaster
on a large scale, it hoped that
these problems would all go away
automatically with an upturn in
the economic cycle from recession to recovery. The ministry
sought to bring on a recovery using the instruments of cyclical
economic policy, continually cutting official interest rates and, re-
luctantly, increasing government spending. But there was no quick
upturn. The bold stock market rescue, designed to be a decisive,
one-off intervention, became instead just the beginning of a protracted Okurasho campaign to artificially levitate a falling market.

■ Indirect directives

Tribal peoples on Pacific Islands were astonished to see aerial drops
of military supplies for troops during World War II. Naturally, they
looked for opportunities to share in the bounty. Some spent many
years after the end of the war waiting for the next load of cargo to
drop from the skies, neglecting their usual lives and earning themselves the title of cargo cultists; so it was in the Tokyo stock market.
Once the Okurasho had effectively declared its intentions on the
1992 intervention—and in the absence of any fundamental reforms—the ministry became the natural focus of market attention.
According to Noboru Kawai, an economist at the brokerage firm
Morgan Stanley Japan, "We've had a change in sentiment, but it has
no underpinning in economic fundamentals." The Nikkei's rise in
late 1992 and early 1993 reflected only "an increase in the number
of investors willing to take short-term advantage of the govern-
ment-manipulated market."[39]

The ministry denied that it was doing anything at all. Yet the markets seethed with gossip of its latest actions and plans and targets. Undoubtedly, the Okurasho was held responsible for things it did not do. As one Securities Bureau official said: "The director-general is sometimes very frustrated because he is being criticized for something that didn't exist, but it's very hard to prove that it didn't exist."[40] But that is the risk in launching covert operations, as the U.S. Central Intelligence Agency might testify. Once an institution is known to conduct covert operations, its hand is seen in everything and its denials are disbelieved. However, there is little point in trying to deny the reality of the ministry's ongoing efforts to support stock prices. Ministry officials sometimes acknowledged their PKO activities to reporters in background briefings, but never in detail or for the record.[41] Officials were active in all sectors—discouraging sellers, prodding buyers, and allocating more public-sector savings to stock market investments. Nobumitsu Kagami, formerly a senior executive at Nomura and now an academic, recalls how pressure was applied to the brokers: "The Ministry of Finance would ring us up and ask, 'What are you doing?' They are smart enough not to make a direct request, but when they ring up and ask, 'Who's selling?' it's very easy to understand what's in their minds. During these conversations we always have in the back of our minds the power over us, particularly their most powerful tool—the power to decide whether we can open new branches."[42]

Generally, ministry officials met with a cooperative response. A senior executive of Japan's biggest private-sector investor—indeed, the biggest anywhere—the Nippon Life Insurance Co., said that his company complied with a ministry request to exercise care in its stock dealings "because we do not invest in stocks, we invest in a system, and we are acting in the best interests of that system."[43] So when, for example, the Nikkei fell below 16,000 points in November 1992, the Okurasho phoned the life insurance companies and other big institutional investors and asked them why they were not buying. The following day, the volume of trading rose by nearly 80 percent and the Nikkei gained 785 points.[44]

The ministry calls such conversations "hearings," and officials readily admit that they hold them in person and by phone. But they maintain a coy fiction that these hearings are conducted to elicit

information from market players rather than to give them directives. An official in the Securities Bureau of the ministry says:
"When the market [was] falling, it is true that some officials held
hearings to ask about the causes, but we did not conduct any guidance on stock prices. Private-sector people may in their own minds
interpret the purpose of the hearings as a request from us—everyone has freedom to interpret the meaning."[45]

In reality, it was hard for any firm under the ministry's direct
regulatory supervision to defy it. But it did meet occasional resistance from those who were not. For example, the Okurasho took its
campaign directly to the top level of the Japanese corporate sector;
it addressed the biggest of the big-business associations, the Keidanren, in November 1993. The head of the ministry's Securities Bureau, Sohei Hidaka, opened his speech to the assembled executives
with these words: "If stock prices are important, companies should
restrain themselves from selling any." A senior executive of Nissan
Motor Co. decided to confront the bureaucrat, but only with some
trepidation. The businessman told the mandarin: "I know that if I
make this statement, it will rebound against me later. But corporate
executives have no faith in official policies." On meeting resistance,
Mr. Hidaka did not retreat, but he did defer to the executives' right
to make business decisions, modifying his approach: "We want you
to bear our request in mind."[46]

At the very top level of the industry, the former chairman of
Nomura Securities, Yukio Aida, gently mocked the Okurasho's
claims of nonintervention. "The Finance Ministry says it does not
attempt to buoy stock prices, but, in reality, stock prices move ab-
normally."[47] And the movement was indeed abnormal. An official in
the Okurasho's Securities Bureau readily agrees: "It is true that
stock prices moved in a relatively narrow band—between 16,000
and 21,000—for the three years after the 1992 announcement. But
that had nothing to do with the Okurasho."[48] In fact, the ministry's
PKO defined the lower edge of this range, forming the floor of
support.

Consider the behavior of public-sector funds. First, the fund
managers—for example, the Post Office Life Insurance Bureau's
fund management division—have themselves confirmed that they

conducted support buying, as distinct from investing according to the normal investment criteria.[49] And second, the actual flows of their cash support this statement. The funds' accounts do not disclose details of how members' funds are invested, but there are some proxies that allow us to get an idea of their behavior.

After August 1992, the trust banks' stock investment patterns changed abruptly. Until that point, they had sometimes sold equities and sometimes bought them when the market was falling. But from August 1992 through 1995, a new and fixed principle applied; whenever the market was falling, the trust banks entered the market as consistent net buyers.[50]

Another interesting new pattern was that the pension fund trusts operated by the trust banks—the type of account in which many public-sector funds were placed—emerged as Japan's most stock-hungry new buyers from 1992 onward. These trusts increased their stockholdings at a rate faster than any other class of Japanese investor. Until 1992, their behavior was unexceptional; in 1990 they had sold 5 percent of their equities, and the next year they increased their holdings by 3.9 percent. But from 1992 onward their appetite for stock quickened noticeably. They increased their holdings by 14.7 percent in 1992, by 14.5 percent the next year, by 26.1 percent the next, and by 19.4 percent in 1995 for an average annual rate of increase of 18.7 percent. By contrast, the comparable rate for all financial institutions was 2 percent, for business corporations 0.07 percent, for individuals 3 percent, and for securities firms minus 5 percent. Abnormal indeed.[51]

It is also interesting to see that these trusts developed a special passion for bank stocks. In the three years from 1993 through 1995, they increased their holdings of bank equity at a voracious annual average rate of 38.6 percent. Again, this was way out of line with the general trend of Japanese investors; financial institutions on average increased their bank stockholdings by 3 percent, business corporations cut theirs back by 1.8 percent, and individuals sold at an annual average rate of 1.4 percent.[52] The trusts' deep interest in bank stock occurred as the net profits of the banks collapsed under the strain of their mountains of souring bubble-era loans.

How much public-sector money was channeled into stocks? The

level of disclosure is too poor to allow any exact reckoning. But we know two pieces of information that provide floor-to-ceiling guideposts. We know the floor because we know the actual investment activities of some disclosed operations of the funds. From 1992 through 1995, this amounted to net new stock buying of 9.1 trillion yen ($91 billion). We know the ceiling because we know the maximum limits permissible under the regulations governing the funds. For the same period, this totaled 14.1 trillion ($141 billion). In short, public-sector funds invested somewhere between 9.1 trillion yen and perhaps as much as 14.1 trillion yen in Japanese stocks in the four years following the launch of the PKO.[53]

■ Intervention—beneficial or ethical?

Whose money was it? Were the buyers consulted? Did they make any profit on their involvement in the support operation? The answer to the first question is that the money was never the property of the government. There were three sources. First, the money drawn from the postal life insurance system is generated by premiums paid by individuals who take out life insurance, plus the investment returns on that money. Ultimately, the funds are to be used to meet claims when policyholders die. Second, the cash from the national pension system is contributed by workers and their employers to fund the pensions of workers when they retire. Third, the money extracted from the postal savings system represents the savings of ordinary Japanese who, eventually, will want their money back, plus interest. So all of this money is only entrusted temporarily to public-sector agencies on behalf of individual Japanese citizens.

The answer to the second question is no. There was no consultation and there is no real mechanism for accountability. None of the depositors or investors was asked whether the funds' investment charters should be extended to include supporting stock prices. Presumably, at least in the case of depositors in the postal savings system, if they wanted to use their money to buy stock, they would not have put it into postal savings accounts. Their representatives—the elected government—were not consulted on their behalf, either. Although ruling-party politicians were deeply involved in establishing the PKO behind the scenes, there was no opportunity for public debate or scrutiny of the decision in any of its various elements. This, in part, explains the reluctance of the ministry to officially confirm the existence of the operation; it is impossible to be held accountable for something that does not exist. In official terms, the decision to liberalize the public-sector funds' stock investment was simply to allow them to diversify their investments and to have the freedom to pursue the best possible returns.

It is also noteworthy that while none of the funds involved in the PKO was actually deposited with the Finance Ministry, it was able to marshall them with relative ease because all postal savings, all national pension funds, and most postal insurance funds are invested through the Okurasho's Trust Fund Bureau, which acts as agent for the institutions into which the money has been deposited.

The answer to the third question is inconclusive. It is impossible to know whether the funds deployed in the PKO generated a profit or a loss for their ultimate owners. Even in the case of the funds that are known to have been invested, no dividend is payable for the first five years, and so we must wait until the end of the decade before we can begin to get even a glimpse.

However, the Liberal Democrats' Mr. Tsushima has a thought on this matter: "I was asked if it was proper for the agency concerned to put money into a volatile market. My answer is that if people in the public sector, as well as the private sector, consider the stock market is at its lowest, and there is some potential for growth in the economy, it's quite natural for people to put money into the market."[54] Officials have used the same basic argument—that the best time to buy stock for profit is when prices are at a low point so that investors capture the gains when they rebound. This is generally true. But in this case, how do we know that stock prices had hit their low point? It was the government that declared the low point, not the market. In the absence of intervention, the market might have fallen much further. Those managing the public-sector funds might have been buying overpriced stock, but they had no choice. Nor is it possible to guess at the performance of the PKO funds by observing the movement of the overall market; fund managers commonly sell their better-performing stocks to take their profits but hold their unsuccessful stocks to avoid crystallizing losses.

The PKO worked in the short term by averting a sudden and serious crisis in Japan's financial system. Did it work in the medium term in restoring the market to health or in reinvigorating the sectors it was designed to protect—the economy in general and the banking system in particular? We'll see.

■ Confession of an entrepreneur

It was 1991 when the Long-Term Credit Bank's willingness to indulge its most heavily leveraged client finally ran out. The bank overran the small office of EIE International and its staff of fifty, dispatching a special task force of thirty bankers to contain the disaster now unfolding. EIE and its associated companies had total debts amounting to a little over 1 trillion yen ($10 billion), but the value of its assets—land and stocks and French impressionist paintings—was collapsing. A good deal of shouting went on in the office over the next two years. The bankers managed to sell the corporate jets and one or two other assets, but otherwise they made little progress in recasting the financial Frankenstein into which they had breathed the life force of unlimited funds.

Mr. Takahashi and his entourage had spent more time filing flight plans for their aeronautical excursions than they had planning how they might be able to service their debts.

The problem was extremely simple. Mr. Takahashi and his entourage had spent more time filing flight plans for their aeronautical excursions than they had planning how they might be able to service their debts—much more. His irrepressible lieutenant, Dr. Ishizaki, confesses:

> We never drew up a plan for servicing the debt. I do take a lot of responsibility, and I have a lot of remorse for concentrating absolutely on capital-gains-type investments and ignoring the ability to service debt. I did put EIE in the position when the bubble burst—and we could

no longer just flip a property over and make a killing—that we couldn't service our debt. Our portfolio should have been more balanced with cash flow. But in those days, talking about 6 percent yields just wasn't in vogue. That was our big mistake, there's no doubt about it.

However big a mistake Mr. Takahashi and Dr. Ishizaki had made, the Long-Term Credit Bank seems to have made an even bigger one; the entrepreneurs had been playing with the bank's money.[55]

∎ Flying on one engine

The recession grew worse. The government fired up the two engines of economic policy. The first to be put into action was monetary (interest rate) policy. The official discount rate was cut from 6 percent in 1990 to 4.5 percent the year after, and within another two years it was at 1.75 percent, a record low. The Okurasho pushed the pace of these cuts faster, repeatedly prodding the Bank of Japan to cut rates before it was ready.[56] But something was wrong. This engine was being operated at top capacity but seemed to have no effect—investment was stagnant. "Who generates the final demand that sparks a recovery?" asked an economist at the Nomura Research Institute, Richard Koo. He argued that it is usually the sector of the economy that is most sensitive to interest rates, real estate and construction. "It has been the first to respond to a decline in interest rates, and its orders for supplies rippled through the economy; corporate investment and other business activities picked up."

But this mechanism wasn't working any longer, said Koo:

Within this sector, banks are burdened with too many loans they cannot collect on to finance new deals . . . the whole financial community has become negative toward loans for real estate and construction, and this has seriously weakened the impact of interest-rate reductions. . . . This stimulation will not work when the balance sheets of the real estate and construction sector have deteriorated seriously. . . . The twin-engine airplane of Japanese economic management has suffered a temporary shutdown of its monetary engine, leaving just the fiscal [government spending] engine to keep it aloft.[57]

During the late 1980s the Finance Ministry, wanting to spare fiscal policy, made monetary policy do all the work of stimulating the economy. That excessive dependence on one arm of policy was a prerequisite for the creation of the speculative bubble. Then, in 1989, the Okurasho decided to start raising interest rates—not so much because it thought the economy required it but because the ministry wanted to create scope to cut rates again later to protect the "main castle"—fiscal policy.

The ministry was obliged to turn increasingly to fiscal policy, the second engine, the main castle it had sought to protect, as a source of stimulus for the sickly postbubble economy.

But now the Okurasho was discovering that the bubble had disabled monetary policy. And the effect was that the ministry was obliged to turn increasingly to fiscal policy, the second engine, the main castle it had sought to protect, as a source of stimulus for the sickly postbubble economy.

The ministry was forced not only to introduce a supplementary budget in 1992 of 2 trillion yen but to supplement it with a 10.7 trillion yen special stimulus package. The next year, the supplementary budget was 2.3 trillion yen and the special stimulus was 13.2 trillion yen. The recession deepened; the tempo of fiscal policy was obliged to quicken. In 1994 there was not only a supplementary budget of 2.1 trillion and a special stimulus package of 9.4 trillion yen, there were also tax cuts worth another 5.85 trillion yen. In 1995 there was a 2.7 trillion yen supplementary budget, another round of tax cuts, and a special stimulus package of 14.2 trillion yen plus a second supplementary budget estimated at 4.7 trillion yen. All in all, the headline value of this fiscal relaxation was 73 trillion yen ($730 billion)—the equivalent of the entire general account national budget for the year of 1994. While all of this extra money was being dispensed to try to stir a little activity and life into the recessed economy, on the other side of the ledger, tax revenues slumped.

To finance the growing gap between revenues and outlays, the government was obliged to issue more debt; the value of outstanding government bonds blew out from 166 trillion yen ($1.66 trillion) in 1990 to about 213 trillion ($2.13 trillion) in 1995. In proportion to the total economy, the national debt swelled from 38.5 percent to 43 percent of GDP in 1995.[58] What did this mean? The national debt was larger than it had been at the time the ministry started its heroic reconstruction of the budget in 1985. It was, in fact, a new record. It was an awful irony, but the ministry's indulgence of its fiscal obsession in the late 1980s had—by helping to create the bubble economy and its disastrous aftermath—contributed to the most serious deterioration in the government's fiscal position since World War II.

The ministry's indulgence of its fiscal obsession in the late 1980s had contributed to the most serious deterioration in the government's fiscal position since World War II.

The Okurasho had relied too much on monetary policy in the 1980s, and now it could not rely on it at all. It had been obsessive in protecting fiscal rectitude, and now fiscal rectitude had been compromised more seriously than at any point since the war.

■ Benefiting from the recession

The costs of these policy failures were enormous. However, the members of the Okurasho did not have to pay them. The Okurasho managed to create yet more amakudari opportunities for itself in the recession. As it was in the good years, so it was in the bad. While the bursting of the bubble economy splattered the ugly prospect of unemployment across most other sectors of the society, it actually contained something of a bonus for the men of the ministry.

The recession put a great deal of stress on the banking system. And when a Japanese bank is in trouble, one of the common consequences is that a Finance Ministry amakudari will be placed in an important position within the bank. As a consequence, there was a greater number of Okurasho men heading banks during the post-bubble recession than at any time since World War II. The influx of these retired officials into banks more than doubled from eight in the three "bubble" years to nineteen in the three years after. In 1983, the presidents at 30 of Japan's 150 private-sector banks were Okurasho amakudari. A decade later their number had swollen to thirty-six. Before the arrival of the bubble years, amakudari officials from the ministry ran one-fifth of the private-sector banks in Japan. After the bubble had burst, one-quarter of the banks in Japan's private sector were counted among the Okurasho's shadow empire. The other area of growth for amakudari at this time was the credit co-op industry, to which Mr. Takahashi's Tokyo Kyowa Credit Co-op belonged. This sector was in even more distress than the banks. The total number of notified amakudari movements from the Okurasho into financial institutions was thirty-nine in 1992 and forty in 1993, each a new record.[59]

Far from bringing the Okurasho to any moment of reckoning for its policy failure, economic recession and bank distress actually rewarded the ministry with an improved climate for well-paid, postministry employment. Economic mismanagement on a grand scale might have been professionally embarrassing for the Okurasho, but it in personal terms it was positively helpful, thanks to the amakudari system.

Economic mismanagement on a grand scale might have been professionally embarrassing for the Okurasho, but it in personal terms it was positively helpful, thanks to the amakudari system.

■ Did the amakudari system help?

Did this increased presence of amakudari do any good? In fact, how helpful had the amakudari in the banking system been *during* the inflation of the bubble? Did these Okurasho old boys use their special insights to forsee the dangers ahead? Did they warn the banks of the risks or alert the policy makers at the ministry to the disaster in the making?

Throughout the entire period of the relationship between the Long-Term Credit Bank and Harunori Takahashi and his EIE group, from courtship, through consummation, and into discord, a

Finance Ministry amakudari was employed on the bank's board in the position of auditor. The ministry's old boys had in fact occupied this position continually since 1980. A second auditor's position at the bank was likewise continually occupied by an amakudari official from the Bank of Japan.[60] Yet the LTCB had consistently and recklessly financed the most outrageous case of bubble-era profligacy known, lending Mr. Takahashi so much money that he became one of the bank's biggest customers in five years. In addition, the bank participated in dubious side deals with Mr. Takahashi's credit co-op. It is entirely clear that at least in this case the amakudari mechanism did not restrain the bank from exercising vast imprudence.

And, according to the Okurasho itself, as told by Isao Kubota, the amakudari did not provide the LTCB with intelligence on the true state of affairs in the banking sector during the expansion of the bubble.

> In general, the amakudari do not go into the operations side of their banks. Some become presidents, but they're exceptions. Generally, they remain as advisers to give advice when asked. . . . We should have had closer consultations with the marketplace. There was a room in charge of market developments set up in the banking bureau, but this bureau was the last to establish such a unit, and [it was] not very active. We should have gone out into the streets and talked to the people engaged in lending. We knew there was unusual growth in the money supply, and we should have demanded to know why.[61]

In short, at the beginning of the bubble, amakudari were presidents of 30 of Japan's 150 banks, yet they provided ministry policy makers with no notable insights into how bank lending was contributing to the accumulation of a large speculative bubble in land and stock prices.

■ Hindsight

And what of the Exxon building in New York that Mitsui Real Estate pursued with such determination during the bubble years? At the time of writing, it was still Mitsui's. But its market value was estimated at perhaps half of Mitsui's $610 million outlay, just a fraction more than Exxon had originally asked for the building.[62] And so it was with most of the investments that most of Japan's companies had made across most of the world in those years. Mr. Suzuki, recalling the Japanese life insurance officers' triumphant tour of U.S. real estate in the late 1980s, observed in 1994: "If you went on the same tour now, it would be a very quiet time."[63]

It had been clear to *Forbes* magazine as early as 1987 that the Japanese speculative bubble resembled past episodes of market irrationality around the globe. The same comparison actually appeared in a report sponsored by the Okurasho—but not until 1993, six years later. The report of a ministry-appointed panel of wise men listed the Dutch tulip craze, the Roaring Twenties boom in the United States, and the South Sea Company crisis as examples of "bubbles that took place against the backdrop of a sudden surge in economic performance . . . the same classification seems applicable to the recent asset-inflated expansion in Japan."[64]

JAPAN BECOMES THE RISK

The morning of April 26, 1995, was crisp and cool in the Hosenji Temple in northwestern Tokyo. A funeral was in progress. The gathering was to mourn the death of one of Japan's financial aristocrats, Yoshihito Amano, sixty-eight, who until his recent and terminal illness had been president of a financial institution specializing in home loans. Lending was Mr. Amano's second career, however. His first was spent in the career-stream service of the Okurasho, representing his ministry in Switzerland and the United Kingdom in a fast-moving succession of promotions that climaxed in a senior appointment in the Minister's Secretariat.

The eulogy was a memorable one. The man who delivered it, Kazuo Okajima, thought so, too: "A fine calligrapher wrote it out in formal style on a traditional scroll. It was one of the best speeches I ever gave and people acclaimed it. I was just pleased that I was able to write a good speech for my friend."[1] He shared more than friendship with Mr. Amano. Mr. Okajima, too, served in a top post in another major home-loan company, or *jusen*. And he, too, was a former elite official of the Finance Ministry, having moved through assignments in the Budget Bureau, the Economic Planning Agency, and, finally, the Minister's Secretariat.

If it seems an odd coincidence that the two should have such similar trajectories through the ranks of the ministry and then into amakudari posts in jusen then it may seem even more remarkable that the careers of both men were closely paralleled by that of yet another black-suited mourner at the Hosenji Temple that spring morning, Takashi Otsuki. He, too, had moved onto the fast track at the Finance Ministry, into the Minister's Secretariat and the Banking Bureau, before beginning a succession of four amakudari posts that led him finally to the position of president at yet another of Japan's seven top jusen. It was more than coincidence that these three shared Okurasho backgrounds and jusen leadership—six of the seven jusen have a history of appointing Finance Ministry old boys to senior positions.[2] The mourners were in grief at the death of their friend, but they grieved for more—the death of the jusen, the death of an industry. "Mr. Okajima gave a very sad speech," recalls one of the mourners. "He talked about how hard Mr. Amano had worked at the jusen to try to rescue it, but there was no hope of reconstruction." And while the doctors said the cause of death was cancer of the bladder, his friends knew otherwise: "I think that one of the reasons for his early death was that he had to tackle the jusen problem. . . . It was his heavy responsibilities and the heavy nature of the job."[3]

After lending a total of $114 billion, the jusen confronted the fact that as much as $76 billion had gone bad.

The top seven jusen, after lending a total of 11.4 trillion yen ($114 billion), were confronting the fact that an amount officially estimated at 7.6 trillion yen ($76 billion) had gone bad—two out of every three yen they had loaned.[4] The industry, technically insolvent and hopelessly indebted, was in the process of being wound up by the government in circumstances so acrimonious that they proved fatal to an entire Cabinet.[5] The recriminations were in full cry, and Mr. Okajima seemed to think that his departed friend may have been fortunate to escape: "When someone is dead, he is never criticized. The media all talked about Amano as an honest man who was about to solve the problems of his company. . . . I came to the jusen industry two years later than Amano, but the media portrays me as evil."[6]

■ Mr. Jusen

The jusen industry began with the Okurasho and ended with the Okurasho. The jusen were conceived in the 1970s as a way of improving the flow of funds for housing to ordinary Japanese. The big banks already dabbled in the field but saw the small-lot lending as too inefficient and unglamorous to conduct it with any great fervor. The jusen were designed to change that. The man who claims credit for the original concept is Keiichiro Niwayama, a career-stream Finance Ministry official who left the ministry to take up an amakudari position in the Small Business Finance Corporation. He discussed his concept with one of the biggest of the commercial banks, the Sanwa Bank, whose managers liked the idea.

Mr. Niwayama left the ministry to head the first of the jusen, Nippon Housing Loan Co., in 1971. "I started the business at the request of Sanwa Bank. All the other jusen that followed were based on my idea, too." He won the nickname Mr. Jusen. Why did a giant bank want a bureaucrat to run its new business? "My experience in the Okurasho was very helpful for many reasons. I had worked in the banking inspection division and also in the Finance Bureau, and I had a relationship with the U.S. Securities Exchange Commission. . . . I didn't ask for the Okurasho's help and they didn't give me any."[7]

This is not the way the Sanwa Bank remembers it. According to a bank executive: "There were nine mother banks involved in setting the business up, and because of the difficulty of choosing a president the banks asked the Okurasho to supply a president for the company. And it was the ministry that provided Mr. Niwayama."[8] Other banks and financiers followed suit almost immediately—within six months another three jusen had been established.

Why did the other jusen also feel obliged to install Okurasho old boys as president or chairman? Mr. Niwayama suggests that "while there were no regulatory barriers to entering the business, a lot of banks thought that there were, and that it was a condition to have an Okurasho amakudari—and maybe it was a result of indirect suggestion by the ministry." Another former ministry bureaucrat, Tomomitsu Oba, explains it this way: "At the time, many banks and life companies wanted to establish jusen and the competition was tough.

It was necessary to get the blessing of the Ministry of Finance. Therefore, the banks and life companies asked the ministry to supply the president or the chairman as a way of winning [its] blessing. And the ministry continued to send second and then third men to the jusen to replace the original ones."[9]

■ A false start

The jusen were an immediate success, but they were met by an immediate challenge. Within a year, the Okurasho and the big banks decided that the banks would increase their own direct lending for home finance—a competitive affront to the jusen. A banker recalls: "All the banks got into the home-loan market at the same time because the ministry suggested it to us as the most efficient way to advance the level of home ownership."[10] The big commercial banks supplied 29 percent of all housing loans to individuals at the time the first jusen opened its doors in 1971, but within four years they expanded their lending aggressively to account for 38 percent of the market. The jusen then had 4 percent of the market.[11] Mr. Niwayama believes that the banks' decision made his brainchild redundant:

The jusen, almost from the moment of their birth, were squeezed out of the home-loan market.

> When the banks entered, there was no competition. The banks had huge funding and ours was very limited. Originally, our customers were referred to us by the founding banks. But these customers were now becoming the banks' customers. Now, it can be said that the jusen should have shut down immediately. The banks had completely reversed their position within one year, and it was very difficult for the jusen to meet their original purpose. But we couldn't stop business after just one or two years, so we decided to switch instead to larger borrowers. And that was the real start of today's problem; it started twenty years ago. It is very regrettable that the Okurasho pushed the banks toward . . . home loans [for] individuals.[12]

So the jusen, almost from the moment of their birth, were squeezed by their founders, the banks, out of the home-loan market. The jusen's share of the market did continue to expand to a 1980 peak of 7 percent, but they were then dealt another heavy blow. The government's home-financing organ, the Housing Loan Corporation, a public-sector corporation operated by the Okurasho, pushed forcefully to expand its lending, too, and doubled its volume of outstanding home loans to individuals between 1980 and 1986. The Housing Loan Corporation's share of the market swelled from 23 percent at the time the jusen were founded to 33 percent in 1986. This figure continued to grow until hitting its 1993 peak of 37 percent.

The fledgling jusen were trapped between the giants of the private sector and the public sector. Under this twin assault, the jusen's market share fell back to 4 percent in 1986. During the years of the bubble economy, it was 3 percent or less. Their original purpose—home financing for individuals—constituted 99.5 percent of their business in 1975 and was still a high 95 percent in 1980 despite the competitive pressure of the banks. But the arrival of the Housing Loan Corporation proved decisive; by 1986 home financing accounted for 51 percent of their lending and by 1990 it was just 22 percent.[13]

■ "Financial garbage cans"

Instead of pursuing home buyers, the jusen pursued just about anyone who would agree to borrow their money. As the hyperliquidity of the bubble years worked its way through Japan's economy and saturated the system with ready finance, the jusen became increasingly desperate to find borrowers. The founding banks used their jusen to finance some of their most risky and unsavory clients, firms that the big banks would not fund directly. The jusen became what one newspaper described as "financial garbage cans."[14]

The role of the jusen was further perverted in 1990, when the Okurasho issued its administrative guidance to the finance industry to restrict its total volume of lending to the real estate sector. The instruction, otherwise comprehensive, exempted the jusen. The finance sector was therefore able to circumvent the restriction by funneling money through the jusen—and that is exactly what it did. The total value of loans to the jusen from banks and others rose from 11.7 trillion yen ($117 billion) at the time the restraint was imposed to 14 trillion yen ($140 billion) a year later, an increase of 20 percent. Virtually all of this extra money for the jusen came from the agricultural cooperatives, cashed-up associations of farmers in search of high returns.[15] So in the last moments of the bubble economy, the jusen were frantically lending money to the most speculative elements in the Japanese economy.

In the last moments of the bubble economy, the jusen were frantically lending money to the most speculative elements in the Japanese economy—for pachinko parlors and sex hotels!

Prudence was not a principle in evidence as the jusen made their lending decisions. All seven top jusen commonly made loans against collateral with a value lower than that of the loan itself. They made loans to borrowers whom they knew to be using false names. They loaned money for speculative stock buying, for *pachinko* parlors—pachinko are Japan's equivalent of slot machines—and for sex hotels. Many loans were made to companies associated with politicians. Most of the jusen loans made after the 1990 restriction were paid to the companies of criminal syndicates. At the time this final orgy of reckless lending was taking place, the position of president or chairman at five of the seven top jusen was held by a former elite officer of the Ministry of Finance. At two of the jusen, both the chairman and the president were ministry amakudari.

At the firm headed by Mr. Jusen himself, Mr. Niwayama, investigations showed that loans were approved "mostly without credit analysis."[16] And the biggest single borrower from his company was an Osaka-based real estate company, Sueno Kosan, whose spokesmen refused to comment when asked about the accuracy of widespread media reports that the company's ultimate owner was a criminal syndicate. Its total debt to the Nippon Housing Loan Co. was 89 billion yen ($890 million), of which 80 percent was declared nonperforming by mid-1995.[17] Other jusen had also loaned money to the company; its total borrowings from jusen were some 187 billion yen ($1.87 billion).[18] The company transferred ownership of its best properties so that the mortgages held against them became defunct.[19]

■ The ministry's delayed response

The Okurasho was well informed about the lending practices of the jusen, and by 1990 it was seriously concerned. It was five years later that the jusen slid into insolvency. An investigation by a team of politicians in 1995 found that surveillance of jusen management by the Finance Ministry and the Bank of Japan was "nonfunctional." Why did the ministry exempt the jusen from its lending restraints in 1990? What was the ministry doing in the five years that followed?

A senior official in the ministry's banking bureau, Sei Nakai, says that the officials responsible for supervising the jusen knew exactly how bad their management was. They also knew that since 1990 the financial sector had been using the jusen to circumvent the ministry's lending restriction. Ministry statements in the Diet as well as documents released by the ministry confirm this. They also show that the ministry took no action, but they do not explain why. Mr. Nakai offers this explanation:

> The leader of the jusen industry was Mr. Niwayama. [From the time he founded the Nippon Housing Loan Co.] he did not obey any instruction from the ministry. He was very critical of the ministry, and the directors-general of the Banking Bureau all stayed away from him. That is the reason that supervision was so loose. If we had touched any of these issues of supervision, Mr. Niwayama would come and say very harsh words to the director-general. That was the real cause of this jusen supervision. Because he would criticize the director-general in public and spread bad words [about him] to all the ministry old boys. Mr. Niwayama is very noisy and rowdy."[20]

So when in 1990 a politician from the ruling Liberal Democrats urged the then chief of the Banking Bureau to bring jusen lending in check, the official instead sought to put the onus of action onto the politicians, urging them to pass legislation to restrain the jusen.[21] The ministry, it seems, had the courage to regulate the banks, the life insurance companies, and all other species in the financial forest but was afraid to confront the jusen and its leader, a former ministry official of considerable seniority with the power, perhaps, to influence the amakudari future of the director-general himself. If Mr. Nakai's explanation is the true reason for the Okurasho's failure to confront the jusen—that a serving ministry official was so intimidated by a senior former official that he was rendered incapable of carrying out his duties—it is a very serious indictment of the amakudari system.

The first decisive attempt to solve the jusen problem came not from the regulators of the industry but from its chief owners—the banks. In May 1992, the main mother bank of Mr. Niwayama's Nippon Housing Loan Co. drew up a plan to liquidate the company's nonperforming loans. Under the plan, a liquidation company was to be created to take over all nonperforming loans, which at the time had a face value of more than 1 trillion yen ($10 billion). The liquidation company would spend some ten years to recover as much of the company's money as possible. Losses—estimated by Sanwa at the time to ultimately total 450 billion yen ($4.5 billion)— were to be borne by the founding banks. The jusen company, purged of its bad assets, would continue operating throughout the liquidation.[22]

The Sanwa Bank took the plan to the Okurasho. The ministry refused permission. A bank executive later suggested that the ministry had been trying to avoid giving the impression that the first and biggest of the jusen had been a failure because this might unsettle the public. Sanwa also proposed a more modest fallback plan, involving a restructuring of the jusen's debts, but told the ministry that this was not realistic because the company would fall into bankruptcy within two years. A broad range of banks approached the ministry with liquidation plans—including some asking for loan support from the central bank but none asking for direct budget allocations—but all were rejected.[23]

Instead, the ministry counterproposed its own plan for restructuring Nippon Housing Loan and, in 1993, obliged the banks to implement it. Under the Okurasho plan, the founding banks cut the interest rate on outstanding loans to the jusen to zero; other banks cut the rates they charged the jusen to 2.5 percent; and the agricultural financial institutions cut theirs to 4.5 percent. This became the model restructuring plan, and it was imposed on all seven major jusen.

This support was estimated to cost the banks and other jusen creditors 1.29 trillion yen ($12.9 billion) a year in forgone interest. As this scheme was designed to stay in place for a minimum of ten years, the cost of salvaging these companies was to be a minimum of 12.9 trillion yen ($129 billion).[24] But it proved exactly as Sanwa Bank had warned: restructuring was doomed, and within two years Nippon Housing Loan and all the other jusen were insolvent. All that had happened in the intervening two years was that the ministry, by delaying a solution, had increased its final cost. By mid-1995, Nippon Housing Loan's tally of irrecoverable bad loans had increased from 450 billion yen to 800 billion yen, an increase of 78 percent.[25] The total cost of disposing of the jusen problem had grown so large that the Finance Ministry decided that it would need to use public funds in the amount of at least 1.3 trillion yen ($13 billion), including a direct allocation of 685 billion yen ($6.85 billion) from the budget. The money was not for the protection of depositors—the jusen did not have any—but for the partial compensation of creditors, particularly the farmers' cooperatives, or *nokyo*.

> **The total cost of disposing of the jusen problem had grown so large that the Finance Ministry decided that it would need to use at least $13 billion of public funds.**

Why was the ministry so slow to confront reality? There are several reasons. One was the terror of public exposure and blame; if decisive action could just be postponed, the normal two-year staff progression would airlift the responsible official into his next assignment, leaving the problem for his successor. Another was the matter of bureaucratic inertia; the ministry's chief priority had long been to prevent financial institution failures. In any contest between established precedent and present need, the bureaucratic instinct is to give the advantage to precedent. In any struggle between fixed policy or new reality, every bureaucratic nerve-ending strains in favor of the existing policy. A third reason may have been fear of confronting the formidable Mr. Niwayama. A fourth was institutional and political cowardice.

The jusen owed large sums to the nokyo. The nokyo are the bricks in the structure of farmers' support for the dominant political party, the Liberal Democrats. Local nokyo leaders are big community figures. Each commands generations-old loyalties from the families in his district. He can deliver many thousands of votes on the day of the national election. Or he can deliver them to another candidate. Because of this, the nokyo command the attention and the patronage of the Liberal Democrats. This made it politically difficult for the Finance Ministry to take decisive action to wind up the jusen. Any such liquidation would have delivered losses to the nokyo. And the nokyo had instant and privileged recourse to the political system. It was far easier for the ministry to postpone decisive action. And when decisive action finally was unavoidable, it was easier for the ministry to propose that the nokyo losses be repaid from the public purse than it was to confront angry nokyo leaders and their anxious allies in the Liberal Democratic Party.

The Okurasho, through skillful manipulation of a political investigation of the jusen, succeeded in winning political endorsement for its plan to use public funds. The prime minister of the day, Ryutaro Hashimoto, pointed out that the proposal was even more intensely controversial than the government's 1989 introduction of consumption taxes. It fell to a former prime minister and Okurasho old boy, Kiichi Miyazawa, to spell out the obvious: "If the jusen mess had been properly addressed [in 1992], the bad debts would not have been so huge, and there probably would not have been any need to dip into taxpayers' money."[26] The proposal to use budget financing dominated the national discourse for months and delayed passage of the budget.

So it was deeply ironic that the Ministry of Finance should now ask the banks to accept responsibility for the jusen failure with a wave of top-level bank resignations. The Okurasho had blocked the banks' efforts to liquidate the jusen at an earlier stage in favor of its own abortive plan, yet now demanded executive resignations as the price of its new plan. The banks had proposed real responsibility—a prudent and orderly winding up of the jusen at minimum cost to the public. The Okurasho's rejection of this idea led directly to a messy, public, and protracted political argument. This, in turn, increased the costs of the jusen failure, ruptured national affairs, imposed extra burdens on the taxpayer, and raised the level of uncertainty in the financial system. After obstructing the exercise of true responsibility, the Okurasho now demanded the token responsibility of banker resignations. The bankers challenged the ministry's authority and refused to resign, a display of spirit that might have been more helpful two years earlier.[27]

After obstructing the exercise of true responsibility, the Okurasho now demanded the token responsibility of banker resignations. The bankers challenged the ministry's authority and refused to resign.

The jusen represented much that was wrong with Japan's financial system. It was a system that had developed a reliance on opaque collusion between private firms and the public regulator rather than a clear framework of objective rules. This reliance was so entrenched that the banks felt unable to open a new business or close it without ministry approval—even if no approval was needed under the law. The system dulled market signals and accountability and instead attuned firms to the wishes of the regulator and encouraged them to take shelter behind it. It was a system that through the structure of amakudari further confused the role of the public and private sectors and ultimately compromised both. And it proved incapable of change, even in the face of impending disaster. And the ministry, which had shown itself to be politically courageous when defending its institutional self-interest, proved to be a political coward in pursuit of good policy. The ministry that took pride in its rigorous defense of the public purse actually offered the public purse up to the politicians in the hope that this would deflect their anger. But while the nonperforming assets of the jusen accounted for a sixth of all such assets in Japan's troubled banking system of the mid-1990s, it was not *the* banking system. It was only an outgrowth of the system and did not enjoy the implicit Okurasho guarantee possessed by banks and credit co-ops. By itself, the jusen might have been set aside as an exceptional industry without any particular lessons for the banking system as a whole.

■ The beginning of the end for the ministry's banking policy

It took that embodiment of bubble-era values, Harunori Takahashi and his EIE International, to actually convince the Okurasho that its entire banking policy was unsustainable. After the Long-Term Credit Bank had overrun EIE's office and failed in its attempt to salvage its finances, it despaired of ever resuscitating the company. The bank complained that Mr. Takahashi had been completely un-cooperative. The LTCB then did something it had never done be-fore, indeed something that had been done by only one other estab-lishment bank in Japan's postoccupation history: it walked away from one of its biggest clients. In July 1993, the Long-Term Credit Bank announced its withdrawal of all support for EIE. It disclosed 190 billion yen ($1.9 billion) in exposure to the company, making loan loss provisions for just under half this amount and declaring a plan to recover the rest through the sale of collateral.[28]

This threatened to put a serious crimp in Mr. Takahashi's style. But reality did not come crashing down on him. Mysteriously, in-stead of courtrooms and penury there were golf courses and luxury. "His life is still elegant and beautiful," marvelled *Aera* magazine. "His golf scores have actually improved since the banks first tried to take control of EIE, and his complexion is better."[29] His personal assets remained intact and his liberty was unthreatened. The EIE office on a Ginza backstreet remained open. Its staff complement of fifty was inexplicably undiminished despite the company's miserable cashflow, vast unserviceable debts, and the well-publicized bankers' walkout. What was going on? Where was the money coming from? Years later, EIE's managing director, Hidetoshi Oshima, said there was no mystery to it: "After the banks withdrew support, the only place Takahashi could turn for funds was the credit unions."[30]

Mr. Takahashi not only had direct control of the Tokyo Kyowa Credit Cooperative, he also had considerable influence over the Anzen Credit Cooperative through his friendship with its proprietor, who appointed Mr. Takahashi a director. Mr. Takahashi busily authorized loans to himself and his other companies far beyond the restraints of prudence and the limits of the law. By the end of 1994, Tokyo Kyowa had loaned 37.6 billion yen ($376 million) to Mr. Takahashi and his interests—40 percent of all the institution's outstanding loans. Anzen (which translates as "safety") extended another 28.9 billion yen ($289 million), one-third of its total loan book. This was common at the time. Forty percent of Japan's credit co-ops were run by executives who simultaneously operated other businesses, creating similar conflicts of interest. The ministry outlawed this practice after the crisis had passed. Thirty-nine percent of all credit co-ops had loaned illegally large concentrations of money to a single client. This was not a failure of regulation but of supervision.[31]

> **Tokyo Kyowa had loaned $376 million to Mr. Takahashi and his interests— 40 percent of all the institution's outstanding loans. Thirty-nine percent of all credit co-ops had loaned illegally large concentrations of money to a single client.**

But what about the Long-Term Credit Bank, which, as we have seen, had put up half of Tokyo Kyowa's capital and also put sizable sums on deposit? Now that it had withdrawn its support for Mr. Takahashi and EIE, what did it do with its investments in his credit co-op? The answer is that it did nothing, leaving the money in place. An LTCB executive said that the reason for this decision was that the regulatory authority with frontline responsibility for the co-op, the Tokyo Metropolitan Government, had asked the bank to leave its money in place to prevent the collapse of the institution. Mr. Takahashi's outspoken officer, Dr. Ishizaki, had a different explanation:

> Anybody who believes that the LTCB really just walked away from Takahashi is pretty naive. The LTCB has been saying, "We have nothing to do with EIE," but they've been propping them up through the back door. They walked out through the front door, but then they supported Takahashi through the back door. That's why there wasn't a single complaint from the Ministry of Finance, the Bank of Japan, or

EIE's other bankers. . . . That's why nobody was fired, why the bills kept getting paid. There was a secret agreement, and the focal point of it was the Tokyo Kyowa Credit union—the LTCB supported Takahashi through the credit union."[32]

Dr. Ishizaki's claim seems to be supported by an interesting detail of Tokyo Kyowa's accounts. The amount of money that the LTCB had on deposit with Tokyo Kyowa—a peak of 37.6 billion yen—matched almost exactly the sum the credit co-op had on loan to Mr. Takahashi—37.5 billion yen.

Even so, this support was not enough. The collapse of the two co-ops was only a question of time. The Ministry of Finance and the Bank of Japan saw the inevitability of the event. And it was at this point that the Okurasho finally realized that its entire banking policy was no longer realistic.

■ The end nears

Until this point in 1994, the Okurasho's approach to the banking system had not changed since World War II. It operated the system as a government-supervised cartel in a formation known as *gososendan*, the escorted convoy system.[32] Prices—in the form of interest rates—were closely controlled by the ministry in unofficial but binding consultation with the banks. Even after the banks were legally granted full freedom to decide their own interest rates, they continued to set them in concert at agreed levels.[34] The banks also worked intimately with the ministry in deciding the level of services they offered customers and even the salaries they paid their staff. This kept the convoy of banks big and small in close formation, traveling at the same speed regardless of size and true horsepower. In exchange for sacrificing some competitive freedom, the banks gained the protection of the Okurasho, gunships which barred new entrants to the system. The ministry also extended an unqualified guarantee against failure, promising implicitly to use its full armada of powers to keep all banks afloat. The cartel structure suppressed competition based on price and service, leaving volume as the only available channel for competition.

This system seemed to work well under conditions of rapid economic growth, but consider the consequences in a slow-growing economy; the banks wanted to lend as much money as possible but had complete impunity from the ultimate consequences of poor lending decisions—that is, failure. The bubble economy accentuated the competition based on volume, regardless of risk. The bursting of the bubble, and the economic stagnation that followed, denied the banks the regenerative powers of a high-growth economy. The problems of the system were abruptly made obvious. And the ministry was not prepared.

Several times postwar—most recently in 1977—the ministry had sought a rationalization of banks, concerned that Japan was "overbanked." But it was frustrated by resistance from the banks in league with sympathetic politicians.[35] And the Okurasho certainly never sought a reorganization through bank failures. Indeed, that was the very outcome the ministry consistently sought to avoid. The Banking Bureau's deputy director-general, Sei Nakai, said, "Previous directors-general of the Banking Bureau thought that their most important task was to prevent bank failures. We made our public believe in the safety of their deposits. But at some time we should have changed that perception gradually. We should have allowed failures and shown how risk operates. This shows we are not so smart."[36]

Rather than shaping the development of the banking system, the ministry now found itself responding to forces already in place—and doing so in great haste. The first public evidence of any official rethinking appeared in late 1994, when the governor of the Bank of Japan, Yasushi Mieno, said that it might be necessary and even desirable for some financial institutions to be permitted to fail.[37] This created a sensation among the monetary cognoscenti. And although the Okurasho said nothing publicly, it was around this same time that it decided to rewrite its banking policy. Mr. Nakai explains: "We decided to change our policy because of the case of the two [Takahashi-affiliated] credit unions and a changeover of director-general [of the Banking Bureau]. The problem became too big to sustain, and we recognized the need to dispose of some financial institutions. We started the policy with the two credit unions. We started quietly preparing a clean-up scheme."[38]

The Okurasho and the Bank of Japan announced in December 1994 that to preserve order in the financial system, the authorities were establishing a new government bank charged specifically with taking over the business of the two Takahashi-affiliated credit co-ops. The co-ops were no longer viable and would be wound up. The system of deposit insurance would have automatically refunded all deposits up to the value of 10 million yen ($100,000), but the establishment of the new bank would ensure that all depositors were repaid in full. This was an event without precedent in postwar Japan. It meant that the Okurasho was withdrawing its implicit guarantee of all financial institutions regardless of circumstances. For the first time, institutions and their managers would confront the full consequences of their mistakes. But depositors were to be protected in full; the government had created a new bank to take over the liabilities of the failing bodies. The two failing institutions were pronounced insolvent with 110 billion yen ($1.1 billion) in nonperforming loans, more than half their total loan portfolio. Each and every yen of their loans to Mr. Takahashi and his interests was classified as bad or doubtful, accounting for 60 percent of the total.

The Okurasho withdrew its implicit guarantee of all financial institutions—an event without precedent in postwar Japan.

Under the ministry's plan, much of the 150 billion yen in capital required for the new rescue bank—named the Tokyo Kyodo Bank—was to come from the Long-Term Credit Bank and other private-sector institutions. But it was also to be subsidized with 50 billion yen ($500 million) in public monies from the Tokyo Metropolitan Government and the Bank of Japan. Nobody mourned the loss of the two credit co-ops, but the announcement of taxpayer subsidies of depositors unleashed national outrage.

■ Reality descends

Mr. Takahashi, until this moment unknown to the Japanese public, instantly became a nationwide figure of contempt and ridicule. The media and the opposition demanded to know why the taxpayers should be required to pay for Mr. Takahashi's carelessness and bad management. It was at this point that the full weight of reality descended upon Mr. Takahashi. As soon as the new bailout bank opened for business, its management brought charges against him for criminal breach of trust. He conceded that his tenure as proprietor and executive director had not been a total success: "I am a businessman, and I am not so good at managing financial institutions."[39]

The outrage preoccupied the government. Both the finance minister and prime minister were targeted by the opposition. As more information was uncovered, the government sank deeper into a state of discomfiture. The questions mounted. Who was responsible for the decision to charge tax payers, and why had it been made? Why was the system of deposit insurance not enough? Why was the government protecting large-lot depositors above and beyond its legal obligations? Who were these rich depositors? The socialist prime minister, Mr. Murayama, was embarrassed at the disclosure that one of his closest sources of political support, the All Japan Prefectural and Municipal Workers' Union, called *jichiro*, was a major depositor. The Liberal Democrats squirmed at the revelation that one of their members, a former Cabinet minister, had received some 37 billion yen ($370 million) in loans from one of Mr. Takahashi's companies.[40] Another Liberal Democrat was revealed to have been living in an apartment owned by Mr. Takahashi.[41]

The Long-Term Credit Bank was not spared either. Mr. Takahashi managed to do the bank considerable damage when he was called before the Lower House Budget Committee of the Diet to give testimony that was broadcast live around the nation: "I was unhappy when I heard that there was to be a publicly funded rescue. The credit union had LTCB staff and LTCB money, so naturally I assumed that if worst came to worst, we would be bailed out by the LTCB." He implied that the bank had used the credit union as a clandestine means of bestowing favors on politicians. For example, he said that the Tokyo Kyowa credit co-op had made a large loan to a golf club associated with a former finance minister because the LTCB had requested it. After a public grilling by legislators, the LTCB's president resigned in an act of contrition.[42]

But some of the harshest criticism was reserved for the Okurasho. How long had it known that the credit co-ops were in trouble? Why did it not act earlier? When it did finally act, why did it see fit to use taxpayers' money? It eventuated that the Tokyo city government had known for a long time. "It knew about the situation since 1989 and kept quiet," said EIE's managing director in 1995. "For six years, the patrol car knew the speed limit was being exceeded."[43]

When the LTCB abandoned EIE in July 1993, the city regulators asked the Okurasho to assist in a joint audit of the two co-ops, and it obliged. City officials acknowledged that it was already clear that their finances were out of control at the time of the first joint audit, a year and a half before their eventual demise. Neither the city nor the Okurasho took any action.[44] A Finance Ministry official conceded in Diet testimony that the ministry had been too optimistic: "We were aware of the worsening financial situations of the two credit unions, but we didn't think the situation would worsen to the extent that the metropolitan government could no longer control [the problem]."[45]

"**Probably no-one outside [the Okurasho and the Bank of Japan] feels that rescuing these two cesspools of swindle and financial skulduggery is even desirable, much less 'necessary and essential.' . . . The whole thing has the distinct fragrance of a massive cover-up operation.**"

The Finance Ministry and its plan were attacked for being arrogant and presumptuous, conceived in secret, and imposed by fiat, for using tax money to pay for ministry incompetence. Its case—that the stability and soundness of the national financial system were at stake—was dismissed in terms such as these: "Probably no-one outside [the Okurasho and the Bank of Japan] feels that rescuing these two cesspools of swindle and financial skulduggery is even desirable, much less 'necessary and essential.' . . . The whole thing has the distinct fragrance of a massive cover-up operation."[46] Some of the most senior figures in the government joined the chorus of condemnation, including Ryutaro Hashimoto, then minister for International Trade and Industry, formerly finance minister, later prime minister.[47] The opposition powerbroker—and the man who had once vacationed in a Takahashi resort—Ichiro Ozawa, threatened to bring a motion of no confidence against the minister of finance. Mr. Ozawa correctly identified the policy implication of the case: "The Okurasho's theory that this is just a once-off case, an exception, is not convincing to the people. It is a larger question of crisis management of the financial system."[48] Just as significant for the Okurasho was the fact that these politicians had been regarded as two of the ministry's most important political allies. The final blow to the authority of the ministry came from the Tokyo Metropolitan Assembly, which voted to block any contribution to the Okurasho scheme.[49] From the national level to the local, the ministry was defied and its competence questioned.

■ A lack of courage

The Finance Ministry had taken the first step in introducing the Darwinian principle of the survival of the fittest to Japan's postwar banking marketplace. It was not criticized for this. Instead, it was criticized for failing to extend that principle more widely. The focus of attack was that the depositors in the two co-ops were not being asked to share any of the risk but instead were to receive the full protection of the State at the taxpayers' expense. The ministry had thought it was taking a very radical step; the public thought it was not acting radically enough. Once again, it seemed, the ministry was doing too little too late.

The Banking Bureau's Mr. Nakai reflects on the episode:

> This scheme got a lot of criticism. The public's opinion was that the Okurasho should have tackled the problem much earlier and the cost would have been lower. That's true. The Okurasho didn't have the courage. In the view of ministry director-generals, the greatest virtue of the director-general was to prevent failures and to stop turmoil. Simply, they didn't have enough courage [to change policy earlier to tackle the problem]. That's why they resorted to saying that the land-price decline would stop."[50]

Wishful thinking supplanted policy action and persisted until a crisis coincided with the appointment of a new director-general.

The change of policy, some five years after the bursting of the bubble economy, had come far too late. The former governor of the central bank, Satoshi Sumita, suggested that the Okurasho should have foreseen the need to revise its bank policy in 1991—when it lifted its controls on lending to the real estate industry—to prepare for the looming problem of bad loans.[51] The ministry's policy inertia repeatedly turned big problems into still bigger problems. Land prices continued falling, bankruptcies continued apace, the stock market continued to stagnate, the banking system continued to amass more bad loans, and it was quite clear in the marketplace that failures lay ahead. The financial system was alive with intelligence and rumors of banks in distress through 1993 and 1994; after the collapse of the Takahashi credit unions, this kind of talk intensified. The contrast between a stricken industry and its apparently implacable supervisor increased the level of uncertainty. It was clear that the industry was in trouble, but it was completely unclear what the Finance Ministry intended to do about it.

But the market did know that the problem weighed heavily on the ministry's mind. For instance, it was during this time that an analyst at a major Japanese research institute issued a study comparing the ways various countries had handled their own banking crises. Soon afterward, he found a senior official of the Banking Bureau on the phone with a question about his research. The economist, gratified that his work was being scrutinized by senior policy makers, said he would be happy to help. The question was this: "What excuses did officials in these other countries use to explain themselves to the public?" The economist hung up the phone in a state of depression.[52]

> The Okurasho's change of policy, some five years after the bursting of the bubble economy, had come far too late.

By mid-1995, the Okurasho had put Japan's banks into a bizarre kind of paradox; they dominated the ranking of the world's biggest banks, they were based in the world's major creditor nation, yet they were being charged a risk premium when they sought to borrow money on the international market. It was called the Japan premium, but it might more aptly have been dubbed the Okurasho premium. The Finance Ministry's implicit guarantee of the banks had effectively un- derwritten them and allowed them access to cheaper money on world markets. Now that it was clear that the old policy was finished, and with no new policy to take its place, the world bank- ing market raised the cost of money accordingly.

The U.S.-based credit rating agency Moody's Investors Services downgraded three of Japan's major twenty-one city banks to a notch above the status of junk bonds.

The implications of a change in policy were enormous: "If you took away the Government guar- antee of the banks, a quarter of the Japanese financial system would disappear," remarked the bank analyst at Jardine Fleming Securities in Tokyo, David Snoddy.[53] He elaborated: "By normal international standards, there aren't many good banks in Japan. Net interest mar- gins, a common measure of bank profitability, averaged just 111 basis points [1.11 percentage points] in fiscal year 1994 for the eleven money center or "city" banks. In the same period, to cite just one example, Chemical Bank of the United States clocked in rather better at 361 basis points. Nor are the Japanese banks well capital- ized. . . . Given the relative weakness of the Japanese banks, it is an inescapable fact that most nonJapanese institutions deal with dozens of banks here in Japan that they wouldn't touch in their home markets, simply because they assume that the [Ministry of Finance] is, ultimately, standing behind the Japanese counterparty."[54]

The U.S.-based credit rating agency Moody's Investors Services downgraded three of the major twenty-one city banks to a notch above the status of junk bonds—in other words, verging on being unsuitable for investment. The banks were Nippon Credit Bank, Chuo Trust Bank, and Hokkaido Takushoku Bank. Moody's ex- plained its change of thinking:

Our rating action reflects the three banks' weakening fundamentals and growing uncertainty regarding the Japanese authorities' ability to pro- vide safeguards for overall stability in the banking system. Given the continuing deflation of asset values in Japan, Japan's forbearance policy may eventually need to be replaced by more aggressive resolution methods involving larger losses . . . than currently envisioned by the banks and the authorities.[55]

■ A new policy

After the liquidation of the two Takahashi credit co-ops, the ministry picked its way gingerly forward in its new and belated embrace of reality—the reality that some failed institutions must be allowed to die. But it would allow this change only under two conditions: first, that depositors remain protected; second, that the death of the institution not pose any risk to the financial system as a whole. To meet these conditions, the ministry knew that ultimately it would need more taxpayers' money. Introducing a change of policy in the midst of a crisis was bound to be much more expensive than changing the policy to prevent one.

First, it decided to raise the level of alarm. During a Diet session in June 1995, the director-general of the Banking Bureau, Yoshimasa Nishimura, revealed that the true dimensions of the problem were much greater than the ministry had so far admitted. Until now, the official figure for nonperforming assets at the twenty-one major banks had been the figure that the banks were required to disclose in their accounts; it stood at 12.5 trillion yen ($125 billion) in March 1995, or 3.3 percent of their total loans. The ministry now told the Diet that its estimate of the true level of such problem loans was 22.5 trillion yen ($225 billion)—80 percent higher than the official figure.

The reason for the difference was the roughly 10 trillion yen ($100 billion) in loans that had been restructured because borrowers had fallen into difficulty but that had not met the narrow definition of problem loans used in Japanese accounting standards.[56] And for the banking system as a whole, including all 150 banks (the small regional banks, too), the ministry estimated the total value of problem loans to be 40 trillion yen ($400 billion). This put the problem loans at the equivalent of 5.8 percent of all outstanding loans by private-sector banks, similar to the 5.6 percent ratio in the United

States at the peak of the U.S. savings and loan crisis in 1991.[57] And it was widely known that the U.S. authorities had been obliged to use taxpayers' funds to solve that problem. Mr. Nishimura later agreed that his motivation was tactical; he had wanted to send a message that the problem required "serious consideration."[58] The ministry estimated that about half of this total would ultimately prove to be irrecoverable.

However, the banking cognoscenti also knew that the figure of 40 trillion yen was tactical rather than truthful. Informed estimates of the real size of problem loans started at around 60 trillion yen ($600 billion), as estimated by U.S. rating agency Standard and Poors and analysts at Nomura Research Institute. In the view of a U.S. bank research company, Veribanc, they finished at levels as high as 140 trillion yen ($1.4 trillion). Whatever the precise figure, the market agreed on two points: (1) that the Okurasho was still underestimating the problem, and (2) that it was a very, very big problem, "potentially the largest non-performing loan problem in global history," according to the head of research at SBC Warburg Securities in Tokyo, Mark Faulkner.[60] The market was not confident that the Okurasho knew what the real scale of the problem was. "Banks have two sets of bad-loan numbers, the ones for external use and the ones strictly for internal use," said Takashi Ishizawa, chief researcher at the Long-Term Credit Bank's research institute. "What the Ministry of Finance gets are the external numbers."[61]

Once the ministry had sent its message, it announced its plan for cleaning up the problem loans in the banking system.[62] The plan was vague, and the stock market was disappointed, but Mr. Nishimura saw it as an important moment: "For some, it may seem like we're just crossing a small river with this report, but I felt like Caesar crossing the Rubicon."[63] Thus the ministry, in the later half of 1995, prepared to allow a bank to go out of business for the first time in its postwar history.

■ A bank collapses

The case of the Hyogo Bank, the biggest regional bank in Japan, epitomizes the effects of the Okurasho's temporizing—euphemistically known as a policy of forbearance—on the ultimate costs of the banking crisis. The bank was based in the prefecture of Hyogo, headquartered in the port city of Kobe. By 1995 it had declared assets of 3.6 trillion yen ($36 billion) and had been in business for fifty-one years. Its major stockholders thought it had been in business too long.

The ministry prepared to allow a bank to go out of business for the first time in its postwar history.

The biggest of these were the Sumitomo Bank, the Long-Term Credit Bank, and the Industrial Bank of Japan. On behalf of the other stockholders, in 1992 Sumitomo asked the Okurasho for permission to liquidate the regional bank in an orderly manner. The stockholders had decided that the Hyogo Bank was beyond redemption, and they were not prepared to commit any more time or money to prolonging its life.

The ministry said no. This was consistent with its policy at the time of allowing no bank to fail. The Okurasho argued that in its assessment, Hyogo Bank had unrecoverable bad debts of 230 billion yen ($2.3 billion) and that these could be charged off the balance sheet by using the bank's own profits over the next ten years. The shareholders disagreed. They estimated the true level of unrecoverable bad debts to be 700 billion to 800 billion yen, ($7 billion to $8 billion). The bank was terminally ill. Ministry officials told the Sumitomo Bank that it should consider absorbing Hyogo Bank, as this had long been a standard fallback in earlier rescues. But while Sumitomo was prepared to close the smaller bank down and write off the value of its 4.99 percent stockholding, it was not prepared to throw more good money after bad by absorbing the entire structure. The ministry was adamant that Hyogo be kept afloat, however, and instructed stockholders to continue supporting the regional bank and thereby preserve confidence in the national financial system.

And, in the ultimate test of the credibility of its own policy, the ministry sent one of the authors of that policy to preside over the Hyogo Bank's rehabilitation. A former director-general of the

Banking Bureau was appointed president of the bank. It was a tremendous investment of ministry prestige in the policy—and in the bank. After two years, the bank's condition had only worsened, and then an act of God interposed in the form of the Kobe earthquake in January 1995. This contributed to the bank's stock of bad loans, but still the ministry persisted in its pretense at rehabilitation. Finally, the quickening pace of withdrawals in the last days of August made it clear that a run was imminent, and on August 30, 1995, the regulators announced the liquidation of Hyogo Bank, with estimated unrecoverable bad debts of 790 billion yen ($7.9 billion). The bank's total capital amounted to only one-fifth of this sum.[64]

In a strict sense, the bank did not fail; its obligations were to be assumed by a new bank to be established by the authorities using capital contributed by thirty major banks and other businesses based in Kobe. Who was to run the new bank? The president was recruited from the private sector, but the Finance Ministry reserved a position as managing director for its amakudari. Even the liquidation of a bank could not extinguish the ministry's claim to an amakudari post. Instead, it was transferred to the new entity.[65]

The Hyogo Bank's liquidation marked the first postwar collapse of a Japanese bank. This made it very clear that the Okurasho could not resuscitate a dying bank and that its powers to coerce healthy banks to absorb sick ones were limited. There was a market, and market forces did operate, even if the Finance Ministry did not believe in them. It had required a major earthquake to subdue him, but even a former director-general of the ministry's Banking Bureau had proved to be, ultimately, mortal. By delaying the bank's demise, the ministry had increased the cost and consequences of the event. The old policy of forbearance—supporting sick banks until economic growth and a reorganization restored them to health—had worked in a fast-growing economy. But Japan was now in a prolonged recession. The global banking community saw in the case of the Hyogo Bank the confirmation that the old policy was finished, but it was still unclear exactly what the new policy might be. The Japan premium rose sharply.

■ Chest-high in cash, low on credit

In early August 1995, a run on the troubled Cosmo Credit Coop-erative, the largest in Tokyo, had forced it into failure. A few weeks later, on the same day the liquidation of Hyogo Bank was an-nounced, a run on another credit union, the Osaka-based Kizu Credit Cooperative, obliged the authorities to take control of it as well. The national TV news was dominated by footage of lines of depositors, queuing for blocks, sleeping overnight in the streets, trying to recover their savings at the front door of credit co-ops while armored vans stuffed with cash from the central bank hur-riedly unloaded small mountains of plastic-wrapped yen at the back door. Sums of 40 billion to 60 billion yen ($400 million to $600 million) were being withdrawn in cash from individual institutions in a single day. The TV news showed chest-high stacks of cash lining the walls of credit co-op branches, clerks handing out great bundles of 10,000-yen notes as quickly as they could rip them open. Occasionally, managers would climb atop the counter to appeal for calm. Branches stayed open until late in the evening handing out money. Their staffs, in small delegations, emerged onto the streets with bullhorns to apologize to waiting customers and then got down on hands and knees to bow in abject contrition. The TV cameras loved it; the anxious customers, stoney-faced, did not. Mr. Nishimura had wanted to point out that the banking problem re-quired serious consideration. The point was now well established in the national psyche.

Sums of $400 million to $600 million were being withdrawn in cash from individual institu-tions each day.

Hysteria, however, was avoided. There were no scenes of chaos at the Hyogo Bank—depositors seemed quite satisfied by the authori-ties' assurances that their money was safe even though the bank itself was to be liquidated. The finance minister, Masayoshi Take-mura, seeking to reassure the nation, declared that the demise of the Kizo Co-op and the Hyogo Bank marked the end of the process: "This will put an end to a chain of announcements of liquidation programs. Such case-by-case solutions have reached a climax. We have overcome the difficulty and can head toward the stabilization of the financial system."[66]

By the time he made this statement, the known failures were officially estimated to require about 900 billion yen ($9 billion) from the Deposit Insurance Corporation to refund depositors who would otherwise lose their savings. This meant that the system was exhausted—at its March 31 balance date it had total available reserves of 876 billion yen—so the central bank quickly announced that emergency loans of up to another 500 billion yen would be available to the deposit system, if required. The Finance Ministry took steps to reassure overseas bankers and regulators, repeatedly telling them that no bank with international obligations would be allowed to fail. The Bank of Japan made well-publicized assurances that it would supply liquidity to the overseas operations of any Japanese banks that stood in need of foreign currency.[67] Within Japan, bank depositors generally remained calm and accepted the reassurances of their government. There were, however, indications of nervousness at the margins of the system. A popular magazine, the *Shukan Shincho*, ran a story in October 1995 listing the potential collapse of three major banks, seven regional banks, and two more credit co-ops by the end of the year. Depositors increasingly moved their holdings into cash and highly liquid deposits, and there was rumored to be an increase in the popularity of safes. At least three mass-market guides on how to understand bank risk and disclosure were in print by early 1996.[68]

But outside Japan, the nervousness was not at the margins but at the center. The international credit-rating agency Moody's Investor Services downgraded the standing of the banks in the world's major creditor economy to the same average as that of the banks in the Third World communist dictatorship of China. Both countries' banks won an average rating of D.[69] The Japan premium, which began midyear as a market penalty on Japanese banks of 7 to 8 basis points, or 0.07 to 0.08 percentage points, had risen tenfold by the end of the year. This was estimated to eat into the profits of the six major commercial banks by 6 billion to 9 billion yen each ($60 million to $90 million), or the equivalent of about 2 percent of their core business profits for the year.[70]

Fearing the prospect of failure, major banks around the world conducted careful assessments of their exposure to the new Japanese risk. Some gave credence to the Okurasho's pledge that no bank would be allowed to fail; others doubted the ministry had the power to enforce this guarantee and cut back their dealings with Japanese counterparts. In the U.S. Congress, the House Committee on Banking and Financial Services convened hearings on the Japanese banking crisis. The International Monetary Fund's annual report on international capital markets in August 1995 challenged the policy of forbearance: "The weakness of the financial system, burdened by nonperforming loans, may become a drag on the economy . . . the losses may not be recovered with forbearance, but may snowball instead." The London-based magazine *The Economist* ran an editorial titled "Something Nasty in the Woodshed" and subtitled "The Markets Are Having Nightmares about Japan's Financial System."[71]

The Japanese banking problem had the potential to disrupt world markets and economies.

One such nightmare was spelled out by the chief economist at the Deutsche Bank in Tokyo, Ken Courtis. He started by pointing out the near-universal analysis underlying global nervousness about Japan—that the entire Japanese banking system was technically bankrupt, with estimated unrecoverable bad debts of 50 trillion to 55 trillion yen ($500 billion to $550 billion) against collective equity of only 42 trillion yen ($420 billion). This meant that even if the Ministry of Finance was able to keep all the banks afloat, the banks might still be forced into taking extreme measures to deal with their bad debts. He explained how this might spill over into world markets. Japan had supplied 60 percent of all net global capital exports in the year to April 1995, pumping money chiefly into the big debtor economies of the North American Free Trade Area—the United States, Canada, and Mexico. The banking crisis now threatened to break this happy cycle, as Mr. Courtis, speaking for the Deutsche Bank, explained: "We think that as the crisis deepens, the Japanese banks will be trapped into liquidating their U.S. bond portfolio," valued at some $200 billion, or 20 trillion yen. The resulting fear was that interest rates in the United States and all markets worldwide would go "haywire."[72]

In short, the Japanese banking problem had the potential to disrupt world markets and economies even if there were no more actual bank failures. The U.S. Federal Reserve, appreciating the gravity of the risks, struck an agreement to provide Japanese banks operating in the United States with liquidity, if necessary. This was, in effect, putting up a liquidity buffer to protect U.S. markets from any possible shock.[73] It was both a sensible precaution and a demonstration of the very precarious position of Japan's banking system.

■ Propping up the property market

Property values fell so precipitously that by mid-1995 there was more debt owed on land in Japan than the land itself was worth, according to an analyst at the Swiss-owned brokerage firm UBS Securities. In other words, the specter of negative equity was upon Japan, and UBS estimated the shortfall to be about 80 trillion yen ($800 billion). In the country that had boasted so many land millionaires five years earlier, at least 15 percent of all home owners now had negative equity in their properties. This continuing evaporation of value was the fundamental reason for the bad-debt problem of the banks, and the Okurasho tried to counter it at the same time that it attempted crisis management of the banking system.

Property values fell so precipitously that by mid-1995 there was more debt owed on land in Japan than the land itself was worth.

By mid-1995 the official figures showed that commercial property prices had halved since their peak in 1991. This was serious enough. But court-supervised auctions of property seized in bankruptcy proceedings showed that commercial property prices had actually fallen much further. The Tokyo District Court presided over some 4,000 auction sales of repossessed real estate in 1994, property with outstanding mortgages of 2.36 trillion yen ($23.6 billion). The court's minimum sale price was an aggregate of just 530 billion yen, suggesting that the lenders were prepared to accept a return of just 22 percent of the money they had loaned for the properties and to write off the other 78 percent.[74]

This is an important point. The ministry's estimate of the scale of the banking problem was based on the assumption that 40 percent of the face value of the problem loans would be recovered from sale of the collateral securing those loans. The court auction statistics suggested that this was wildly optimistic.

The Finance Ministry decided on two main measures to try to support the property market. Both were, typically, dirigiste. As the banking problem approached crisis proportions, the ministry started pumping taxpayers' funds directly into the land market. It had already allocated money to the property market indirectly through spending on public works. Some 20 percent of all public works spending went toward buying land. In 1994 the Finance Ministry also started to make special additional allocations through its emergency economic stimulus packages—2.8 trillion yen in 1994 and another 3.23 trillion yen in 1995.[75] There was no evidence that this had any significant impact on prices, which continued to fall.

The ministry also discouraged companies from making property deals in which sale prices seemed to be too low, arguing that such transactions might prove disheartening to the market. This stance was, of course, designed to help support the market and to protect the banks. It did not; it merely encouraged companies to circumvent the restriction or to give up the idea of buying property. In some cases, property transactions went ahead at prices roughly in line with the official price statistics. But the disclosed part of the deal would be only one element; the buyer and seller traded other assets elsewhere, which had the effect of reducing the true sale price to much lower levels. In general, the ministry tried to discourage companies from disclosing any price information on deals involving prime real estate.[76]

As we saw in the case of the stock market, too, the more that property prices fell, the more the ministry interfered with the market, driving it away from true market forces. The denial of accurate information made the market more opaque, and interference with transactions made deals more difficult. Prices, both official and real, continued to fall.

But one of the greatest problems was not just that prices were severely depressed but that it was often difficult to sell commercial or industrial land at all. As the Long-Term Credit Bank's Mr. Ishizawa said: "We are not able to sell our collateral anyway, so we just write it off at somewhere close to the official land price levels." The parking-meter index told the story of the market's immobility. Banks across Tokyo turned repossessed land into parking lots while they settled down for a long wait for buyers, and sales of parking meters at Nippon Signal Co. rose fivefold from their 1991 levels to 500 a month by mid-1995, mainly on sales to banks.[77] Much of the land the banks did sell was sold through artificial schemes designed to conceal problem loans or to crystallize limited losses to create tax deductions.[78]

Banks across Tokyo turned repossessed land into parking lots while they settled down for a long wait for buyers, and sales of parking meters at Nippon Signal Co. rose fivefold— mainly on sales to banks.

The man responsible for Japan's biggest program of land sales, Shoichi Takata of the JR Settlement Corporation—the company charged with the ongoing retrenching of the debts of the old national railways—represented the consensus among economists and industrialists when he suggested that two things were necessary for the reliquification of Japan's frozen property market. First, the government needed to remove regulatory interference and taxes from land transactions. Second: "The main point for the government is to stimulate the economy itself."[79]

■ Taking profits

The banks, unable to rely on sales of collateral, came to depend on three other sources of income. First, they sold large volumes of their stock portfolios, taking their "hidden profits" and using them to write off bad loans. Most of their stocks had been bought long ago at very low prices, so there was a fat profit to be made on selling them. In the year to March 1994, for example, the major twenty-one banks harvested 2.42 trillion yen ($24.2 billion) in profits in this way, and these profits accounted for 63 percent of all the problem-loan write-offs by the banks in that year. In the year after, banks took an extraordinary 4.09 trillion yen ($40.9 billion) in stock profits, and this supplied three-quarters of the resources for problem-loan write-offs for the year.[80]

The problem was that they immediately bought virtually all of these stocks back again. And because they bought them back, naturally, at current prices, they were tying up precious capital in stocks.[81] So they were replacing low-yielding bad loans on their balance sheets with low-yielding stocks. Rather than employing these assets in profitable new lending, the banks locked the money away in long-term stock investments with dividend yields of less than 1 percent. The result was unfortunate and ironic. According to Salomon Brothers' bank analyst Alicia Ogawa, although the banks had the satisfaction of cutting back their bad-loan burdens, they tied up so much money in stock investment that the twenty-one major banks actually increased the proportion of capital tied up in assets producing little or no return. In March 1993, 5.5 percent of the banks' capital was dedicated to supporting low-yielding assets. Two years later, despite writing off 9.3 trillion yen ($93 billion) in problem loans, the proportion of capital tied up in low-return assets had risen to 7.9 percent.

According to a report from Salomon Brothers Tokyo, "these unrealized gains on securities are turning out to be a source of new balance sheet problems as many banks succumb to the temptation to sacrifice future profitability for sake of cosmetic improvement in bad debt numbers. . . . Because the funding cost is higher than the yield on these assets, most of the banks' stock portfolios should be regarded in the same category as nonperforming assets."[82] Why did the bankers buy the stocks back? Partly to preserve their relationships with the companies that issued the stock—that is, they wanted to remain stockholders in client companies—and partly because they were under ministry pressure not to undermine the stock market by acting as net sellers.[83] Overall, the effect of the banks as stock investors in the marketplace was absolutely neutral; in March 1990 the banking sector owned stocks accounting for 25.9 percent of the total market value, and five years later the figure stood at 26.0 percent.[84]

Another major source of bank profits during this reconstruction phase came courtesy of the ultralow level of interest rates. Thanks to the easy credit policy of the Okurasho and Bank of Japan—with the official discount rate cut through a succession of record-breaking lows that took it to 0.5 percent in September 1995—the banks' cost of funds fell far below the level at which they were able to lend the money out. Although the economy was stagnant and the banks made only feeble efforts to cut their running costs, they were able to make huge windfall profits from the ongoing relaxation of interest rates. For example, in the first half of fiscal 1995, the twenty-one major banks managed to screw down their operating costs by a negligible 0.2 percent, yet their operating profits ballooned by 66 percent to 2.4 trillion yen ($24 billion).[85]

The banks also got help from the central bank, which transferred trillions of yen into bank profits by staging a tremendous bond-buying operation beginning in July 1995. It wanted to achieve that most controversial of aims—the deliberate use of public funds to subsidize the banks. But because it was done through the bond market rather than the national budget, it was barely noticed. The Bank of Japan stepped up its annual rate of bond buying from 1.4 trillion yen in 1994 to about 10 trillion to 12 trillion yen ($100 billion to $120 billion). This surge in demand pushed bond prices up sharply, and while all bond holders benefited, the banks were the chief target and the primary beneficiaries.[86]

■ The end of an era

The consequences of Japan's banking crisis in 1985–95 could not be buried safely with the jusen and their leaders. They could not be neatly handed over to the prosecutors of Mr. Takahashi for just disposal. They could not be happily written off with the bad debts of the banks or billed to taxpayers as a one-off surcharge for the privilege of a smoothly functioning financial system. The banking crisis reflected fundamental and continuing problems in Japan's policy-making and administrative systems.

Against all Okurasho efforts to hold it at bay, risk had arrived in the banking system. It had always been present, but high-speed economic growth for half a century had outpaced and overpowered it. This experience had created a sense of complacency in the banks and in their regulatory masters. The implicit government guarantee of all banks had made them cocky, and this sentiment, mixed with the excitement of the bubble economy, created a dangerously intoxicating cocktail of lending recklessness. The regulators who should have checked this behavior had instead happily exploited the opportunities it presented for postministry employment. After the damage had been done, the Okurasho failed to anticipate its consequences. This multiplied the costs of its original mistakes.

In 1995, in belated recognition of all that had transpired, the ministry renounced its implicit guarantee of all banks and gave notice that it would, after a five-year interval, withdraw its guarantee of the security of all deposits.[87] After the immediate crisis had passed, the Banking Bureau expected the ministry's new policy and the natural evolution of the market to bring about a steady rationalization of the banking system, weeding out perhaps 10 or 20 of Japan's 150 banks by the year 2000.[88] The gososendan was being slowly scattered as market forces attacked and overpowered the bureaucratic gunships holding the banks together in tight formation. The strong banks seemed destined to pull further and further ahead of the weak.

But these are the minimum necessary adjustments forced on the system. More change will occur in the economy and the financial system, more problems and more opportunities will emerge. The Finance Ministry's response to the banking crisis did not create what Japan evidently needs: policy-making structures that facilitate understanding of the markets, anticipation of change, and the active shaping of policy.

As soon as the ministry had decided that it would change its banking policy, a new scandal broke out illustrating just how much the ministry needed to learn. On August 8, 1995, the president of one of Japan's major national banks, Daiwa Bank, took the director-general of the Banking Bureau, Mr. Nishimura, to dinner. In the course of the conversation, the Daiwa head disclosed that the bank had a problem. The joint general manager and executive vice president of the bank's New York branch, Toshihide Inoguchi, had lost $1.1 billion in unauthorized bond trading. The losses had been accumulating for eleven years.

The ministry's Nishimura suggested the bank investigate the affair. He took no further action. The bank continued to trade in the U.S. markets and raise funds. Forty-one days later, Daiwa Bank informed U.S. regulators of its losses. After another eight days, it informed the market. American authorities were angry, and the bank paid heavily for withholding the information; it was ordered to close its U.S. branch. The Finance Ministry was unrepentant. Its top official said that Mr. Nishimura had "quickly instructed the bank to investigate the incident, and it is understandable that his actions went no further than that." He blamed the bank for the failure to inform U.S. authorities.[89] The affair confirmed the fact that the ministry's first loyalty was to its relationship of patronage to the banks rather than to the integrity of the system, the proper functioning of the market, or the principles of international cooperation.

THE RISING PRICE
OF FAILURE

Japan was the world's biggest exporter of money during the second half of the 1980s. In the last three years of the bubble economy, Japan sent a net total of $133 billion, or 13.3 trillion yen, overseas.[1] But when the bubble economy burst, companies and institutions were racked by recession and the stock market collapse—they lost the capacity to export money and instead started bringing their overseas cash back home to help repair the damage to their balance sheets. Japan immediately reversed its position and became a net importer of funds. In the four years after 1990 this reverse flow of funds back into Japan turned into a torrential net total of $380 billion, or 38 trillion yen.[2]

This tremendous accumulation of money created an explosion in demand for yen, and the currency appreciated steeply. The Okurasho sought to offset some of this pressure by increasing the government's role in recycling Japan's surpluses—it sent the Bank of Japan into the market to sell yen and swap them for dollars, the opposite of what was going on in the private sector. In 1993, Japan's central bank bought an estimated net $24 billion worth of U.S. dollars, another $21 billion the year after, and an astonishing $57 billion the next.[3] This was some ten times the total American currency bought by U.S. and German authorities combined. "Nowadays, monetary authorities are an important part of the recycling; central bank intervention is an important way of smoothing trade-balance recycling," Bank of Japan's Kengo Inoue pointed out.[4]

■ "Criminal" damage to the life insurance companies

But it was not enough. The yen had been appreciating almost continually since it was unhitched from its fixed relationship to the dollar in 1973. Now, despite the best efforts of the authorities, it entered one of its more determined upsurges, appreciating from its 1990 average of 144 to the dollar to 102 in 1994 and 95 in 1995—a gain of 34 percent in five years. We have seen how the implosion of stock and land prices damaged the economy and the banking system. The yen's surge was yet another channel through which the trauma resulting from the bursting of the bubble was transmitted across Japan. The cost to the greatest of Japan's private-sector investors, the life insurers, was appalling.

In the last year of the bubble, 1989, 15 percent of life insurance companies' assets was invested in bonds and stocks overseas and another 1.3 percent in international real estate—a total worth 19 trillion yen ($190 billion). Each time the yen moved a notch higher against other currencies, the value of these overseas assets fell in tandem.[5] The life insurance companies had become accustomed to losing money on their foreign investments. This was partly because the yen had grown stronger for most of the post-1973 period and partly because they were woefully slow to use any sort of hedging techniques. But until now it did not matter; the life insurers had such tremendous hidden profits from their holdings of Japanese stocks that it was easy for them to absorb their losses from investment abroad.

Now they had lost this protective buffer as well as their tolerance of risk; their overseas losses wounded them deeply.[6] They were trapped in a vicious cycle. The higher the yen rose, the more money they lost on their overseas investments, and the more they sold, repatriating the proceeds and putting yet more upward pressure on the yen, they cut the value of their overseas holdings yet further. The Nomura Research Institute estimates that in the ten years from 1985 to 1995, Japan's institutional investors suffered a total of 50 trillion yen in foreign exchange losses ($500 billion), most of this borne by the life insurers.[7] An executive in charge of foreign investment at a top Japanese life insurance company in 1994 gestured to his colleagues in the overseas division and made a confession: "We are the criminals of this institution." He then indicated the dozen mounted photographs and commissioned paintings around the walls showing the firm's once-prized property possessions in prime sites in New York, London, Sydney, and elsewhere: "And these are the wanted posters."[8]

Between 1985 and 1995, Japan's institutional investors suffered a total of 50 trillion yen in foreign exchange losses.

From 1991 onward, the life insurance companies were trapped in an awful dilemma, and as the years went by the dilemma grew in severity and urgency. It was this: they were obliged by contract to pay their policy holders and investors yearly returns of about 5 percent, but they were actually earning much less. This situation was entirely new to them. Until the 1990s, assisted by the high rate of economic growth, they had effortlessly bettered their performance targets for the postwar era.[9] But now, because of the recession and the banking crisis, official interest rates were eased, and in 1992 the yield on government bonds began to fall below the minimum returns the life insurance companies needed. In addition, slumping stock and land prices and the effects of the strong yen pushed their returns decisively below the 5 percent threshold. This new shortfall—known as negative spread—worsened, and in 1994 their returns ranged from 1.3 percent to 3.5 percent.[10]

To fill the gap between what they earned and what they owed, these companies started doing what the banks were doing—taking profits on their stock portfolios. Then they began trying to liquidate some of their real estate holdings. At the same time, they cut the returns they promised on new policies to 3.75 percent from 1994 onwards. But they were still locked into paying the higher rates on existing policies.[11] None of these measures was enough, and eight of the seventeen major life insurers recorded current deficits in 1994. When the stock market slumped again in 1995—to levels similar to those which had inspired the price-keeping operation of 1992—the hidden stock profits of even some of the biggest life insurers evaporated. An air of desperation took hold, and the companies lobbied the Okurasho for emergency help.

The ministry had already relieved some of the pressure on the industry by waiving some accounting requirements. But now, with rating agencies downgrading the firms, it was quite clear that the industry was indeed suffering what the chairman of the Life Insurance Association of Japan described as "a very difficult situation."[12] So the ministry agreed to the industry's request to break its promises to policy holders and investors and to cut their guaranteed returns. For instance, the guaranteed minimum yield on group pension accounts was cut—first from 5.5 percent to 4.5 percent in 1994 and then from 4.5 percent to 2.5 percent in 1996.[13] And this was done uniformly by all the life insurance companies. Like the banks, the life insurers are an Okurasho-supervised cartel, traveling in the escorted convoy system. Naturally, the cut in returns was stiffly resisted by those who stood to lose, such as the Pension Fund Association, which represented millions of workers. The association refused to agree to the loss of benefits for its members.[14] But once the Okurasho had struck a deal with the life insurers, it was a fait accompli.

■ More than one way to save a pension system

The Okurasho insistently sounds the alarm of the aging society, using it to warn against profligacy in government spending: "The aging of the population is expected to proceed more rapidly hereafter . . . we should try to stem the growth of government bonds outstanding so that we do not leave future generations saddled with a massive debt."[15] There is a striking contrast between the warmth of this concern for future generations on the subject of fiscal policy and the ministry's disregard for them—and indeed for present generations, too—when it comes to the issue of pensions.

For many years, the aging of Japanese society had foretold trouble for the pension system. In 1994, for instance, the number of people receiving public pensions rose by 5 percent, while the number of people contributing to the system rose by only 0.4 percent.[16] Tokyo University's Professor Kazuo Ueda estimated in 1987 that those over age fifty would receive more in pension benefits than they had paid into the system. People aged fifty would be paid back the same in value that they had contributed. But people in their twenties or younger could look forward to pensions worth only half the amount that they would have paid in during their working lives.[17] In 1993 the Organization for Economic Cooperation and Development (OECD) calculated that without any major changes, the public pension system would face a shortfall twice the size of the national economy—about 1 quadrillion yen ($10 trillion)—merely in paying pension benefits to people already in the workforce.[18]

In 1993 OECD calculated that the public pension system would face a shortfall twice the size of the national economy merely in paying pension benefits to people already in the workforce.

The Okurasho, together with the Ministry of Health and Welfare and the ruling coalition—the Liberal Democrats, the Socialists, and Sakigake—responded to this looming problem with two main measures. The retirement age was to be moved from sixty to sixty-five, and contributions to the two major national pension funds were to be raised. The ratio of payments into the main fund—employee pension insurance—was to be doubled. From 14.5 percent of monthly salary, the contribution rate was to be gradually increased until it reached a very high 29.6 percent in 2025, the burden shared equally between worker and employer. This would, of course, cut into workers' disposable incomes and depress consumption. It would also chew up corporate cash flow. Yet the changes should guarantee a fully funded pension system. This was the sensible and inevitable solution. Or was it?

The government response to the problem ignored one of the fundamental attributes of a pension system. It looked at the system the way you might consider a safe—counting the amount of money hoarded away in it and comparing that with the amount eventually to be drawn out. But pension funds are not safes. They are not places for simply storing funds but for increasing them; they are investment vehicles capable of generating returns. But the government did not seriously explore the possibility of squeezing better returns out of the pension system. Ironically, because the existing returns had been appallingly low, the potential for improvement was high.

Consider some of the possibilities. The OECD estimated that by improving the yield on public pension assets by 1.5 percentage points a year, the shortfall in the public pension system would be reduced from the equivalent of 200 percent of Japan's economic output (or GDP) to 74 percent.[19] The Nomura Research Institute reckoned that if the annual rate of return on corporate pension funds reached 8.5 percent, the funds would become self-financing and no extra contributions would be required.[20] And the Pension Fund Association calculated that a 1 percentage point increase in the yield on pension assets would cut the required contribution to corporate pension funds by 20 percent.[21] In other words, there is a very direct trade-off between performance and contributions—the better the performance of a fund, the less its members need to pay into it. So why did the government only demand an increase in contributions and neglect returns? For the answer, we need to look at who manages the money.

■ The money club

Japan's total pension assets were valued at around 200 trillion yen ($2 trillion) in 1994, a pool of money almost twice as large as the comparable collection of funds in the ten main European countries.[22] This money was, and still is today, invested by four different institutions. In this system, roughly half the total funds are channeled directly through the Okurasho's Trust Fund Bureau, and their management is controlled or substantially influenced by the Okurasho.[23] Less than 1 percent of Japan's pension money is managed by investment advisory companies. Virtually all of the rest is managed by two groups of institutions: trust banks and life insurance companies.[24] Each of these is a cartel operating under the supervision of the Okurasho. So some 99 percent of Japan's total pension assets is under the management or control of the Okurasho or its client cartels.

These managers have produced very poor returns on the pension money they hold in trust for the Japanese workforce. The Trust Fund Bureau pays a rate of return very close to the yield on government bonds.[25] And because it has a legislated monopoly on control of the money, it is not subject to competitive pressure to do any better. In 1996 it was paying annual interest of 3.3 percent. And consider the returns on corporate pension funds managed by the life insurers and the trust banks. In the nine years from 1985 to 1993, corporate pension funds produced annual average yields of 5.54 percent. During the same period, U.S. corporate pension funds yielded an annual average of 16.65 percent—outperforming their Japanese counterparts by an average 11.11 percent.[26] Even when adjusting this figure to account for the higher level of inflation in the United States, the life insurance companies and trust banks in Japan were still underperforming by 9 percentage points a year.[27]

From 1985 to 1993, Japanese corporate pension funds produced annual average yields of 5.54 percent. During the same period, U.S. corporate pension funds yielded an annual average of 16.65 percent.

These fund managers have no incentive to improve the returns they offer clients. One reason is that there is so little competition, with almost all the business concentrated in the hands of just fifteen institutions in a pair of closed cartels. Partly because of this, companies often chose pension-fund managers not according to performance but according to relationship.[28] Consequently, the life insurers and the trust banks worry more about maintaining relationships with the fund managers than about managing funds profitably. Another reason for the lack of incentive to improve returns is that, as we have seen, even when these institutions failed to meet their required targets, they were able to use the protective authority of the Okurasho to release them from their obligations. In such an environment, where there is no incentive to improve and no sanction for failure, the trust banks and the life insurance companies have failed to develop any real investment expertise.

Their fund managers have customarily been general-duty salaried staff who are cycled through different jobs every couple of years, perhaps working in personnel one year and funds management the next, and then moving off to an assignment in sales after that. U.S. and other overseas-based investment companies and banks have expressed amazement for many years at the poor levels of invest-ment sophistication of their Japa-nese counterparts. As Noboru Terada, executive director of the Pension Fund Association, ob-serves: "There's no incentive for investment managers to advance their level of sophistication. Be-cause there's a lot of regulation in the market, . . . there's less competition between investment man-agers."[29]

> U.S. and other overseas-based investment companies and banks have been amazed for many years by the poor levels of investment sophistication of their Japanese counterparts.

■ Minimal change under maximum pressure: Part 1

If it performs so poorly, why did Japan persist with this insulated, cartel-like system? It was not for lack of diagnosing the problem. As the Sanwa Bank Research Institute urged in its study of the issue: "To relieve the burden on future generations, a number of measures should be aggressively adopted within the current framework. These include improving the yield on pension fund assets through the introduction of the principle of competition."[30] And it was not for lack of pressure. The Ministry of Health and Welfare, which manages a major fund but was forced to channel the bulk of it through the Okurasho and to observe that ministry's regulations and restraints, had asked the Finance Ministry for reform of the system for years.[31] The Pension Fund Association, representing some 1,500 major corporate funds, spent years lobbying the Okurasho for removal of restrictions on fund management.[32] The U.S. government also asked the Finance Ministry to move toward a more performance-oriented system in the belief that this would improve the prospects for U.S. funds managers. Even the Okurasho's advisory bodies recommended such changes.[33] The ministry resisted.

Why? According to Tokyo University's Kazuo Ueda, it was "an

obvious attempt to protect entrenched interests." Specifically, the ministry was protecting the two cartels it oversees, the life insurance companies and the trust banks. And it was protecting itself; allowing the Ministry of Health and Welfare to directly invest the funds of its big *nenpuku*, or Pension Welfare Service Corporation fund—instead of investing through the Okurasho's Trust Fund Bureau—would shrink the total pool under the Finance Ministry's control.[34]

Consider the equation that confronted the Okurasho. On one hand were four overlapping interests: first, the interests of Japan's workers, present and future, who must finance the pension system; second, the interests of Japan's future pensioners, who must eventually live on the proceeds of their pensions; third, the future vitality and flexibility of the economy, which diminishes as workers and companies lock up increasingly large chunks of income in pension plans (and Japan suffers no shortage of savings); and, fourth, the interests of the potential new funds managers, Japanese and foreign firms that stood to earn profits if allowed to manage more pension money. And on the other hand, there were two overlapping interests: first, the existing private-sector fund managers, the life insurance companies and the trust banks, and second, the Okurasho itself as a major fund manager. The ministry weighed these two sets of interests and judged in favor of itself and the companies under its regulatory aegis. The ministry did make small concessions to allow some competition at the margins of the system in 1987 and 1990, but the structural suppression of competition remained essentially unchanged.

Ultimately, however, change was forced on the Okurasho. The damage done by the trauma caused by the bursting of the bubble created extra, irresistible pressures on the system. Not only did yields fall, but unrealized losses built up in the pension system. By the early to mid-1990s, most corporate pension funds had unrealized losses that were the equivalent of 15 percent of their total assets.[35] In November 1994, an Osaka spinning-industry pension fund went bankrupt, the first to do so in nine years, and there were predictions of more to follow. The number of companies notifying contributors that they would be forced to make premature increases in pension-fund contributions rose six fold, to sixty-eight over the two years to late 1995, a sure sign of serious distress.[36] And the

Ministry of Health and Welfare disclosed cumulative losses of 698 billion yen ($6.98 billion) in 1995 in the nenpuku pension fund, losses for which it blamed the Okurasho's management system.[37] A system built in the high-growth years of postwar Japan with a relatively young population was not able to endure the tensions and losses building up in the system in postbubble recession: "The system will not be able to survive in its current state," was the 1995 verdict of Atsushi Seike, a professor of commercial science at Keio University.[38]

This deterioration in the system combined with intensive lobbying for change. From April 1996 on, a number of changes were introduced. These included a loosening of the stranglehold of the life insurance companies and trust banks, although they will still enjoy a captive market of at least 50 percent of corporate pension fund assets. This easing should allow investment advisory firms, Japanese and foreign, to play a larger role and provide some fresh competition and new expertise. And managers were allowed extra flexibility in allocating funds. In addition, from 1997 on a new accounting system will for the first time oblige fund managers to disclose the true market value of their assets—they will have nowhere to hide losses. All of these changes should increase the emphasis on improving the returns on funds. However, the great omission in the reforms concerns the public pension system—the Okurasho's Trust Fund Bureau remains squarely in control of the great bulk of funds. We will revisit this issue later in the book.

Once again, it was a case of reform by crisis. Nothing short of crisis—not demonstrated failure, not national interest, not concerted pressure—was able to persuade the Finance Ministry to introduce serious reforms to an outmoded system.

■ Japan's manufacturers emigrate

An extraordinary migration of Japanese industry took place in the first half of the 1990s. An average of 1 percent of its manufacturing base moved overseas every year. This was roughly the equivalent of relocating the entire economy of Singapore every twelve months.[39] Why were Japanese companies moving their factories? In a word, it was the yen. The strong yen, rising inexorably, made Japan one of the world's most expensive manufacturing centers. This put a big competitive burden on exporters competing in the world market.

In the first half of the 1990s, an average of 1 percent of Japan's manufacturing base moved overseas every year. This was roughly the equivalent of relocating the entire economy of Singapore every twelve months.

So the nation's most prized sector simply moved away from this disadvantage, relocating to countries where manufacturing costs were cheaper. "Japan is the most expensive country in the world," declared the president of electronics manufacturer Aiwa Co., Hajime Unoki, in 1995, "from communications costs to electricity and highway transport costs. By moving overseas, we can make things cheaper thanks to lower infrastructure costs. We wouldn't dream of increasing domestic production [in Japan]." Of its total output, Aiwa increased its proportion manufactured overseas to 80 percent.[40]

Until the mid-1990s, Japanese manufacturers had managed a small miracle of aggressive competitiveness. In 1986 their threshold of export profitability was 207 yen to the U.S. dollar; they made money on export sales if the yen fell below this level and would lose money if the yen rose above it. But the yen, of course, did strengthen, appreciating dramatically through the rest of the 1980s. Japan's exporters successfully scrambled to keep up, extracting stunning and continual new efficiencies from their operations so that in early 1995 they were able to export profitably at an exchange rate of 108 yen to the dollar. In nine years, they had practically halved their break-even point on exports.[41] In 1994, with the yen trading at 105 to the dollar, a leading U.S. industrialist, General Electric's chief executive John Welch, told American managers that they should feel humbled by this achievement: "Think about it. An enormously resourceful Japan, handicapped by a strong yen, still exports a record $350 billion of merchandise in 1993, grows to what some consider the world's largest manufacturing economy, and is talking about cost reductions of 30 to 50 percent. I could make the case that the powerful yen is the best thing that ever happened to Japanese competitiveness."[42]

One result of their successful efficiency drive was that Japan's manufacturers did not need to shift much manufacturing capacity overseas. The proportion of Japanese manufacturing conducted in other countries slowly crept up from 3 percent in the year of the Plaza Accord, 1985, to 6 percent in 1993.[43] But as the postbubble years advanced, the yen's appreciation tested the limits of manufacturers' ingenuity—the exchange-rate problem seemed to exhaust the remaining corporate willpower. There was a surge in the movement of production offshore. In 1993, companies planned to raise the share of their overseas production gradually to 9 percent over the five years ahead. The yen's abrupt advance accelerated the movement—the figure hit 9 percent just two years later, and the trend gave every sign of continuing; the former top official of the ministry of International Trade and Industry, Shinji Fukukawa, forecast a ratio of 15 percent by the year 2000.[44] This phenomenon was widely deplored as the "hollowing out" of the industrial base.

The yen overpowers Mazda

The transfer of manufacturing out of the country was perhaps most visible in the champion of Japanese industrial success, the car industry. Until 1995, it cost about the same to make a car in Japan as it did in the United Kingdom. But in just a couple of months, as the yen moved sharply higher against all currencies, including the pound sterling, Japan became 20 percent more expensive.[45] Nissan became the first car manufacturer to close a plant postwar, shutting down its Zama factory in April 1995 and cutting its car-making capacity in Japan by 12 percent. New Japanese car factories sprouted around the world. In the three years from 1992 through 1994, the proportion of Japanese cars assembled in other countries rose from 26.5 percent to 31 percent.[46]

The yen continued to smash through a succession of highs every year, and by 1995, when it reached 80 yen to the U.S. dollar, Nissan's executive vice president Yoshikazu Kawana hinted at the despair in the industry: "This exchange rate is just too much. It's more than any company can be expected to handle."[47] At that time, the break-even point for Japan's car exports was 109 yen to the dollar.

In 1993 Japan's car industry for the first time manufactured more automobiles in the United States than it exported there. By 1995 it was exporting 1.3 million cars from Japan to the United States, and producing 2 million cars a year in the United States, making there 50 percent more than it shipped there.[48] The exchange rate had transformed the economics of car making. The more nimble the company, the bigger the rewards.

Mazda was too slow. It had put its faith in the power of Japanese know-how and technology; its gleaming new high-tech plant in the Japanese town of Hofu, near its home base of Hiroshima, opened in 1992, reputedly the most efficient car plant in the world. But it was just as vulnerable to the yen as every other car plant in Japan: "It's a great plant," quipped an analyst, "but in the wrong country."[49] In mid-1995 it was operating at 30 percent of its capacity. Mazda was more dependent on exports than its major competitors—exports accounted for 60 percent of sales, compared with Toyota's 37 percent and Nissan's 41 percent—and so 60 percent of its output grew less competitive with each strengthening of the yen. It was more brutally damaged than its competitors in proportionate terms. Every time the Japanese currency appreciated by 1 yen against the dollar, Mazda lost another 7 billion yen ($70 million) in profits. By the time it realized its error, it was too late—Mazda could no longer afford to build new plants overseas. It already had problems in positioning itself in the Japanese market, and the recession was punishing all the carmakers. The rising yen was the final, crippling blow.

Every time the Japanese currency appreciated by 1 yen against the dollar, Mazda lost another $70 million in profits.

One of the company's allies and its main underwriter, Nomura Securities, in 1995 gave the company's stock the lowest rating possible and told clients that at then-prevailing exchange rates, it was "very likely" that the company would not return to profitability. A Mazda executive said: "We are asking the Japanese Government to take more measures to deal with the strength of the yen. Their measures so far have had no effect."[50] This vulnerability combined with the recession to finally force the company to confront a choice between collapse and the surrender of its independence. Ford Motor Co. took effective control of Mazda in 1996 and installed an American as chief executive. It was the first instance in postoccupation Japan of a leading Japanese manufacturer being taken over by a foreign firm.[51]

Alarmed at the yen's strength, the carworkers' unions commissioned the Mitsubishi Research Institute to estimate the effects of a persistent exchange rate of 85 yen to the dollar. The answer? The car companies would cut output in Japan by 1.5 million cars a year, or 14 percent, as they moved more production overseas over the five years to 2000. Some 160,000 jobs would be lost in Japan.[52] The car companies did not wait for this exchange rate to become permanent—by the end of 1995 they were planning to move yet more production abroad.

The 100- and 200-yen industries

A perpetual frustration for Japan's manufacturers is that while they must be relentlessly efficient and hypercompetitive in tough world markets, they have to do business in an economic landscape crowded with fat, lazy industries grazing on government handouts behind fences of official protection. Keio University's Heizo Takanaka puts it this way: "The dual nature of the economy pits industries with high productivity—which can compete in international markets even with the yen as high as 100 yen to the U.S. dollar—against low productivity industries that are operating on a 200 yen to the dollar level, surrounded by protective regulations. The 200-yen industries survive by clinging to the 100-yen industries."[53]

The 100-yen sector is represented by the companies that have earned Japan's postwar prosperity—manufacturers like Toyota, Matsushita, Honda, Kyocera, and Sony. And to their continuing irritation, they are obliged to buy many of their services and other "inputs" from the chronically inefficient 200-yen sector, which includes practically all of the nonmanufacturing industries in the economy. We have heard already Aiwa's Mr. Unoki complaining of the high cost of Japan's communications, electricity, and highway transport industries. Sony Corporation's chairman, Norio Ohga, made this lament:

> In Japan today, manufacturing just doesn't pay. Since the Government refuses to deregulate, things like beef and rice don't get any cheaper and Japan's purchasing power parity is stuck at 180 yen to the dollar. [That is, the same amount of goods and services that $1 dollar can buy in the United States cost 180 yen in Japan, even though at the time, in 1995, $1 dollar was actually trading for just 90 yen.] Since we have obligations to our shareholders, we've got no choice but to move manufacturing over-seas.

Although the above statement is not strictly accurate—beef prices fell dramatically after imports were liberalized under U.S. pressure in 1989—it is certainly true that the entire food sector is a notable underperformer. The consulting firm McKinsey & Co. found in a 1993 study that while productivity in Japan's steel, automotive, metals, and electronics industries were well above U.S. levels, in food Japanese productivity was just 33 percent that of the United States.[54] Why? One reason is that the manufacturers have no choice—they are forced to be competitive with a tariff protection at home of 4.9 percent, among the lowest in the world. Japan's agriculture industries, on the other hand, have no need to be competitive—they luxuriate in average tariff protection of 88 percent.[55] It is widely known that consumer prices are obscenely high in Japan compared with the rest of the world, with the cost of living in Tokyo about 80 percent higher than that in New York, for example.[56] The flabby inefficiency of the nonmanufacturing sector in Japan accounts for the great bulk of this price gap, a penalty on Japan's consumers and on the efficient parts of its economy.[57]

When the strong yen made imports cheaper—the obverse of the syndrome confronting exporters—the benefits were hoarded by the importers, the distributors, and the retailers, with benefits of only about 1 yen in every seven passed on to consumers. And those consumers include the manufacturers. Indeed, the pass-through rate of these currency benefits in 1995 had been unchanged since the early years of the bubble economy.[58] The costly and inefficient rigidities of the economy had not improved in a decade. The frustrated president of the world's biggest steel producer, Takashi Imai of Nippon Steel, complained that "protected by regulations, the nontradeable goods [goods and services not traded on world markets] industries have low productivity, and high consumer prices prevail in Japan as a result, further widening the internal-external price gap. . . . If Japan is to have the capacity to adapt to the strong-yen era, its economic structure must be reformed."[59]

Japan would become a remittance state; the rich and successful manufacturers operating overseas would send money home in the form of corporate taxes, and the government would redistribute this money to prop up the hopelessly uncompetitive local industries left behind in Japan.

Despairing that the 200-yen sector could be made efficient, giving up on any hope that the government was serious about reforming the the Japanese economy, the manufacturers increasingly decided to abandon it. The policy platform of the dominant opposition party of 1995, the Shinshinto, or New Frontier Party, stated the logical conclusion of such an event: "The high yen is forcing export-oriented industries to move more and more elements of production overseas. If this trend continues, the only industries left at home will be low-productivity enterprises protected by numerous regulations."[60] Japan would become a remittance state; the rich and successful manufacturers operating overseas would send money home in the form of corporate taxes, and the government would redistribute this money to prop up the hopelessly uncompetitive local industries left behind in Japan.

■ Minimal change under maximum pressure: Part 2

As the yen appreciated to the level of 90 to the dollar in March 1995, the minister of international trade and industry, Ryutaro Hashimoto, declared a state of "near crisis" for Japan's manufacturing sector. A month later, as appreciation approached the 80-yen level, he warned that the exchange rate threatened manufacturers with "a fatal blow."[61] Of eighty-four top exporters surveyed at that moment, fifty-nine said they were planning to expand their production overseas.[62] When the 80-yen threshold was hit a few days later, the finance minister, Masayoshi Takemura, confessed to "a sense of crisis."[63] In the Okurasho itself, executive-level attention was fixed on the exchange rate whenever the yen threatened to broach a new height; the latest rates were displayed on the electronic boards, which flash key market indices into the ministry's top-level offices. Here there was a sense of crisis indeed.

One reason for the Finance Ministry's concern was the terrible consequences of yen appreciation on the economy. Official and private-sector estimates agreed that a 10 percent rise in the value of the yen against the dollar depressed the rate of Japan's economic growth by about 0.5 percentage points, snuffing out some 2.3 trillion yen ($23 billion) of potential economic activity.[64] In the first few months of 1995 the yen climbed by 20 percent. In an anemic economy struggling to regain momentum, this was enough to wipe out any hope of recovery. This did not happen once but twice to Japan in the first half of the 1990s; first in 1993 and then again in 1995, helping to keep the country mired in four years of near-zero growth, its longest postwar stagnation. Japan's customary postwar solution to recession—to export its way out—was no longer available. The Okurasho's deepest fear was that it would be obliged to respond by loosening government spending and going deeper into debt.

The accelerating yen, by eroding the profits of exporters, also tended to damage their stock prices and thereby punish the entire stock market. For example, the Nikko Research Center estimated in 1995 that a strengthening of the Japanese currency by 1 yen against the dollar eroded the current profits of the manufacturing sector by 3.8 percent and that of all companies by 1.74 percent. And, as we have seen, a strong yen took a very high toll on the overseas investments of Japan's life insurance companies, too. In the meantime, the Bank of Japan frantically intervened in the market on the ministry's behalf and bought an estimated $14 billion worth of U.S. dollars in

March and another $12 billion in April—an average of $600 million a day.[65] Indeed, on some days in the Tokyo market the central bank was reported to be the only buyer of any significance—but to no avail. The Finance Ministry asked major institutions to refrain from selling dollars for yen, but, again, to no effect. Some ministers started to talk about addressing the foreign exchange market's concerns by setting numerical targets for the trimming of Japan's $130 billion current account surplus, but the Okurasho's top official, Jiro Saito, immediately ruled out any such possibility.[66]

With the politicians and industrialists clamoring for action, the Okurasho in April 1995 put together a special yen-busting policy package. The package was designed to achieve two main objectives: first, to stimulate economic growth, second, to deregulate the economy to force a streamlining of the inefficient "200-yen sector." The first part of the package played to the cycle of the economy, while the second addressed its structure. The chairman of the Japan Research Institute and a former economist at the Bank of Japan, Mikio Wakatsuki, described the event:

> On April 14, the Government compiled a six-sector, 24-item package of emergency economic measures to cope with the strong yen. At the same time, the Bank of Japan lowered the official discount rate by 0.75 percentage points to an all-time low of 1 percent. However, the market's response was indifferent, and the exchange rate surged further in the middle of the following week to an all-time high of 79.75 yen [to the dollar]. This cool market reaction was due to the fact that the "emergency" package was regarded as mostly rhetoric and short of concrete contents. . . . Most of the currency package contains economic measures that are necessary regardless of the strong yen. That these "emergency" measures are needed in the first place is one reason that the yen's value has surged so dramatically.[67]

As the president of Germany's central bank, the Bundesbank, said: "We are living in a world where the credibility of a country's policy is playing a crucial role. Every country should be aware of being tested minute by minute, hour by hour, by the international markets."[68] The Okurasho failed.

Toyota Motors vice president Hiroshi Okuda expressed the dismayed reaction of manufacturers to the authorities' efforts:

It appears that Japan does not make a move unless it faces a crisis. . . . If the auto industry is to shoulder the negative aspect of the high yen, it will have a grave impact. . . . Export-oriented firms are at a loss. The reality is that they are silently watching developments. If they are determined to rely on neither the state nor industrial circles nor anyone else, many firms will leave for foreign countries. Most Japanese firms will become selfish . . . they will be able to survive as corporations, but the Japanese economy will be in a critical situation. . . . In the past, when the coal industry declined, the next wave of industries, such as heavy industry, emerged. Now, there are no new industries that can replace the auto and electronics industries. It is urgently necessary to consolidate a job-creating mechanism by nurturing the venture industry . . . using deregulation as a breakthrough. In the Government's emergency high-yen package, the Government brought forward the timetable for the five-year deregulation promotion plan by two years, but the market's evaluation is that it is not sufficient. I can only say that there is a lack of a sense of alarm.[69]

It was merely one more ineffectual effort among the many made by the Okurasho in the previous decade to stem the appreciation of Japanese currency. In fairness to the Okurasho, it does not have direct regulatory control of most of the economy and so does not have the direct authority to enact structural reform simply by re-writing relevant regulations. The Transport Ministry is responsible for the transport sector, the Agriculture Ministry for the farm sector, Ministry of International Trade and Industry for energy industries, and so on.

■ Minimal change under maximum pressure: Part 3 (or how to terrify Americans)

If the Finance Ministry wanted to do so, could it galvanize economic reform? The ministry does have some powerful levers for change available to it—available exclusively to the Okurasho. Consider four of them.

First, through the budget it subsidizes many of the inefficiencies in the economy. Second, through its control of the chairmanship of the Fair Trade Commission it tolerates many cartels and other anti-competitive practices in the corporate world. Third, through its control of corporate accounting rules it sets the benchmarks for corporate transparency and private-sector performance. And fourth, through its supervision of virtually all institutional investors, the banks, and the stock market, it has available to it all the mechanisms of corporate governances, those systems which direct company behavior.

The ministry has tremendous potential to change the fundamental parameters for the operation of industry and hence the structure of the economy. And if the Okurasho chose to pull these levers at critical moments of national alarm, such as the yen crisis of 1995, it could exploit that alarm. It could play to political and industrial concern to win support at home. And, as economic reform would also coincide with the U.S. agenda, Japan could expect the strong endorsement of its major international partner as well.

The Finance Ministry did none of these things. In a replay of the yen's great upswing in 1993, the Okurasho failed to make any convincing move toward structural reform of the economy. To compensate for its failure to reform, it turned instead to politicking to solve its problems. In 1995, as in 1993, it cut a deal with the United States to adjust the exchange rate. This deal reversed the course of the yen and eased the pressure on Japan's manufacturers, its stock market, and its banks. It relaxed the systemic pressure on Japan to restructure its economy.

The ministry achieved this quite simply—by terrifying the United States. The freshly appointed head of the International Finance Bureau, Eisuke Sakakibara, told the U.S. Treasury that Japan was on the brink of a major banking crisis.[70] Japan's hard-pressed banks were increasingly likely to liquidate their $200 billion of U.S. bond holdings, which would send U.S. interest rates up sharply, bring on the market nightmare described in chapter 5. The United States could disarm this economic and political bomb by agreeing to

cut the value of the yen against the dollar. The well-informed
American economist David Hale described what happened next:

> The U.S. Treasury contacted a variety of people in the private sector
> about their views of Japan's financial situation and sent key officials to
> Tokyo to discuss the outlook with Japanese bureaucrats. . . . As a result,
> the day after the [U.S. Federal Reserve Board] eased U.S. interest rates
> by 25 basis points [0.25 percent], the Bank of Japan also eased and there
> was joint U.S.-Japan intervention to push the dollar higher. The inter-
> vention was intended to show clear U.S. support for a stronger dollar in
> order to help stabilize the Tokyo stockmarket and boost the Japanese
> economy. Japan then followed up by announcing a series of measures to
> boost capital outflows.[71]

As a former U.S. official put it: "The Ministry of Finance sold us a
bill of goods, and we bought it."[72] This sale won Dr. Sakakibara
considerable acclaim at home.

But while deals with the Americans certainly helped to ease the
pressures on Japan in the short term, they did nothing to change the
underlying structural problems in the economy that actually generated those pressures in the first place. For manufacturers, the medium-term future of the yen looked daunting. The new president of
Sony said that he "wouldn't be surprised [to see] 50 yen" to the
dollar eventually, for an appre-
ciation 37 percent above and beyond its all-time high.[73] The Japan Research Institute estimated
that failure to address the structural causes of "hollowing out"—
the shift of manufacturing out of
Japan as companies sought to escape the high yen—would perpetuate the cycle, leading Japan
into a phase of low growth and rising unemployment, with a net
total of 4 million jobs disappearing from the economy in the years
to the end of the decade and unemployment rising from 3 percent
to 8.2 percent.[74] The Prime Minister's think tank on economic is-

**Unless Japan addressed its "hol-
lowing out"—the emigration of
manufacturers to escape the
high yen—it could expect to
lose 4 million jobs by the year
2000.**

sues, the Economic Council, ended 1995 by issuing a plan stating that "the current social and economic structure of Japan has been unable to cope" with the "tide shifts" occurring in modern Japan. This had created problems among which the first was "retardation of new industries and industrial hollowing."[75]

■ Another "hollowing out"

One of Japan's best-known filmmakers internationally, Juzo Itami, has risked his personal safety to continue making his critiques of Japanese society in Japan. His face was slashed in a gang attack over an unfavorable portrayal of the Japanese Mafia, the *yakuza*, and his life has been threatened. But there are some risks he is not prepared to take. He does not finance his work in Japan. Instead, the maker of *Tampopo* and *Taxing Woman* has set up his finance company in New York. He is one among the fast-growing group of people who have decided that even though Japan may be the world's largest creditor nation and awash in cheap cash, the restrictions on its efficient deployment are just too great.

This is a paradox; Japan is the main source of global credit, but not the main market for it. When companies and institutions, both Japanese and non-Japanese, borrow money from Japan's banks and institutions, they prefer to sidestep the Tokyo market and go outside Japan to the Euromarket. And they prefer it by a margin of 3 to 1.[76] The reason? Simply an excess of regulation in Japan, which increases the cost and complexity of doing business there. Many of the borrowers who do raise their funds in Japan are poor credit risks who would have trouble operating on the Euromarket. Yoshiaki Miwa argued in his 1993 book that the Okurasho's distrust of market forces has diminished the very markets it seeks to control.[77] The markets have sidestepped this and, like the manufacturers frustrated with the pace of reform at home, moved abroad. But only the best can make the move. The uncompetitive part of the economy, once more, is left behind.

All of Japan's capital markets were beset by the "hollowing out" that followed the bubble economy. One of the first to draw the parallel between the hollowing out of manufacturing and that of the financial markets was a Finance Ministry old boy, Tomomitsu Oba. He pointed out that when manufacturing declined in the United States and the United Kingdom, some of the lost activity in those economies was offset by growth in their financial services industries. But Japan was a victim of a "dual hollowing." He said: "In the financial sector, employment is actually declining as U.S. and European financial institutions abandon the Tokyo market in favor of Hong Kong and Singapore."[78] Among others, institutions like America's Merrill Lynch and J. P. Morgan, Canada's Bank of Montreal, and the French bank Credit Lyonnais moved all or part of their trading out of Tokyo in the early 1990s.

There are three recurring Okurasho mantras: the need for stability, the importance of protecting investors, and the need to discourage speculation.

Mr. Oba's Japan Center for International Finance surveyed foreign banks and brokers to find out why. The survey of 145 foreign financial institutions with offices in Tokyo found six dominant reasons for dissatisfaction with the Japanese capital as a financial market. Five of them were the direct result of Okurasho regulation or practice. The five reasons were:

1. lack of diversification in the capital markets
2. the number of limits on transactions
3. the heavy burden of filing reports to the authorities
4. the presence of firewalls (legal divisions between different types of business in the one company)
5. inadequate public disclosure by financial firms

The only unhappiness that was not a direct result of ministry practice was the difficulty in recruiting finance specialists. And of the 145 foreign firms, how many thought the ministry was making satisfactory progress in deregulating the markets? Not one. To them, Tokyo's international importance was in decline—and it would likely continue to decline in the years ahead.[79]

The governor of the central bank, Yasuo Matsushita, although an old boy of the Okurasho, felt compelled to register his protest: "Recently, a concern has been raised whether Japan's financial and capital markets have been 'hollowing out.' This is not only a matter of declining market turnover; the problem has its roots in a growing awareness that Japan's financial and capital markets, compared to overseas markets, are not responding sufficiently to the financing and investment needs of the economy."[80]

Finance Ministry suspicion of market forces obliges Japan's financial institutions to conduct their new and most prospective business overseas. For instance, the Sumitomo, Sanwa, Fuji, Sakura, and Dai-Ichi Kangyo banks all set up their derivatives trading centers in Hong Kong and other regional centers outside Japan.[81] The ministry was reluctant to endorse financial derivatives for the stated reason that they could increase market volatility, but the markets believed the real reason was the ministry's fear that these new products would dilute its control over the stock market. They lost the control anyway—the business simply moved overseas and investors can still write derivatives contracts related to Tokyo stocks—and they lost the potential benefits of the new business, too. So the power they sought to preserve was illusory, but the lost business was real. Of twenty-five financial instruments commonly traded in the United States and Europe in 1993, only twelve were approved for trading in Japan.[82]

There are three recurring Okurasho mantras that its officials chant to defend regulation of the capital markets: the first is the need for stability, the second is the importance of protecting investors, the third is the need to discourage speculation. These were paramount considerations in the controlled economy before and after World War II and were perhaps useful guidelines in the postwar reconstruction phase, when scant savings had to be allocated carefully to key sectors of the economy. But the hard evidence of the period 1985 to 1995 says that even if these three goals still have validity, the ministry's method of achieving them no longer works. As a direct consequence of the Okurasho's approach to both economic policy and market supervision, Japan's economy and financial systems became the very embodiment of instability, investor loss, and speculation. All three of these vices were more rampant in Japan during this period than in any other industrialized nation. Eco-

nomic policy making according to unchecked institutional convenience helped generate the wild swings of Japan's bubble boom and
the ensuing bust. In the financial system and the markets, the effects
of this misjudgment were amplified by a dogged dependence on
rigid regulatory control rather than market disciplines.

■ PKO: the results start coming in

The Okurasho's bold confrontation of market forces in the Tokyo
stock market—the price-keeping operation, or PKO—forestalled a
major and sudden crisis in Japan's financial system. It did not restore
the market to health. The government, haunting the marketplace
for three years to prevent collapse but never promoting reform, may
have contributed to the medium-term stagnation of the market.
The former Nomura chairman, Mr. Aida, says: "The ministry does
not realize that by sending out signals that indicate 'do not sell,' it is
giving signals that say 'do not buy.' The ministry does not realize
how the market mechanism works."[83] Hideo Sakamaki, who was
then president of Nomura, went a step further, warning that three
years after the launch of the PKO intervention, Japan was in danger
of witnessing "the death of equities."[84]

There was no evidence of revitalization of the stock market. After
an anemic recovery to around 21,500 points in 1994, the Nikkei in
1995 again collapsed to around 14,500—a level approaching its
1992 low. Partly, this reflected the state of the economy and company profits. It was also a symptom of the deadening effect wrought
by official intervention and of an inherent lack of energy in the
market. An analyst of the Nomura Research Institute, Yasuyuki
Fuchita, argued that the Tokyo stock market's major problem was
not the collapse in prices or volumes but the fact that "the quality of
the markets [had] deteriorated due to the introduction, after the
economic bubble collapsed, of controls and practices that violate
market principles."[85] The Bank of Japan's governor, Mr. Matsushita,
suggested that in denying companies access to investors' capital the
PKO's suppression of new stock issues retarded the development of
new industries in Japan:

The value of stock issues in the U.S. corporate sector since 1990 . . . [has been] almost five times as much as that in Japan during the same period. Particularly noteworthy is that the U.S. firms continued to issue stock aggressively in 1991 and 1992 when the recession hit the economy. . . . Such active functioning of the capital market in the U.S. is said to have contributed much to the development of venture firms in new fields . . . while also facilitating the restructuring of existing firms, and to have eventually led to the current economic recovery. In contrast, Japanese stock prices . . . have remained stagnant on the whole . . . However, there is no reason why firms should refrain from issuing stocks simply because stock prices are stagnant. . . . Such times clearly provide ideal fund-raising opportunities for entrepreneurs wishing to launch new businesses.[86]

The Government's National Land Agency published a 1994 survey that found Tokyo falling significantly behind other centers of international finance. It prescribed a cure: a liberalization of the financial markets, improved standards in accounting and legal infrastructure, and lower rents.[87]

The Okurasho's response to the clamor for reform was to conduct its own study of the "hollowing out" problem. The Securities Bureau tested the hypothesis by narrowing its appraisal of the Tokyo markets down to five specific numerical indicators. It found that two of these did suggest problems and made some cautious moves to address these specific indicators. The other three indicated no problem according to the Securities Bureau and so it was assumed that the problem of the "hollowing out" of Japan's capital markets had been solved.[88] This narrow, selective, and grudging approach seems to confirm the ministry's reluctance to deal seriously with the issue. The International Finance Bureau, however, had a different view. "There is a kind of hollowing out going on in Tokyo," said a senior official, "as activities move to other markets." But the International Finance Bureau was unable to persuade the Securities Bureau of the urgency or magnitude of the problem.[89]

In the final analysis, the PKO—unaccompanied by significant supporting reforms of the market and the economy—probably contributed to lingering stock market stagnation. In combination with other ministry policies, it may have converted an abrupt convulsive crisis into a longer slow-grinding one. Just as the ministry tried to cut deals with the United States to contain currency crises rather than deal with the underlying flaws in the Japanese economy, so it seems to have used the PKO as a way to ease pressure rather than seriously address problems. In both cases, the problems remained.

A CRISIS OF IDEAS

One of the Finance Ministry's most senior officials wrote a long magazine article in 1995 to launch an attack on one of his closest friends. The director-general of the International Finance Bureau, Eisuke Sakakibara, conducted the equivalent of a public vivisection. Upon prying open his friend's psyche, Dr. Sakakibara found all sorts of unsavory things there and held them up to vilification for his readers: immaturity, bitterness, arrogance, an inferiority complex, the subordination of reason to passion. Who was this friend and what dreadful crime had he committed?

The target of Dr. Sakakibara's attack was in fact a charming and soft-spoken scholar, Yukio Noguchi, a professor of economics at Hitotsubashi University and, at fifty-five, a year senior to Dr. Sakakibara. As youths the two had entered the career stream together, having both studied at Tokyo University and developed their political consciousness there. Both joined radical left-wing actions in the heady days of 1960, when students protested Ampo, the U.S.-Japan security treaty. Professor Noguchi had not planned to become a civil servant, however. He recalls being approached by a high-powered

To Noguchi, Japan's economic structure was an aberration, a "1940 economic structure" based on the needs of World War II, "a total-war economy."

official as a potential recruit, "and when I regained consciousness I was an Okurasho bureaucrat." He soon left to pursue a successful academic career. His crime was to write an influential book arguing that Japan's economic structure was an aberration, a "1940 economic structure" based on the needs of World War II, "a total-war economy."[1] Elsewhere, in a discussion with a fellow professor, Noguchi said:

> The common understanding about the contemporary history of Japan is that Japan's defeat in World War Two brought about an enormous discontinuity between the prewar and postwar periods, . . . but I don't think there was such discontinuity as far as the economy was concerned. . . . Only the economic agencies were left intact while the Japanese Imperial Army and the Ministry of Home Affairs were disbanded. The prime example of that is the Okurasho. . . . Despite Japan's defeat in the war, the war-time system survived and until today has decisively affected economic progress in Japan. I refer to that system as the 1940 system. . . .
>
> There are three features of the Japanese economic system to point out: one is Japanese-type firms featuring lifetime employment and seniority-based wages; another is industry-by-industry labor unions; and the other is the indirect financing system centering on banks. Those three have played a key part in leading economic growth. But they were all adopted around 1940 as part of the war-time economic system. . . .
>
> What was the fundamental thinking that has supported such a 1940 system? It consisted of two elements. One is the principle of giving priority to producers. The other is the rejection of competition. These two elements have been undertaken and transmitted down to today. . . . It has been said that cooperation is more vital than competition. That thinking has been accepted as conventional wisdom by postwar corporate managers. . . . The government's aim was to adopt a privately owned but state-managed system. Rejection of competition, restrictions on it, and a warranty guaranteeing the survival of producers, in my view, are still the features of the 1940 system. . . .
>
> The 1940 system was designed for total battle, targeting a clear object. For that purpose, Japanese-type firms and the indirect financing system have worked well. However, the challenge for Japan today is developing creativity. There is no model here that would lead to that goal. So Japan

must find it by trial and error. The 1940 system cannot respond well to this challenge. This is the most crucial problem. . . . So deregulation has made no progress, and nor can new industry emerge. The Japanese economy remains confined by a stifling straitjacket.[2]

■ An abnormal nation

Professor Noguchi's argument, launched in midrecession, resonated with many in Japan. His book was a best-seller and spawned a small industry of debates, discussions, magazine articles, journal pieces, and other books. It characterized the entire economic structure as a historical aberration: "Some people point out that it is not easy to change the Japanese socioeconomic system because it is time-honored in Japan. But it did not have a long history. It emerged during an emergency—the war. It is then quite a unique system, so it is possible to change it."[3] By discrediting the contemporary economic system, his argument provided the ideal intellectual launching pad for a renewed reform movement in Japan.

Among those who seized on Professor Noguchi's thesis were Japan's multinational businesses and reform-minded politicians. Shusei Tanaka, an intellectual, a member of the Lower House of Parliament, and a senior adviser to Japan's only reformist prime minister, Morihiro Hosokawa, slotted the argument about the 1940 economic system into the larger political framework. Mr. Tanaka wrote:

The 1940 structure, if put in other words, was a system for national unity. Above it a firm and solid framework called the Emperor system existed. That framework later changed into the occupation structure and then into the Cold War structure. Under each framework, the 1940 structure was effective for pursuing the respective goals of each period, using the system of national unity formed through cooperation among the government, bureaucracy, and business circles. However, after the end of the Cold War the 1940 system has lost its direction. A system that has lost its goal and authority is no longer valid as a mechanism in human society.[4]

Most significantly, Noguchi's theory buttressed perfectly the manifesto of the real political force in Japan's reformist coalition, Ichiro Ozawa. Mr. Ozawa, formerly an important powerbroker in the Liberal Democratic Party, led the corps of breakaway dissidents that ended the party's thirty-eight-year rule and was instrumental in forging the reformist Hosokawa administration. In his potent 1993 book, Mr. Ozawa argued that Japan was an aberration in the world. It had conceded strategic leadership to the United States during the Cold War, and its politicians had reverted to a single function—supervising the distribution of wealth generated by high-speed growth. "Politics," wrote Mr. Ozawa, "has been reduced to the task of apportioning the dividends of Japan, Inc." The Cold War was over, but still Japan persisted with this system, "and Japan therefore remains unlike 'normal nations.'" As part of the revolution he prescribed, Mr. Ozawa wanted an overhaul of the economic system. The bureaucracy had operated a "factory-management approach" of centralized control over industry and its financing. While this was fine for Japan's catch-up industrialization, it was now obsolete:

"Politics," wrote Mr. Ozawa, "has been reduced to the task of apportioning the dividends of Japan, Inc."

> The failings of management-style administration are clearly revealed in the travails of our financial administration, which recently attracted attention with the collapse of the bubble economy. Every aspect of the finance industry, from the building of new bank branches to the establishment of deposit interest rates, was carried out under the strict regulation and supervision of the Okurasho. . . . The ministry also gave detailed guidance on every action taken by individual financial organs. Again, we return to the image of the foreman managing his factory."

But the factory had become too big and complex for the Okurasho to manage under this antiquated system. The result was an accumulation of bad debts and "serious crimes" in the banking industry. "The administration of the financial industry must be changed from the bottom up," prescribed Mr. Ozawa.[5]

■ "A failure of legitimacy?"

Professor Noguchi's economic critique was intimately and happily compatible with Mr. Ozawa's political blueprint. This gave it a tremendous practical power as a force for reform. Both saw Japan as an aberration in need of serious correction. While Professor Noguchi saw Japan's "total war" economic structure as an aberration in the history of Japan, Mr. Ozawa saw the overall Japanese politicoeconomic system as an aberration internationally. Both believed that an excess of bureaucratic meddling in the economy was at the core of contemporary Japan's abnormal structure and was an obstruction to future development of the economy. Both wanted the economy in general and the financial sector in particular to be governed more by market forces and less by bureaucrats—and that constituted a direct assault on the Okurasho.

Dr. Sakakibara saw Noguchi's ideas as a direct attack on the ministry: "Noguchi, as an influential opinion leader of a 'reform' group . . . is speaking loudly and clearly about the need to break away from the Okurasho and Japan's bureaucratic system."[6] And while he might have said precisely the same of Mr. Ozawa, it was more politically prudent to say it of his old friend, the academic, than of one of the country's most powerful men. Professor Noguchi, while very important in his own right, was also a proxy target for the Okurasho, a means of attacking the Ozawa manifesto and its intellectual basis without actually mentioning Mr. Ozawa.

Arching over the entire debate was the grand theory propounded by the Japanese-American Francis Fukuyama in his 1992 book *The End of History and the Last Man:* that "liberal democracy may constitute the end point of mankind's ideological evolution and the final form of human government." Strong nation-states had failed to endure because of what was "in the final analysis a failure of legitimacy—that is, a crisis on the level of ideas." Mr. Fukuyama perceives a universalist convergence on a single source of legitimacy—the sovereignty of the people. This concept has both political and economic meaning, investing individuals as voters with the right to choose their governments but also as workers and consumers with the right to choose jobs and products. There is no room in the

Fukuyama convergence for the survival of strong nation-states or their footsoldiers, strong bureaucracies.[7]

There is no room in the Fukuyama convergence for the survival of strong nation-states or their footsoldiers, strong bureaucracies.

These three dimensions of the argument crashed like a series of waves on the intellectual defenses of the Okurasho, each wave larger than the one before, each reinforcing the others; Noguchi's assertion that the Japanese economic structure had become aberrant and obsolete, Ozawa's contention that the political, social, and economic structures of Japan were abnormal and interim, and, finally, the Fukuyama argument that all countries have been evolving irrevocably under the twin impulses of democratic politics and market economies into a universal model where the individual is sovereign and where the bureaucracy is the servant, not the master. None of these developments boded well for the preservation of power at the Okurasho.

■ Defending the abnormal

Dr. Sakakibara conceded that the Noguchi view had come to occupy the mainstream position in Japan's public discourse, and he decided that it was vitally important to counter it. And so he vigorously took up the case against his friend and his theory, thereby implicitly attacking Ozawa and Fukuyama at the same time. The magazine article he wrote heralded only the beginning of Dr. Sakakibara's campaign: "The thesis on the 1940 economic structure conceals a taste of bitterness of Noguchi's being in his second adolescence," Dr. Sakakibara wrote.

> This experience strangely recalls his first adolescence, featured by my memory of him dashing onto the Diet grounds through its south gate in 1960 as one of the demonstrators opposed to the Ampo [U.S.-Japan Security Treaty] following Susumu Nishibe [now a popular critic], who was waving a blue flag.
> On closer reflection it may be only natural that the memories of the

two "adventures" overlap each other, for the pattern of thought underlying these two events was exactly the same, although there were ideological changes—the first action based on Marxism and the second on neoclassical economics. The thinking pattern at work in both events was his belief that there was a universal model to be found and "reform" to be aimed at, based on comparing that model with Japan's current conditions. . . . In other words, it is an advocacy backed by the impatience that comes from immaturity, arrogant elitism, and complex passions mixed with a kind of inferiority complex toward Europe and the U.S.[8]

Dr. Sakakibara does not dispute the existence of the 1940 economic structure. Where he differs from Professor Noguchi is in whether it is abnormal. Dr. Sakakibara argues that Japan's style of capitalism is quite consistent with Japanese history and values. Classical capitalism was the aberration in Japan, not the norm; it had existed for perhaps only twenty years or so in the entire history of the country, in the first quarter of the twentieth century. And its short life was inglorious; it had aggravated poverty and created social unrest and rice riots.

At the same time, Dr. Sakakibara marshalled the resources of the ministry to challenge the concept of Japan as abnormal internationally; in other words, to repudiate the Ozawa and Fukuyama theses without mentioning Mr. Ozawa himself. "In Japan," explained Dr. Sakakibara, "Fukuyama's universalism/revisionism is dominant in the press, as well as in political and administrative

To Dr. Sakakibara, classical capitalism was the aberration. It had aggravated poverty and created social unrest and rice riots.

circles. At present, 'reform' is coming onto the real stage. At this point we thought it necessary to verify the truth about universalism/revisionism." He assembled a panel of sixteen experts—thirteen academics, mainly from law departments, two bureaucrats, and a private-sector economist—through the ministry's Institute of Fiscal and Monetary Policy, and asked them to compare the Japanese political, economic, and social systems with those of the United States and Europe. Setting aside cultural differences, the task for the group was specifically to "examine whether or not Japan, in spite of such differences, is well equipped with 'modern' mechanisms institution-ally."[9]

The preliminary results, as summarized in an essay by Dr. Sakakibara, were entirely predictable: "From an institutional point of view," he said, "Japan lies in between the European model and the American model." Flowing from this is the implication that Japan is not abnormal. "What is important," concluded the architect of the project, "is to cast aside the 'reform view' based on the outlier-Japan concept and then to position Japan as a model or as a civilization in thinking about what direction it will take."[10]

Dr. Sakakibara does not propose that reform is entirely necessary. In his own work, in fact, he has made some modest liberalizations, chiefly in removing the last vestiges of controls on foreign exchange. But he does argue that reform should be guided by a Japanese ideal rather than a universalist or American ideal. And this implies that a minimum of change is required in Japan. In this way the former Okurasho bureaucrat Professor Noguchi became the leading intellectual force for sweeping reform of the Japanese economy, and his old friend and Okurasho leader, Dr. Sakakibara, became the leading defender of the status quo.

■ The struggle over deregulation

In the United States an estimated 6.6 percent of the economy is classified as falling into regulated sectors. In Japan, the comparable figure is 50.4 percent. And within Japan, the Ministry of Finance presides over one of the most heavily regulated industries: 100 percent of the many fields of the finance industry are regulated. This makes it even more closely supervised than the notoriously overregulated agriculture sector, with its regulation ratio of 86 percent. This helps explain why the Okurasho has emerged as the chief advocate for the status quo, the point of resistance in the national drive for deregulation. By contrast, only 16.8 percent of the sectors in Japan's manufacturing industry are regulated.[11] So it might not be surprising that the Ministry of International Trade and Industry has become, of all the government ministries, the most outspoken advocate for reform in Japan.

In sum, the Finance Ministry is the most important defender of the inefficient 200-yen sectors of the Japanese economy, while the Industry Ministry is the most aggressive agency arguing for the superefficient 100-yen sector (as explained in chapter 6). Can it be purely coincidental that on world markets Japan's banks, brokers, and finance firms are generally considered the equivalent of the Beverly Hillbillies—rich but laughably unsophisticated and seriously uncompetitive—while Japan's manufacturers are respected everywhere as world-class?

The Okurasho's stance on deregulation is extremely frustrating to Japan's competitive manufacturers. The ministry has a powerful influence on their competitiveness. This works through the ministry's direct controls over critical pieces of the economic infrastructure—the tax system and the financial markets, for instance—and also through its indirect controls over, for example, competition policy. "Japanese industry will continue moving offshore to escape these competitive disadvantages until, in the future, the only industry left in Japan will be the Okurasho," says a managing director of the big-business federation, the Keidanren. Yukio Nakamura, whose work includes lobbying the ministry on behalf of Japan's multinational corporations, believes that Dr. Sakakibara's work has been an important source of intellectual protection for the ministry's role: "We agree with Sakakibara that Japan should not change to reach the extremes of capitalism that are found in the U.S., but we do believe that there does need to be a lot of change and a lot of deregulation. The problem is that Sakakibara's arguments have become a cover for not doing anything at all."[12]

The national debate over deregulation went into the practicalities of how it would affect the economy. Every major study, including those by the government, agreed that a major program of deregulation would significantly accelerate economic growth. The Economic Planning Agency, for instance, estimated in 1994 that a national deregulation drive would add half a percentage point to the rate of economic growth every year for at least five years, thereby generating over five years as much new activity as the entire economy of Thailand or Indonesia creates annually. Allowing market forces freer play would also overcome the problem of the "hollowing out" of the industrial structure by assisting in the creation of new industry. Some of the simulations suggested that deregulation would also increase unemployment. The Economic Planning Agency proposed overcoming this side effect with an expanded program of government investment.[13] But policy makers did not really need simulations. Where deregulation did occur in Japan—for instance, with small relaxations in the regulations controlling cellular phones and licenses for retail stores—there was an explosion of activity. The consensus of economists was that the alternative to a sweeping program of deregulation was a permanent new paradigm of sclerotic economic growth and the stagnation of the industrial structure.

The first major contemporary call for restructuring the Japanese economy through deregulation came from the *Maekawa Report* of 1986, prepared by a top-level commission appointed by the prime minister and chaired by a former governor of the central bank. In the next ten years, the government issued nine more major reports either proposing more deregulation or announcing its implementation. During that time, every prime minister spoke of the pressing need to liberate the economy's inherent energy through a serious program of deregulation. Yet the reality never approached the level of the rhetoric. One crude but indicative measure of the deregulation drive is what happened to the number of regulations in force. The first official survey of national regulation was carried out the year before the *Maekawa Report;* it counted a total of 10,054 national regulations in force. In the most recent survey available, carried out in 1994, there were 10,945 regulations in force. In other words, a decade of supposed deregulation had actually increased the number of regulations by 891, or 8.9 percent. Of those ministries which had increased the net number of regulations, the most active was the Ministry of Welfare. Next came the Ministry of Finance. In the nine years from the first survey to the last, the Okurasho increased the number of its regulations in force by 275, or 25 percent.

The Okurasho's standard posture is to resist any proposal for deregulation, but sometimes it has even gone on the offensive to suppress private-sector proposals and to head off demands. This is what happened in 1993 when the Keidanren submitted seventeen requests for deregulation and liberalization to the Government's Office of Trade Ombudsman. The response of the Ministry of Finance was to search out the companies that had initiated the requests and pressure them to keep silent.[14]

A decade of supposed deregulation had actually increased the number of regulations by 891, or 8.9 percent.

Usually, however, the ministry's resistance is based on that great ally of bureaucrats, inertia. Inertia is often the ministry's only line of defense. In November 1995, when Okurasho officials were called before the prime minister's special deregulation task force, for example, the panel wanted to know why the issue of corporate debt instruments known as corporate paper was restricted for the moneylending industry and why it could not be further liberalized. The hearing was held a few days after corporate paper (CP) with a term of two weeks had just been liberalized.

"If two-week CP can be liberalized," asked a member of the panel, "why not CP with longer terms? Regulation leads to higher costs for industry. If you think it is necessary, you should prove how and why."

From among the serried ranks of Finance Ministry officials who had come to face the panel, one spoke: "However," he began, "in Japan the concept of investor self-responsibility is not yet established and the market is not yet mature." This response is a typical counter to requests for deregulation. It is based on bureaucratic paternalism in the first instance and a protectively circular logic in the second; if the market is not mature, it cannot be liberalized; yet if it is not liberalized, how can it ever become mature?

The official then argued that the liberalization of two-week CP was the exception and not the rule: "The reason that two-week CP was liberalized is because, fortunately, we were able to get an adjustment of views among the related parties." The officials failed to answer a question about who the related parties were and what the adjustment might have been.

The panel tried a different tack: "This law was legislated in 1951. It's obviously outdated!"

The officials countered with another stock response: "A law is not bad because of its age—it's alive and well right now."[15]

And so it goes. In all such dealings the Okurasho holds the advantage: the weight of inertia is great, and it operates in favor of the bureaucracy. As a panel member lamented:

> Formally, we have a lot of power. But the problem is this: The Japanese Government is divided into many ministries, and the ministries are divided into many bureaus, and the bureaus into many sections. The bureaucrats always have ridiculous arguments for why the regulations should continue, and we always have heated discussions with them. But a section chief at age 45 represents the entire Government of Japan in his own area of policy. . . . Once he says "no," it is very hard for anyone to change his decision.[16]

■ Virtual regulation

Until 1994, Japan's banks offered a uniform interest rate on ordinary savings accounts of 0.22 percent a year. Then rates were deregulated. And after the long-awaited liberalization? Of Japan's 149 banks, 127 offered rates between 0.22 and 0.25 percent. Professor emeritus Shozo Ueda of Kansai University in Osaka was disgusted: "That's not free competition; that's camouflage. You need a microscope to spot the difference." He points out that there is a tremendous variation in the strength of the banks—the most profitable making about twenty times as much profit per employee as the laggards—and yet the strongest and weakest offered the same rates. "But the concern of the strongest bank is not to offer the best possible rate to consumers, but to maintain the discipline of the cartel."[17]

Professor Ueda protested formally but won no support form the Okurasho. "I'm aware of Professor Ueda's view, but our view is that it's unnatural for different banks to offer different interest rates," said Yoshimasa Nishimura, then head of the Banking Bureau. "Bank savings accounts as a product are very similar. So it's very possible that the banks will offer the same interest rate as a result." And what of the report in the magazine *Kinyu Business* that a secret meeting of top bank executives prearranged rates to avoid "excessive competition"? "That's not a meeting to operate a cartel," said Nishimura, "it's just a forum for exchange of information."[18]

The Fair Trade Commission investigated Professor Ueda's complaint but said it found no evidence to support the claim of anticompetitive behavior. He was not surprised: "The chairman of the banks' cartel is the Okurasho, and the co-chairman is the Fair Trade Commission."[19] The banks were the winners and Japan's consumers the losers; an increase of one percentage point in the average deposit rate would have required the banks to put an extra 3.6 trillion yen ($36 billion) into their customers' accounts each year. And the deposit rates were about 2 percentage points below the rate on overnight call money at the time.[20] The bank cartel survived deregulation intact. Indeed, two years later, they were more uniform than ever; of 149 banks of all types, 147 offered an identical rate on ordinary savings accounts of 0.1 percent.[21]

After the landmark 1984 negotiations with the United States over Japan's financial system, the so-called Yen-Dollar Committee, the Okurasho was obliged to begin a serious program for the liberalization of bank interest rates.[22] It was an agonizingly slow process, with the last formal controls removed ten years later. But even in cases such as this, where deregulation is utterly unavoidable, the Ministry of Finance has shown that it is possible to remove the regulation and yet preserve industry practice much as if the regulation were still in force. The ministry has perfected the art of deregulating in name rather than substance. It might be called virtual regulation.

■ A new miracle?

Beneath the creaking industrial structure of Japan's aging postwar economic miracle are the makings of a new miracle. While the establishment agonizes over the loss of jobs at the mainstays of yesterday's miracle—companies like Nippon Steel and Nissan—

small, aggressive firms that most people have never heard of are creating new jobs, growing their total number of staff by 5 percent a year even in recession. These companies, the firms listed on the over-the-counter (OTC) stock market, are the mainstays of tomorrow's miracle. While the profits of the big companies listed on the first and second sections of the Tokyo Stock Exchange stagnated in recession in 1994, the OTC companies were enjoying profit growth of 20 percent a year. They are "the world's greatest emerging market," according to the big U.S. funds manager Fidelity Investments, and "the most exciting growth market in Asia," according to U.K.-based Barclays Securities. And they are not just growing fast, they are growing something different—a new type of economic activity.

Beneath the creaking industrial structure of Japan's aging post-war economic miracle are the makings of a new miracle: small, aggressive firms that most people have never heard of.

One distinguishing characteristic of these companies is their relative immunity from exchange rate fluctuations—exports account for just 3 percent of their total sales. And they are based on services—only a quarter of OTC firms are manufacturers, compared with half of those listed on the main market.[23] In short, the OTC market represents the prospect of a new and promising industrial structure for Japan. And it is precisely for this reason that the Ministry of International Trade and Industry wants to promote new listings on the market, listings that have been drastically restricted.

How restricted? Researchers at the Sanwa Bank took a sample of the 455 venture businesses listed in a handbook of innovative new Japanese businesses, the *Nikkei Venture Business Annual 1994*, and then applied the listing criteria of the OTC market to them. Only 23 percent qualified. The same companies were then passed through the filter of listing criteria for the comparable market in the United States, the NASDAQ. Three times as many—71 percent— made it.[24] And those companies which had the greatest difficulty getting listed in Japan were the newest ones. On average, it takes a company five years just to get through the screening process for the OTC market; an OTC company is, on average, seventeen years old by the time it lists.[25] "We are worried that we may not have much time," said one Industry Ministry official. "We may be missing a window of opportunity, and if we do miss it, looking ten or twenty years from now, Japan might not have many healthy industries. We are saying this restraint [on new listings] should be removed. If interesting new companies are listed, it can revitalize the economy. . . . The government must not hinder change in the private sector."[26]

The Okurasho, however, refused to allow a serious liberalization of the OTC market. Although on paper the ministry does not appear to have the jurisdictional powers to do this, it in fact controls the body that operates the market, the Japan Securities Dealers' Association. The reasons it blocks easier access for venture firms to investors' capital? It looks on the market as a haven of speculation. And it considers that the OTC market, by possibly attracting investors' capital from the main market, could weaken prices on the Tokyo Stock Exchange's first section.[27] There is some basis to both of these concerns, but not much.

The first section of the Tokyo stock market is notorious internationally as an intensely speculative market, owing partly to Okurasho tolerance. Is it logical to protect one speculative market for the sake of another? And the Japan Security Dealers' Association has conducted surveys showing that only about one-fifth of the money subscribed to new listings on the OTC market was leaching from the main market.[28] And in any case, the OTC market is just one-twentieth the size of the main market. The Okurasho has been protecting a giant from a pygmy.

After protracted negotiations between the Industry and the Finance Ministries, a compromise was reached in 1995. Some new technology companies that met stringent listing criteria would be allowed to apply to be traded on a new technology section of the OTC market. It was a bureaucratic construct, and it met a bureaucratic fate: it was deeply unattractive to the companies that were supposed to use it. A survey of 766 potentially eligible firms found that only 13 were interested in the possibility of listing.[29] There was a distinct possibility that the new section would host no companies whatsoever, and the Industry Ministry was reported to be asking a few firms to list purely to save ministerial face. In this way the

Okurasho has managed to defend the old economic order at the expense of the new.

■ Maturity or hypocrisy?

The leading intellectual advocate for the Finance Ministry's interventionism, Dr. Sakakibara, has not always held his current views about the value of preserving the unique Japanese approach to regulating the economy. In fact, in 1977, he wrote one of the toughest and most insightful critiques ever published on the controlled nature of Japan's economy. Dr. Sakakibara was actually one of two authors of the article—the other was his friend Professor Noguchi. The piece was titled "Dissecting the Finance Ministry–Bank of Japan Dynasty" and subtitled "End of the Wartime System for Total Economic Mobilization."[30] The authors wrote, "We believe that the economic system which until now has supported high growth is fundamentally a continuation of the war-time system of total mobilization of economic resources." This is remarkably similar to Professor Noguchi's thesis about the 1940 system, his argument that Japan continued to operate a "total-war economy," the argument that Dr. Sakakibara attacked so energetically and so publicly in the 1990s.

The 1977 article continued:

> We propose to interpret the economic structure which has been in existence in Japan since World War Two in terms of two hypotheses. First, although in terms of ideology Japanese society underwent a drastic reorientation after the end of the war, the economic system—particularly the institutional system for financial control—was retained essentially intact. The result was a bipolar structure and an acute gap between understanding and reality. Second, the newly adopted ideology of egalitarianism released energy for economic growth, and this energy, while being controlled by the financial system, gave birth to rapid growth.
>
> These hypotheses interpret the high-growth Japanese economic structure not as a planned economy, a free-market economy, or a mixed economy of the West European type, but as a totally unique structure. . . .

But at the same time, it has been a contradictory and unstable structure that could only be sustained by continued growth. . . . The egalitarianism adopted by postwar Japanese society and the retained apparatus for preferential application of economic controls are two mutually conflicting elements, and holding them together required the acrobatic skill to walk a tightrope. It was high economic growth that dynamically sustained the bipolar economic structure. In this sense, the postwar Japanese economy may be likened to bicycle riding—unless one pedals fast enough, there is a danger the bicycle will fall over.

Financial instruments of regulation were the chief pillar of preferential economic control, this control, of course, lacking legitimacy under the postwar egalitarianism. Control was effective only because the high growth cycle existed. . . . It is thought for this reason that the transition to stable growth will be impossible without fundamental alteration of the economic structure.

The authors saw five central elements in this system of control:

1. Control over interest rates to keep them artificially low.
2. Control over foreign exchange and capital flows.
3. Control of the banking system.
4. The establishment of strategic financing institutions, such as the Japan Development Bank and the Export-Import Bank of Japan.
5. The doctrine of the balanced budget.

Every one of these elements was under the control of the Ministry of Finance. And while the second element no longer exists, the other four, either formally or informally, remain intact.

Also according to this article, the system is illegitimate and unsustainable, an obstacle to industrial transformation. Dr. Sakakibara acknowledges that the article was the prototype of Professor Noguchi's 1940 thesis, the thesis he now opposed so vehemently and with the full support and endorsement of the Finance Ministry's think tank. How does the he explain the total reversal of his view?

When the two men wrote the article in 1977, they had both recently left the Finance Ministry and taken positions on the faculty of Saitama University. Dr. Sakakibara was planning to enter politics.

Japan, rocked by oil crises and revolted by the Lockheed political scandals,[31] was reconsidering itself, and a new reformist political group, the New Liberal Club, was an expression of the mood. Dr. Sakakibara wanted to join. The critique of the Ministry of Finance–Bank of Japan Dynasty was "meant to be a kind of announcement of my running in the race and a farewell address to the Okurasho." But while Professor Noguchi's departure from the ministry proved to be a permanent one, and his view has remained unchanged, his friend and collaborator soon returned. The ministry and the system that Dr. Sakakibara damned from outside he now champions passionately from within. He defends himself against the charge of hypocrisy in later life by pleading immaturity in his earlier years.[32] And their friendship? Could it survive so grand, so public, and so personal a clash? "Sakakibara is one of my closest friends," says Professor Noguchi. "Still."[33]

THE SACRED MISSION

One of Japan's most powerful postwar politicians, Shin Kanemaru, a supreme backroom tactician and for a decade Japan's king maker—a political power-broker whose support is vital when selecting a prime minister—told a gathering of constituents just how far he was prepared to go to win government funding for his rural electorate: "You can't keep everyone happy unless you're prepared to lay your life on the line and go about overturning the desk of the director-general of the Budget Bureau at the Okurasho!"[1] This colorfully captures the superior bargaining position of the ministry and the supplicant status of the politician. The Finance Ministry's role as the honest guardian of public revenues, providing protection from political depredation, is its most valuable moral mantle.

And budget making is the ministry's core power. The Okurasho has an effective monopoly on proposing and compiling the budget. It has the exclusive power to implement it—the ministry collects all revenues and, in practice, authorizes all spending. Its ability to withhold a budget gives it tremendous coercive power over a government. This power has been exposed most nakedly in the ministry's treatment of weak governments. It refused to cooperate with Japan's first and only Socialist government, the Katayama Cabinet of 1947–1948. By denying it funding for a sensitive program, the Okurasho contributed to the government's collapse after only nine months in office. The ministry had no such difficulty funding the next government—a conservative one.[2]

203

After this episode, Mr. Kanemaru's party, the Liberal Democrats, in their unbroken thirty-eight-year tenure in office, developed methods for more successfully managing the Okurasho in budget negotiations. Compelled to coexist for nearly forty years, the ministry and the Liberal Democrats have in the main established a businesslike symbiosis. The ministry has catered to the party's essential political needs, supplying subsidies to groups that are economically inefficient but politically powerful—farmers and fishermen and owners of small businesses. But the ministry has cooperated on condition that the party otherwise allows it broad discretion. A natural tension persists.

The politicians, always tempted to profligacy, have been in continual conflict with the ministry's instinctive fiscal caution. Sometimes the politicians win. Most spectacularly, Prime Minister Kakuei Tanaka blew apart the Okurasho's ban on government deficits with his grand plan to reconstruct the Japanese archipelago with expensive public works in the first half of the 1970s. The ministry acquiesced at the time,[3] but after the event realized that it had been humiliated and public finances plundered. Officials have since described deficits as "narcotic" and "evil."[4] Ruefully, the Okurasho's top officer in 1993 recounted the story to new ministry recruits: "In 1975, in breach of Article Four of the Public Finance Law, deficit-covering bonds were issued. It took us fifteen years to recover from it. I must insist that we never repeat that mistake."[5]

When the consumption tax was thrust on a resentful public, the voters penalized the Liberal Democrats by depriving them of control of the Upper House.

The Okurasho launched a counterstrike. It responded to the Tanaka attack on public finance with an unrelenting ten-year campaign to force the Liberal Democrats to introduce a new and deeply unpopular tax—a tax on consumption. The first time the party attempted to introduce it—in 1979 under Prime Minister Masayoshi Ohira—it provoked extraordinary popular resistance. It was finally denounced by most Liberal Democrat legislators, and Mr. Ohira was forced to retract the idea. He died of stress-related illness soon afterward. A second effort failed in 1987. When the tax was finally thrust on a resentful public in 1989, the voters penalized the Liberal Democrats three months later by depriving them of their control of the Upper House.

■ Political suicide

The Liberal Democrats eventually lost office in 1993. The moment this happened, the ministry gave its tendency toward intimidation full play. It decided to use the advent of the immensely popular government of Morihiro Hosokawa to improve the state of public finances. The new government was elected on a platform of political reform and economic deregulation, but it was at core a conservative, mainstream administration—procapital, progrowth, pro-United States. Its policy goals were not much different from those of the Liberal Democrats. The main contrast was that Hosokawa supported reform in some of the mechanisms for delivering those goals. He wanted a bigger role for the marketplace and a lesser one for regulations, a larger role for politicians over bureaucrats. In sum, he advocated a "responsible revolution."

In 1994, the Okurasho used its budget power to intimidate the new Hosokawa government into announcing a politically suicidal tax policy. The prime minister called an abrupt and wholly unexpected midnight press conference to declare an increase in the consumption tax from 3 percent to 7 percent. Public outcry at this startling announcement obliged Mr. Hosokawa to retract his plan the next day; the episode contributed decisively to the government's collapse three months later.

How do civil servants force a popular elected government to commit suicide? Hosokawa took office promising to cut taxes. This was not just a political ploy but, with the economy in protracted recession, an economic necessity. The Okurasho was prepared to comply. But the ministry imposed the condition that the government pass a law at the same time to raise taxes a year later. Specifically, the ministry wanted the government to increase the rate of consumption tax in 1995. The ministry demanded that

Mr. Hosokawa enshrine both measures in law simultaneously, because it did not trust politicians when they promised to increase taxes at some future date. The politicians, said the ministry, would be happy to hand out the tax cuts to help the economy recover but would fail to implement an unpopular tax increase once recovery was secure. The result would simply be a further deterioration in the national finances.

But Mr. Hosokawa refused to package a tax cut with a tax increase. He argued that wage earners would be less inclined to spend their tax refunds if they knew they were to be followed by a tax increase. The stimulative effect of the tax cut would be lost. The new prime minister resolved to implement his election promise in the budget for the year beginning April 1, 1994. He set a deadline for compiling the budget—the end of December 1993. But the moment he tried to press ahead, indeed on the very day he decided to set this deadline, the Okurasho intervened. Two of Hosokawa's top political aides were waiting for the arrival of the finance minister so they could move to implement the prime minister's orders for the quick compilation of the national budget. They were surprised when the minister failed to appear and, instead, they were joined by the Okurasho's top bureaucrat, administrative affairs vice minister Jiro Saito. Mr. Saito took control of the agenda and blocked the government's attempts to compile the national budget.[6]

Mr. Hosokawa was now in an impossible position. "There were many immediate subjects to be tackled," he later wrote, "such as the national budget, the third supplementary budget, the financial plan for the local government sector, and the February summit between Japan and the U.S. None of them could be settled without reform of the tax system, including a tax cut."[7] The Okurasho was holding the budget hostage. And Hosokawa was running out of time to negotiate. As if this threat to the government were not plan enough, a current affairs magazine, *Sentaku*, reported that Mr. Saito had recently called on the prime minister one night to make a direct threat: "If you announce a tax cut without securing the funding for it, we can delay the drafting of the budget."[8] Asked later whether he had received such a threat, Mr. Hosokawa did not deny it but replied: "Rather than discussing whether there was Okurasho convincing and compulsion, I might say we should first strengthen the authority and power of the prime minister."[9] Mr. Saito in the meantime was lobbying big business and the media personally in an effort to generate support for the Okurasho's tax proposal. He was accompanied by the top official of the Ministry of International Trade and Industry, the junior partner in this campaign to isolate the prime minister.[10] Mr. Saito also pressured the powerbroker of the new government, Ichiro Ozawa, over dinner on one celebrated occasion, setting out the government's options in stark terms.

The prime minister surrendered to the Okurasho. Mr. Saito won the satisfaction of hearing Mr. Hosokawa announce on February 3 a tax cut, to be followed by an increase in the consumption tax—from 3 percent to 7 percent. For cosmetic reasons, the tax was renamed the welfare tax. But Mr. Hosokawa's abrupt and unconvincing midnight announcement made it perfectly plain that the plan was not his own. Asked by reporters the basis for setting the tax rate at 7 percent, he was unable to give one, stammering that it was a "rough estimate" of what might be needed. Mr. Saito, asked by reporters if he were responsible for the tax increase, replied: "No, it was the Prime Minister's decision." This is, of course, technically true. However, it is also true that Mr. Saito left the prime minister no other option.

It was a hollow victory for the Okurasho. The political uproar within Mr. Hosokawa's ruling coalition—which had not been consulted—and among the public at large forced the prime minister to recant the next day. It proved to be a fatal blow to the credibility and popularity of the Hosokawa government, which survived for fewer than three months after the tax debacle. But it was only a tactical setback for the Finance Ministry. It survived, its tax agenda intact, to work on Mr. Hosokawa's successors. The episode did carry some cost for the ministry. The Liberal Democrats suspected that the deal showed a treasonable Okurasho willingness to work with the Hosokawa government and looked for opportunities to take revenge later. This did nothing to interfere with the ministry's campaign to increase the scale of the consumption tax, however. The next Liberal Democrat administration, the coalition Murayama government, legislated for an increase in the consumption tax—

from 3 percent to 5 percent—effective from April 1, 1997. The Okurasho has made it clear that it wants to continue increasing the consumption tax rate.

"You could say that the budget represents the political will of the nation, but actually it's the Okurasho that puts those numbers together—that means they are manufacturing the political will of Japan," says long-serving legislator and former minister Kazuo Aichi, who served in both the Liberal Democrats and in Mr. Hosokawa's coalition, "This is a long-standing political problem."[11]

> "... It's the Okurasho that puts [the budget] together—... they are manufacturing the political will of Japan."

■ The closely guarded power of the budget

The ministry itself is not a monolith. According to one expression, it is all bureau, no ministry. Legal regulatory authority resides with the director-general of each bureau rather than with the vice minister for administrative affairs, the ministry's top bureaucrat, so the bureau sometimes resemble warring fiefdoms. As the most senior ministry member, the administrative vice minister is often the mediator between the fiefs rather than the chief of the institution. But while the Finance Ministry sometimes speaks with many voices, the voice of the Budget Bureau is its most authoritative. The other bureaus defer to it, ministry staff seek to work in it, politicians try desperately to cultivate it. Experience as the bureau's director-general is customarily a prerequisite for candidates for the Okurasho's vice-minister for administrative affairs. "If you're not in the Budget Bureau," some say of this powerful, prestigious office, "you're nowhere." Its reach is great; any matter involving government spending, even relatively small sums, must be filtered through the budgeting process.[12]

The Constitution of Japan does not give the Okurasho a monopoly on writing the budget. Indeed, the Constitution does not even mention the Ministry of Finance; it recognizes only the authority of the Cabinet and the Diet. The ministry's role is based on a combination of convention and legislation. Various governments have toyed with the idea of transferring the budget-writing role from the ministry to a more politically responsive agency, such as the Cabinet. Most recently, in 1993, an advisory body to the prime minister, the Administrative Reform Council [*Gyokakushin*], considered setting up a Cabinet Budget Bureau to take control of the budget, but it panicked in the face of stern and implacable opposition from the Okurasho. As a result, the council failed to recommend that the ministry lose its budgeting powers when it sent its report to the prime minister of the day—the same one who was to fall victim to precisely this power. Mr. Hosokawa.[13] Yet Mr. Hosokawa concluded from his own sorry experience that this was one of the most important challenges confronting Japan.[14]

> **Japan was the most restrained among the deficit nations, the most virtuous among the sinners.**

Do the ends justify the means?

The ministry's fierce fiscal reflex seems to have yielded results. Japan has for many years has been one of the most restrained spenders in the world. For example, in the 1980s, the various governments in power did submit to the temptation to live beyond their means—running government deficits—but they were relatively modest about it. In Japan, government spending outstripped income by an average of 1.5 percent of the total economy, as defined by GDP. By comparison, in the same decade the United States overspent by 2.5 percent, the Group of Seven biggest economies by 3 percent, and the industrialized world as a whole by a little more than 3 percent. This did not make Japan the most prudent spender in the world—Finland and Norway consistently ran surpluses—but it was the most restrained among the deficit nations, the most virtuous among the sinners.[15]

Evidence of the ministry's fiscal vigilance is everywhere. The Okurasho's budget examiners, poised at the cutting edge of fiscal restraint, are among the most fearsome figures in modern Japan. During the high-pressure months of budget compilation, these officials, working eighteen-hour days, often sleeping in the office and seldom returning home on weekdays, carefully study the spending requests and budget proposals submitted by all government agencies. The examiners call before them the officials of these agencies and ask them to justify their requests. They interrogate older men of higher rank, paying no deference to seniority. They keep these supplicants awaiting their convenience in corridors and anterooms at all hours of the day and night.

Finance Ministry stringency has held pork-barrel programs such as farm subsidies and industry assistance from ballooning to grotesque proportions. And there are a thousand small examples of ministry watchfulness. For example, it forced the Defense Agency to postpone the retirement age for troops—for instance, in 1985 colonels had to retire at age fifty-three, but ten years later the age had been extended to fifty-five—to delay paying their lump-sum retirement checks. The Defense Agency, complaining that it would have an army of old men, was powerless to do anything about it.[16] No matter is too small for ministry scrutiny. In 1995 it decided to abolish the subsidy on rice for school lunches.[17] And no distance is too great. The Foreign Ministry administers a grassroots overseas aid program designed specifically to meet the local needs of small villages in poor countries. To keep the program immediate and decentralized, spending is authorized by Japan's embassies abroad—but only up to a limit of 1 million yen ($10,000). Anything above that must be approved by the Okurasho. All of this seems ample license, moral and practical, to justify its monopoly grip on budget making.

During the high-pressure months of budget compilation, its officials work eighteen-hour days, often sleeping in the office.

An abortive attempt at change

But the Okurasho is not as tough as it seems. While it is formidable in trimming the fringes of government spending, it has proved to be ineffectual in changing some of the fundamentals. The structure of Japan's public works spending is a prime example. Allocations became so rigid that they started to look ridiculous. They were so widely criticized that the Budget Bureau decided to participate in a 1993 review by one of the ministry's advisory councils, the Deliberation Council on the Fiscal System. The chairman of the review, Hiromitsu Ishi of Hitotsubashi University, described the problem:

> Over the past 30 years, the Japanese economy has undergone a significant structural transformation. Jolted by the twin oil crises of the 1970s, it left the path of rapid growth for the path of stable growth. . . . Primary industry's contribution to [the economy] dropped dramatically from 9.5 percent in 1965 to 2.2 percent in 1992. . . . The means of transportation, for both passengers and freight, also changed dramatically, shifting from trains and ships to automobiles and airplanes. . . . [But] the allocation of public works has hardly changed at all in 30 years. One could call this a classic case of inefficient resource allocation.[18]

In particular, the public works carried out directly by the central government showed extraordinary inflexibility. And this is a significant program. In 1995 it was allocated 9.3 trillion yen ($93 billion), accounting for 1 yen in every 8 in the national budget. Every year from 1965 until the year of Professor Ishi's inquiry, 1993, the Okurasho carved up this particular part of the budget in the following manner: 68–69 percent to the Ministry of Construction, 20–22 percent to the Ministry of Agriculture, and 6–7 percent to the Ministry of Transport. Professor Ishi was bitingly critical. He declared that the allocations were set not according to the nation's investment needs but according to the number of engineers employed by each ministry. The money for the Agriculture Ministry, for instance, was just the right amount to keep its 18,000 engineers fully employed on new projects, not taking into account the fact that the ministry "builds 'agricultural' roads for the sake of building them, with little consideration for the convenience of users or efficiency of investment."

Professor Ishi and his colleagues on the council's Public Works Subcommittee recommended that the Okurasho abandon mere precedent and instead spend taxpayers' money according to priority. This committee, with Budget Bureau participation, proposed three categories of varying urgency. It suggested, for instance, that improving housing and water supplies should take priority over building more forest roads. Professor Ishi refrained from blaming the Finance Ministry for the awful rigidity that had gripped the system; he said it was a result of the spending ministries colluding with politicians of the Liberal Democratic Party to frustrate rational budgeting.

So what happened when the Liberal Democrats lost power and a new coalition government took office? In 1994, the Ministry of Construction was once more given 68 percent of central government public works money, the Ministry of Agriculture once again given 20 percent, and the Ministry of Transport its customary 6 percent. The Budget Bureau had been empowered by a new policy recommendation, liberated by a once-in-forty-years change of government, yet was not able to engineer a change in interministerial budget allocations of even a single percentage point. Professor Ishi was deeply disappointed. He concluded that the Okurasho had effectively surrendered its budget oversight and that change was impossible without strong political leadership.[18]

■ Japan's "special corporations"

If the Okurasho were serious about fiscal reform, it would be serious about reform of the ninety-two major companies owned by the State, the so-called special corporations. There is room for streamlining the companies and their half-million staff members. Most were established in the 1950s and 1960s. Many have outgrown their original purpose, such as the Japan Raw Silk and Sugar Price Stabilization Agency and the Maritime Credit Corporation. Others seem ripe for privatization, for instance, the Japan National Oil Corporation and the Japan Development Bank. None had been subject to serious review for many years.

There had been *attempts* at review, but they were consistently frustrated by the bureaucracy. For instance, when the third Administrative Reform Council convened a hearing to examine the matter in 1993, all ministries boycotted the meetings. In 1994 Japan's taxpayers paid subsidies of 4.9 trillion yen ($49 billion) to the special corporations. The potential significance of reform was tremendous; these losses are the equivalent of the revenue that would have been generated by a consumption tax of 2.5 percent in 1994.

In the first half of the 1990s, the Hosokawa and Murayama governments, although different in political complexion, both wanted to exploit the revenue potential of a rationalization. In 1994 a political project team in the Murayama government proposed a plan to abolish three special corporations, to privatize twenty-two, and to streamline another twenty-four. The savings to the taxpayer were estimated at 1.7 trillion yen a year, very close to the tax yield of a 1 percent consumption tax.[19] Indeed, Prime Minister Murayama explicitly linked the reform of the special corporations to the consumption tax; the government, he said, would "shed blood" in reforming the corporations in return for the public's acceptance of an enlarged consumption tax. Reform of these fat cats of the economy was politically popular and strongly endorsed by big business.

The Ministry of Finance should have been one of the most enthusiastic campaigners for this reform plan. And at one time it was indeed interested in exploiting the fiscal potential of a program of mergers and reconstruction.[20] But then it became clear that if the special corporations were to be shaken up, some of the Okurasho's own special corporations would be rattled, too. The ministry's interest in the proposal evaporated. When the Cabinet asked each government ministry to submit a proposal for a streamlining of the special corporations, an Okurasho official summarized the ministry position: "All public corporations are necessary. Our report will suggest no changes."[21] The matter might have finished here with the frustration of the prime minister's pledge to shed blood, except that the Liberal Democrats, after their brief nine months on the opposition benches, were now thirsty for revenge after the Okurasho's perceived readiness to forge an alliance with the Hosokawa government.

In early 1995 the Liberal Democrats decided to press ahead with a proposal to merge two of the Okurasho's client special corporations, the Japan Development Bank and the Export-Import Bank of Japan. The politicians argued that the merger would eliminate duplication of services and save taxpayers' money, but their hidden motivation was to punish the Ministry of Finance. How would such a merger punish the ministry? Instead of two well-paid and well-padded positions as bank governors, a merger would leave room for only one. There would also be a shrinkage in the supply of deputy governor positions and directors' jobs. This was, therefore, a direct assault on the retirement options of Okurasho bureaucrats. "This is war," declared a senior Liberal Democrat.

The Okurasho responded with a campaign of high-level lobbying. Administrative Vice Minister Jiro Saito called on a faction leader in the Liberal Democrats and a former Okurasho bureaucrat, Kiichi Miyazawa. (Mr. Saito was apparently oblivious to the irony of this appeal for the protection of a Finance Ministry job entitlement to the man who, as prime minister, had been ignored when he tried to curtail another entitlement—it was Mr. Miyazawa who had ordered the ministry to relax the stranglehold of Tokyo University graduates on jobs in the Finance Ministry.) The politicians were unmoved. Some, including the party's powerful secretary-general, closed their minds completely, even refusing to receive Okurasho officials sent to lobby them. The ministry, seeing that it was losing the argument, tried the time-tested bureaucratic technique of delay.

It turned for help to perhaps the most powerful man in the Liberal Democrats, the former prime minister and faction boss Noboru Takeshita, who was counted as one of the ministry's most reliable allies. Soon afterward, a Takeshita disciple who was then minister for international trade and industry, Ryutaro Hashimoto, presented the ruling coalition with a proposal for a thorough inquiry into all government-affiliated financial institutions. This was a classic ploy, and it was instantly recognized as one. But it went further; Mr. Hashimoto's inquiry was to have no fixed reporting date and was also to examine the issue of the postal savings system. This was a politically intractable issue. By including it, Mr. Hashimoto was seeking to guarantee that the inquiry would lead to a dead end.

For a moment the Finance Ministry's tactics seem to have worked. But Mr. Hashimoto's proposal remained just that. This was one occasion where the bulk of the Liberal Democrats had made up their minds, where the Okurasho could not claim the protection of any special technical expertise or moral authority, and, therefore, where it was destined to lose.[22] The final outcome was a decision to merge two of the Finance Ministry's special corporations, the Export-Import Bank of Japan and the Overseas Economic Cooperation Fund. It was hardly a drastic measure; it was actually a reintegration, as previously the two had been a single entity.

And because the Okurasho resisted the reform so fiercely, it ended up yielding no savings, bringing no fiscal benefit. The merger was to take place in 1999, an unjustifiable delay of four years, and the government projected no savings to the taxpayer. It had become an exercise in pure political punishment. And the Okurasho had utterly failed to use the opportunity to accomplish any fiscal goal. "The plan is meaningless as a streamlining," observed the head of an external advisory body, Hiroshi Kato of the Tax Commission, "because the integration means their operations will actually be enlarged. They should both be privatized." He estimated that a privatization of the Japan Development Bank would yield 2.28 trillion yen ($22.8 billion) in revenue. And what does the Okurasho say about this idea? From the big building at 3-1-1 Kasumigaseki, there is only a profound silence.[23]

■ A paradoxical appearance of power

So while the Okurasho has been important in restraining government spending, the evidence also shows that it is not wholeheartedly committed to the principle of fiscal restraint. It is vigilant in overseeing the annual budget process, yet it has failed to exploit prime opportunities to improve the fundamental structure of Japan's public outlays. In the case of the special corporations, the ministry's motivation is transparent—it simply wants to maximize the number of comfortable postministry jobs for its own members. But what of the case of the allocation of public investment? How can that, and a range of other examples, be explained? Why does the ministry appear to be so earnest in its commitment to the budget process and yet so insincere elsewhere?

The suspicion arises that the ministry employs its fiscal authority as an exercise in power rather than in the pursuit of policy, that it is more interested in establishing leverage than actually achieving a balanced budget or the elimination of the national deficit. In an interesting piece of research, an Okurasho official demonstrated through a mathematical formula that the exercise of austerity certainly increases the Finance Ministry's power over other ministries in the government.

The ministry employs its fiscal authority as an exercise in power rather than in the pursuit of policy.

In a 1979 paper for the Economic Planning Agency, Eisuke Sakakibara, later head of the Okurasho's International Finance Bureau, led a team of six officials in analyzing the annual negotiation for budget funds between the Ministry of Construction and the Ministry of Finance. It measured the relative power of the two ministries, the spender and the financier, in negotiations from 1959 to 1978 over funding for national roads and tollways, and it charted the outcome in graph form. The team found that only two events put significantly more power in the hands of those in the Finance Ministry—oil shocks and austerity campaigns. This is pretty much common sense, but it is nevertheless interesting to find it confirmed in research by an official of the ministry itself. The paper concluded that the Finance Ministry's use of a "dynamic structuralism" model "seems to capture the essence of bureaucratic politics in the Japanese context."[24]

And in his careful study of Japanese budget making, U.S. scholar John Creighton Campbell suggested a hierarchial order of the eight objectives that guide the ministry in compiling the budget. The first has nothing to do with fiscal policy or deficits but everything to do with institutional power: "Protection of the ministry's autonomy, elite status and jurisdictional boundaries." Second is the use of fiscal policy as a tool in economic management, and third the minimization of the size of the total budget in the current year. Surprisingly, perhaps, Campbell's study goes on to suggest that the reason the ministry has failed to deal with some of the fundamentals of government spending is that it lacks the power to get away with it. "The irony of the Finance Ministry's high position," Campbell wrote, "is that the MoF stands so delicately balanced on the peak of the Japanese Governmental structure that a sudden move in any direction would cause it to fall. That is to say, the ministry

The ministry can maintain its power (or its reputation for power) only by refraining from using it.

can maintain its power (or its reputation for power) only by refraining from using it; if Finance officials were to attempt, say, a major transfer of funds from one ministry or policy area to another, not only would opposition sufficient to veto the move quickly arise, but generalized pressures would probably mount." If it exposed itself by taking such a risk, he suggests, the ministry might ultimately lose the budget function to the Cabinet office. "The MoF's real power is less than it appears on the surface."[25]

The intrigue deepens. An academic at the University of Tokyo, Junko Kato, develops the case further, arguing that the ministry uses fiscal restraint as a tactical weapon. It exercises just enough fiscal tightness to create discomfort—to persuade the nation that there is a real problem with public finances and that the ministry is serious about addressing it—but not enough to actually solve the problem. This discredits austerity as the solution. Once this softening-up of the system has been achieved, the Okurasho introduces its proposal for a real solution—an increase in consumption tax. Ms. Kato, an associate professor of political science, traces this pattern in repeated episodes of ministry behavior through the 1970s, the 1980s, and the 1990s. But the introduction and enlargement of a consumption tax is not an end in itself.

On its own testimony, the Okurasho pursues the consumption tax to increase the tax take. Its primary aim is to collect enough revenue to meet the demands of expenditure—in other words, to eliminate budget deficits. But Ms. Kato suggests that this is another case of the Okurasho using the moral authority of fiscal rectitude to shield a baser motive—to increase institutional power, to strengthen itself in its perpetual power struggle with the politicians.[26] How could this work?

In the early postwar years, the various governments in power were prevented by law from going into deficit. Budgets had to be balanced. And, as it was the Okurasho that was responsible for the balancing, this put the ministry in a tremendously strong position. But in 1965 the government rewrote the law. Deficits, financed by bond issues, were permitted on the condition that the Diet approve the scale of each annual bond issue. This shifted a great deal of power from the bureaucrats in the Okurasho to the politicians in the ruling party. By eliminating deficit finance, the ministry would reduce its dependence on the Diet and restore much of the leverage it lost in 1965.

■ Zaito: A giant slush fund?

The deepest insight into the Okurasho's true motives and interests may lie in the way it handles its greatest repository of money, a pool of some 350 trillion yen ($3.5 trillion).[27] This immense aggregation of money in the Fiscal Investment and Loan Program, or *zaito*, is the equivalent of 70 percent of the size of the Japanese economy, or about half that of the U.S. economy.

The deepest insight into the Okurasho's true motives may lie in the way it handles a pool of $3.5 trillion.

What is the zaito? In short, it is a giant public-sector financing system, and a unique one. The forerunner of the zaito system was set up in 1872 to collect the savings of the people and funnel them into financing Japan's industrial modernization. For nearly its entire existence—from 1885 to the present—it has been managed by the Ministry of Finance. This system was also used to finance Japan's militarization in World War II. After the war, and under the supervision of the U.S. occupation, the system was recast into its current form and once more became a money pump, sucking up the savings of the people and channeling them to industry.

New money continually flows into the Okurasho's Trust Fund Bureau for management and reallocation, which is supervised by the ministry's Finance Bureau. The size of these inflows are tremendous; the system is often called the "second budget," and its new lending allocations in 1995 of 48 trillion yen ($480 billion) were about two-thirds the size of the main national budget. The ministry also exercises considerable control over the final stages of the money's outflow. The public finance institutions that receive the money from the Trust Fund Bureau and lend it out in the marketplace are dominated by Okurasho-controlled institutions, such as the Japan Development Bank. The system's annual allocations are subject to Diet approval.[28]

The Ministry of Finance says that zaito "is considered as important as the Budget."[29] But it is quite different. For one, it is not funded by taxes appropriated by the government. Zaito is funded mainly by deposits from individuals, through the postal savings system, the postal insurance system, and the public pension system. These are deposits on loan and ultimately must be repaid with interest.[30] The amount of new money that the system attracts, however, is not limited or defined—it is an open-ended point of collection that absorbs as much as the Japanese public might decide to deposit.

This system created a vast supply of capital for financing the reindustrialization of postwar Japan making loans available at deliberately low interest rates. Normally, this would not be possible— why would people deposit money in, say, a postal savings account if the return were inadequate? But in postwar Japan it was possible because the Okurasho was at the same time suppressing the interest rates available on the alternatives through its regulation of the banking system.[31]

The zaito system was very successful in financing the rapid development of the government's four priority industries of electric power, shipping, coal, and steel in the 1950s and 1960s. It also did much to fund the building of roads, transport, and communications—important industrial infrastructure. In these ways it provided an important base for rapid economic growth. And because the government was able to use zaito funds, it did not need to raise taxes. This kept fiscal deficits down and tax rates low, important inducements to economic growth. But by the early 1970s, the "miracle" of Japan's postwar reconstruction and reindustrialization had been achieved, and the zaito system lost much of its purpose. It switched to financing social infrastructure needs, particularly housing investment. By the late 1980s, the zaito system was allocating more money for social purposes than industrial ones.

By the late 1980s, the zaito system was allocating more money for social purposes than industrial ones.

By the 1990s, it became clear that the zaito system was in need of serious reform. It was some 120 years since its forerunner had been created and half a century since its retooling for Japan's reindustrialization. Now that Japan had become one of the world's largest and richest powers, there was a diminishing need for a system of developmental finance. But the zaito system just kept getting bigger, growing even faster than Japan itself. Its new allocations in 1970 were the equivalent of 5.5 percent of the total economy as measured by GDP. In 1995, this had burgeoned to 9.8 percent.

The system's liquidity pump was not needed so acutely as before, yet it pumped more money than ever, deluging the economy with liquidity. In the early reconstruction phase, from 1955 to 1965, the system, through public-sector finance institutions, supplied 14 percent of all lending (other than lending to the finance sector). In the following decade, this swelled to 20 percent. By 1994 it had reached a preposterous 43 percent. "This sharp increase in public-sector lending indicates that government financial institutions have extended their lending beyond the accepted role of public-sector finance and are moving into the area of private-sector finance," said Yoshio Suzuki, a former central banker and head of the Nomura Research Institute.[32] There is a good case for a thorough review and reorganization of the entire system. Yet the ministry's Finance Bureau says there is no serious problem and no plan for review.[33]

The Okurasho has increasingly used the zaito system as a substitute for budget spending. One of Japan's leading analysts of the system, Atsushi Miyawaki at Hokkaido University, has identified two ways in which this is done. One is to supply funds to repay debts and tide over deficit accounts that would otherwise have to be funded directly from the budget. Professor Miyawaki calls this passive fiscal demand. This includes funding part of the deficits of the former national rail system, the forest management system, and the national hospital system. The other way is to use the zaito system as a substitute for active fiscal demand. This includes funding public investment for the school system and overseas aid. Professor Miyawaki points out that the money for all of this is supplied by postal savings and pensions and eventually must be rapid. The ministry has been gradually and surreptitiously "merging" the two systems—the national budget and the zaito system—he argues, which does "nothing more than postpone the fiscal burden."

"Ultimately," says Professor Miyawaki, "the merging of the two systems will result in either higher taxes or lower returns on postal savings and pensions. Whatever measure is chosen, the people will bear the cost." Exactly how high is the cost? The ministry does not disclose vital information about the zaito system, including the flow of funds between it and the budget program. This opacity has spared the ministry from proper scrutiny. But Professor Miyawaki estimated that in 1992 about 150 trillion yen ($1.5 trillion), or half of what was then the total of zaito funds, have been used as a substitute for spending from the budget. Other experts agree with this estimate.[34]

> **"The merging of the two systems will result in either higher taxes or lower returns on postal savings and pensions. . . . the people will bear the cost."**

The zaito system has become a hidden supplement to the national budget. This makes a mockery of the Okurasho's claims to exert fiscal responsibility and of its drive to cut the issuance of government bonds. The ministry wages a tough public campaign to reduce deficit spending so that it can maximize its power and political leverage. But at the same time it fails to confront inefficiencies and rigidities in public finance and surreptitiously uses public deposits to cover losses and inadequacies. So while it claims to be protecting future generations from inheriting large burdens of public debt by campaigning against large fiscal deficits, it is actually building up large hidden losses within the zaito system. The ministry has failed to confront these problems openly and directly. Perhaps this is because it would reveal the true scale of the problems, exposing it to censure, political vulnerability, and perhaps even reform imposed from outside. Professor Miyawaki puts the problem of the zaito in personal terms: "By the time I retire, I don't think I can expect any public pension."[35] In 1996 he was forty years old.

"By the time I retire, I don't think I can expect any public pension." When he said this in 1996, Professor Miyakawa was forty years old.

A WORLD APART

The jet had lifted off, bearing aloft a pair of senior Okurasho officials on an overseas trip. "When we got in the air and out over the sea, away from Japan," recalls one official, his colleague "called the stewardess over and said to her, 'It's rather stuffy in here, can you please open a window?'" Ministry of Finance officials have long been able to pursue careers to the very top of the ministry without ever setting foot outside Japan because the MoF has traditionally maintained a separate cadre of officials who specialize in contact with foreigners, and they are concentrated chiefly in the International Finance Bureau. Toyoo Ghyoten, the man telling the story, is one of the best known of these.[1] Although he was one of the most influential economic officials in the world, he had seen nothing of the world beyond the physical boundaries of Japan—this was his first time on an airplane. This division of labor has spared the rest of the ministry any need to leave home. One former administrative vice minister declined to be considered for the governorship of the Bank of Japan on the ground that the job would involve too much overseas travel. "I went overseas once," he told colleagues, "and I don't want to have to do it again." Nonetheless, the domestic group usually enjoyed the last laugh. As Mr. Ghyoten attests, even as vice minister for international affairs and apparently the second-ranked man in the ministry, he was obliged to seek the approval of some junior director in the Budget Bureau before he could confidently advance any proposal.[2] The international tribe may have done a lot of flying, but it was the domestic men who paid the airfares. However, the demarcation between the international and domestic officials is gradually breaking down now that all career-stream mandarins are sent abroad to do postgraduate study. Eventually, all senior officials will have lived and studied overseas.

The Tokyo-based Dutch journalist Karel van Wolferen identified within the ranks of Japan's government and companies a set of people he described as "buffers," an intermediary community of English-speaking and supposedly internationalized people who are expected to absorb the shocks that an unpredictable outside world might deliver to their institutions. They were "entrusted with the task of making contacts with foreigners as smooth as possible."[3] And while many Japanese institutions do have people who seem to fit this description, the Okurasho officials who specialize in dealing with foreigners do not seem to have read their job description. They have demonstrated the capacity to be strident and intimidating in dealings with other nations.

In the early 1990s, as the Finance Ministry tried to assert its mastery over market forces on the Tokyo Stock Exchange in the face of collapsing stock prices, it waged a complementary campaign to discourage overseas exchanges from trading securities linked to Japanese shares. In the United States, the Finance Ministry's Mitsuo Sato yelled at and threatened officials of the American Stock Exchange in an effort to dissuade them from allowing the trading of new financial derivatives linked to Japanese equities. (One U.S. official, Ivers Riley, quipped: "I felt a couple of times that I was going to get the rubber hose treatment."[4]) And in Singapore, Mr. Sato threatened officials with the "ashtray treatment." He demanded that the Singapore International Monetary Exchange (SIMEX) conform to Japanese trading regulations in Singapore trading of futures contracts linked to Japanese stock prices. The president of SIMEX, Ang Swee Tian, refused. Mr. Sato resorted to bullying, shouting, and pounding the table. In a rage, he picked up an ashtray and threatened to throw it

The Okurasho was unable to suppress elsewhere the process of financial innovation that it had managed to strangle in Japan.

at the Singaporean official's head.[5] He met with no success in either country. The Okurasho was unable to suppress elsewhere the process of financial innovation that it had managed to strangle in Japan. But all of this is small scale compared with the breathtaking threats the ministry has made to sabotage the U.S. economy.

■ Capital strike

In 1994 the Okurasho threatened a capital strike against the United States—the deliberate withdrawal of the lifeblood of the modern capitalist economy, the world's largest creditor threatening to deny funds to the world's largest debtor. "At a meeting in Washington," recalled a senior economist at the Nomura Research Institute, Richard Koo, "one of the Japanese negotiators said, 'We will have no choice but to tell Japanese investors to sell their U.S. bond holdings. I was there. He said it at a meeting with [U.S. Treasury Secretary] Lloyd Bentsen, congressmen, senators—everyone." And what did the Americans say in reply? "Nothing," says Mr. Koo. "He's one of the core guys in the Ministry of Finance. If he really wanted to do something like that, maybe he could do it. This kind of talk is very dangerous."[6]

Another witness to the ministry's threats was the chief economist for the Chicago-based Kemper Financial Companies, David Hale. He attested to hearing a ministry official making "very outspoken threats" in Washington in 1994. "They know the rise in American bond yields has spooked us, so they know it's a way they can have leverage over us as an economic threat. The only leverage they can get in negotiations is this threat of capital withdrawal. . . . But once you get on this route, you can lose control."[7]

The purpose of these threats was to stem U.S. trade pressure and to discourage the United States from cheapening its dollar as a trade weapon, according to Mr. Hale. As we have seen, a weak dollar and its obverse, a strong yen, penalizes Japan's exports and slows the national rate of economic growth. This, in turn, puts pressure on the Ministry of Finance to spend more money to stimulate the economy, a challenge to the Okurasho's fiscal conservatism.

Both Mr. Koo and Mr. Hale identified the most explicit and

aggressive Japanese official as Eisuke Sakakibara, who had served as
the senior ministry representative in the so-called trade "framework" negotiations with the
United States.[8] The negotiations
had broken down in February
1994, when Japan refused to accommodate U.S. trade demands.
It was the first time postwar that
a Japanese prime minister had
openly defied a U.S. president
over trade demands. Japan's
Prime Minister Hosokawa an-
nounced the breakdown in negotiations by saying that "in this new
era" of post–Cold War, post–Liberal Democrat government, it was
time to "frankly admit what we can and cannot do." Better this than
continuing the forty-year-old masquerade of signing "ambiguous
agreements which can gloss over the problems of the time only to
find them become sources of later misunderstandings." The fight,
however, was not over, only changing venue.

Japan refused to accommodate U.S. trade demands—the first time postwar that a Japanese prime minister had openly defied a U.S. president over trade demands.

American pressure moved from the negotiating table to the foreign exchange markets, and the yen ratcheted up to excruciatingly
painful heights for the Japanese economy, approximately halving
the expected growth rate for Japan's economy that year.[9] The U.S.
logic was clear: if Japan would not redress its $60 billion trade
surplus with the United States by opening its markets, then the
exchange rate would be used to price Japanese exports out of the
U.S. market. The Okurasho decided to fight back. Dr. Sakakibara
was dispatched to Washington.

And what did Dr. Sakakibara say? Asked whether he was threatening the U.S. government with the possibility of a major Japanese
capital withdrawal from U.S. markets, he did not deny it but answered:

It's not Government policy, but if institutions feel the U.S. has major
policy problems then it's natural for them to withdraw their funds. I
don't see any symptoms of that at the moment, but Japanese investors
are reluctant to put money into U.S. markets. And in terms of decades,
Japanese investors will probably put more of their funds into Asia.

I think U.S. officials have been relatively concerned about their markets. And I think markets are extremely important—and you do need to be extremely careful.[10]

If it were to transpire, such a withdrawal of capital could have serious consequences for the U.S. economy. It would depend on the precise circumstances, but an abrupt, large-scale sell-off of U.S. Treasury bonds could push U.S. interest rates up sharply. This happened in March 1987 when panicking Japanese life insurance companies dumped quantities of U.S. bonds, pushing the yield on thirty-year bonds up from 7.5 percent to 9 percent. A large and sustained rise in interest rates could, in turn, slow the U.S. economy and exact a large price in lost activity, profits forgone, and jobs sacrificed. But could it actually happen, even if the ministry tried to carry out such a threat? Does it have enough power over Japanese investors?

When it has suited the ministry's agenda, the Okurasho has successfully encouraged its institutional investors to move many billions of dollars in investment funds between markets. Bill Clinton told a Japanese audience in 1993 that "in the 1980s, when my country went on a huge debt binge . . . Japanese purchases of much of that debt helped to keep our economy going and helped to prevent our interest rates from exploding."[11] Why did Japan's institutions buy this debt? Although it was chiefly an investment decision, they were also encouraged by unofficial Okurasho policy. Mr. Koo recounts: "In the 1980s, the MoF encouraged Japanese institutions to buy U.S.-dollar-denominated securities. And in particular they told the kanpo [post office life insurance bureau] and other public funds to increase their purchases of U.S. securities to slow the appreciation of the yen."[12]

American pressure moved from the negotiating table to the foreign exchange markets, and the yen ratcheted up to excruciatingly painful heights.

A financial economist at investment house Goldman Sachs who was formerly with the Bank of Japan, Tetsufumi Yamakawa, points out that the ministry can use indirect methods: "Pressure can be subtle. For example, when the MoF asked the life [insurance] companies to report regularly their purchases of U.S. Treasury bonds, the institutions felt obliged to maintain their enthusiasm for treasuries—that's an additional factor in their enthusiasm for buying them."[13] Dr. Sakakibara concurs that the ministry did unofficially encourage investment in U.S. securities in the 1980s. And he suggests the conditions under which such unofficial persuasion might work on the market once more: "It's a policy of leaning [with] the wind. And that kind of policy could work again. We could lean with the market, but we couldn't lean against it."[14]

■ The Asia factor

In recent years the Okurasho has been far more solicitous of the countries in Asia. A threshold year was 1991, when the newly appointed top official responsible for dealings with the outside world, the vice minister for international affairs, Tadao Chino, broke the well-established pattern of his predecessors. Instead of first making an introductory trip to the United States, he went to the capitals of Asia.

In the same year the ministry began asserting Japan's credentials as an advocate of Asia by challenging the priorities of the two big international economic agencies, the World Bank and the International Monetary Fund. The ministry argued that the two big multinational agencies were Western dominated and obsessed with supporting the reconstructing former Communist nations of Europe and the Soviet Union. The ministry successfully argued for equivalent support and lending to emerging Asian economies.[15]

The first postwar overseas mission to be led by the Okurasho's topmost bureaucratic official was a mission to China in 1993.

The ministry also decided that it was fed up with World Bank and IMF policy dictates to Asian nations, dictates it believed were narrowly defined, U.S.-style, laissez-faire prescriptions. The Ministry of Finance funded a landmark World Bank analysis of the elements of economic success in East Asia, a report published in 1993 as *The East Asian Miracle.*[16] The result? The first recognition by any of the big multinational agencies that government intervention in the marketplace can be helpful in the right circumstances, that neoclassical, U.S.-style free marketeering is not always the only policy solution.

It was also in 1991, incidentally, that Asia displaced the United States as Japan's biggest export market.[17] It is also instructive that the first postwar overseas mission to be led by the Okurasho's topmost bureaucratic official, the administrative vice minister, was a mission to China in 1993.[18]

In the mid-1990s the Finance Ministry started to encourage Japanese institutions to channel their investment funds to Asia as the priority region. One senior official, Isao Kubota, said that while the Okurasho cannot direct the private sector, "what we can do is show them how other countries are performing well and perhaps recommend that they examine them." The ministry accordingly set up an affiliated advisory body to "determine how Japan should play its role as a supplier of funds to Asian nations."[19] There was no such project studying how to fund any other area of the world.

"Asia is where capital is needed," said Dr. Sakakibara. "The U.S. now doesn't have to worry so much about funding its deficit. It's a big and sophisticated market. . . . In the last couple of years, Japan's investors have been consistently losing money on their U.S. dollar-denominated assets. So I think it's natural for them to be reluctant about new investment in the U.S."[20]

The ministry thinks of Asia as being the site of Japan's natural community and its sphere of influence.

Certainly, the ministry's policy is in close accord with existing trends in the market. In 1989 Japanese investment trusts had 60 percent of their assets in U.S. securities; by 1994 their share had fallen to 13 percent. Their Asian holdings rose from 18 percent to 75 percent.[21] And in 1995 Japanese banks opened twenty new overseas branches—every one of them was in Asia.[22]

But there is more. The ministry thinks of Asia as being the site of Japan's natural community and its sphere of influence. The ministry was instrumental in setting up the Asian Development Bank and remains dominant in its affairs. When ministers from around the world gather for the annual meetings of the World Bank and the International Monetary Fund, Japan's Finance Minister customarily hosts an informal lunch for finance ministers from Asian-Pacific nations. The Okurasho organizes a well-credentialed Asia-Pacific club for Japan's political and policy-making elite. Its members include former prime minister Noboru Takeshita and his protégé, Ryutaro Hashimoto, prime minister at the time of writing. The club meets for breakfast every two months and talks about finance and diplomacy. While it is essentially a pro-U.S. group, it supports the view that Japan must have an independent policy on Asia.[23] A former vice minister for international affairs, Makoto Utsumi, said in 1989 that he was "convinced the U.S. is and should be the lead manager on things—for example the Latin American debt issue," but that "in Asia maybe it is a bit different."[24]

■ The chronic trade surplus

After World War II, the first Japanese official to be invited to visit the United States was Takeshi Watanabe, a forty-three-year-old Okurasho bureaucrat and one of the key links between the Japanese civil service and the U.S. occupation administration of General Douglas MacArthur. Almost half a century later, Mr. Watanabe recalled an interested American asking him a vitally important question during his visit: How could war-torn Japan, with no resources, no land, and a large population, survive? His answer: "We have lost almost all our assets, but we still possess an important asset—the well-educated, hard-working Japanese people. If we could be permitted to import resources and export manufactured goods, then there is no reason we could not survive. I also pointed out that we had something even the U.S. didn't have—a balanced budget."[25]

Japan, of course, succeeded beyond all expectations in developing an export-driven, high-growth economy and became the world's first economic "miracle." It was an inspiration and model for all the later "miracle" economies of East Asia. It was the prototype for the greatest economic transformation of our time, with a formula for growth that was later applied to countries containing half of the human population. Of course, the approach to export-led growth also relied on having markets that would absorb those exports; by keeping their markets open, the nations of the developed world in general and the United States in particular were indispensable to the rapid growth of Japan and all of its imitators.

Japan, the world's first economic miracle, was an inspiration and model for all the later "miracle" economies of East Asia.

The Okurasho can proudly claim credit for many of the elements of Japan's postwar transformation. Two, in particular, stand out; indeed, they are the same elements specified by Mr. Watanabe. First is the doctrine of a balanced budget. Although Japan's early postwar stipulation of a balanced budget was imposed by the United States to contain inflation, it was embraced and enforced by the Okurasho. Even when the politicians of the Liberal Democratic Party managed to effectively end the policy in 1965, when the Diet authorized the issue of government bonds to finance deficit spending, the ministry remained powerfully attached to the doctrine of fiscal discipline. By limiting government spending, the ministry was able to keep tax rates low and give the private sector easier access to the national savings pool. Second is the emphasis on exporting. The national system of industrial finance operated by the Okurasho—both through the banks and through the Fiscal Investment and Loans Program, or zaito system (as described in chapter 8)—funneled low-cost financing into Japan's industrial base and its export sector. The money channeled through these systems was used to build up the industrial infrastructure and to fund the government-designated priority industries and sectors. This was a critical element in Japan's successful export drive.

As history has shown, however, the export drive became perhaps too successful. Japan's trade account went into chronic surplus, and these surpluses became so huge and persistent that by mid-1980s they were angering Japan's major trading partners. The United States accused Japan of being a mercantilist parasite on U.S. markets and the world trading system—exporting to other countries but not allowing other countries the full opportunity of exporting to Japan. It was not only the United States but also the European Union, South Korea, Taiwan, and most of the countries of Southeast Asia that grew increasingly frustrated with Japan's persistent trade surpluses. Sentiment became so intense that the Japanese trade surplus became one of the most disruptive influences in global politics and economics. It was seized on by protectionists, particularly in the United States and Europe, as evidence that the world trading system was not working.

In 1994, the U.S. undersecretary of the Treasury, Lawrence Summers, described it not so much as a question of trade balances but of employment balances. Japan's "excessive" exports had put about 2 million people out of jobs around the world, he claimed. "You know, Japan used to say that as a small island nation it needed to export in order to import. Today Japan needs to recognize that it needs to import if it is to continue to be given the opportunity to export."[26] The world's consumers came to know postwar Japan through its exports of electronics and cars; the world's policy makers and government officials came to know it through the trade surplus those exports produced.

"Japan used to say that as a small island nation it needed to export in order to import. Today Japan needs to recognize that it needs to import if it is to continue to be given the opportunity to export."

What did the Okurasho do in the face of this problem? It had four main avenues on which to pursue a solution. First was its control over the system of trade tariffs and the customs system. Here the ministry played a generally passive role, neither suggesting market-opening measures nor blocking them if other ministries proposed them. Second was its direct jurisdiction over sectors such as banking and capital markets. Here the ministry worked to protect its corporate constituents by keeping foreign institutions out as much as possible, although ultimately relenting. It had little choice as Japanese institutions were already operating in other countries' markets. Third was its indirect power over other sectors of the

Japanese economy—for example, its monopoly on the chairmanship of the main instrument of competition policy, the Fair Trade Commission, which has the power to break cartels and hence open markets. The Okurasho did not volunteer any activity in this realm and generally resisted when the United States raised the issue in negotiations. Fourth, and perhaps most important, the ministry controlled the system of public investment.

How is public investment relevant? It is relevant because it is a basic tenet of economics that the balance between savings and investments is identical to the balance between imports and exports. In other words, if Japan saves more than it invests, it will also have a surplus on its current account. For example, in the five years from 1986 to 1990, net saving in Japan was the equivalent of 19.2 percent of total economic output, or GNP; of this, 16.4 percent was invested in Japan, and this satisfied the investment needs of the economy. The rest—2.8 percent of GNP—was exported as capital. This amount is identical to the size of the current account surplus. Conversely, the United States saved only 2.6 percent of its GNP and yet invested 5.1 percent; it had a shortfall of funds for investment and so imported the other 2.5 percent that it needed. This is identical to its current account deficit.

With Japan exporting and the United States importing huge amounts of capital, Japan came to accumulate the world's biggest stock of overseas investments while the United States became the biggest debtor.

It was in this way, with Japan exporting huge amounts of capital and the United States importing huge amounts, that Japan came to accumulate the world's biggest stock of overseas investments while the United States became the biggest debtor. This way of accounting for national surpluses and deficits—looking at the capital accounts of nations as the mirror image of their current accounts—is standard economics. However, the balance of savings and investment does not necessarily cause the same balance to force its way through to the current account; there is no fixed and agreed cause-and-effect relationship. But it does help to explain structural elements in national balances. For this reason, analysts and international negotiators have turned to the examination of savings and investment in the United States and Japan.[27]

Japanese negotiators and economists have pointed out that the United States must improve its levels of savings. "From the American point of view, the disturbing aspect of [the] statistics is not the trade deficit but the low rates of saving and investment," said perhaps the most influential Japanese economist on this subject, Ryutaro Komiya. "The saving rate in particular, which has been dropping steadily over the past several decades, is a cause for concern. . . . Two effective means of boosting the saving rate are to slash the Federal deficit and reform the system of income and corporate taxation. . . . Only an imperious hegemon would demand that its trading partners make all the effort."[28] Deficit reduction was a core U.S. concern, too, and in the mid-1990s the Clinton administration and the Congress began making some headway on the problem.

In negotiations with Japan, the United States countered that Japan must increase its levels of investment to correct the scale of the imbalances. The United States particularly concentrated on Japan's program of public investment because it falls directly into the realm of the government—that is, it is an area where government can act. This was also an area of concern among many Japanese, and not only because of the need to address the imbalance—many Japanese wanted to see improvements in the standard of public facilities.

For example, a top-level body appointed by the prime minister to examine structural reform of the economy was anxious to increase public investment during deliberations in late 1993, when Japan was in midrecession. This posed a critical test of the Okurasho's approach. The body, the Advisory Group for Economic Structural Reform, was more commonly known by the name of its chairman, Gaishi Hiraiwa, also the head of the blue-chip business federation the Keidanren. The committee also included a senior official from the Ministry of Finance, Yoshihiko Yoshino.

When the private-sector members of the committee proposed substantial increases in Japan's public investment program, Mr. Yoshino objected and simply refused to yield. "He just kept on saying that public investment must not be increased," recalls another member of the group. "When the private-sector members of the group dug in their heels and insisted on the public spending increase, he then insisted that the increase must be financed by new taxes and not by deficit spending. Yoshino got especially excited at the December 13 meeting—he was shouting his head off."[29]

The result was a compromise. The Hiraiwa report called for a review of the public investment program but did not suggest any particular increase. When the government did review the program and announced in October 1994 a new plan to spend an apparently impressive 630 trillion yen ($6.3 trillion) over ten years, the result represented the status quo plus real growth of 3 percent a year (allowing for inflation averaging 1 percent a year). But as Japan's potential economic growth was probably 3.5 percent, this new investment plan could actually result in shrinking the total share of public investment in the economy.

 TIME FOR CHANGE?

When the Ministry of Finance enters a negotiation, it often adopts a military strategy of the former Imperial Japanese Army: "Set the weight bases." The strategy was devised for the defense of a core military base. In a map of this scheme, the vital facility is at the center of a series of imaginary concentric circles. Set along the circles are the outer bases. These are the "weight bases." They are aligned to protect the core base from a direct attack. In a negotiation, as in a war, the outer bases are initial points of resistance. In the face of a determined assault, they are expendable—positions that may be surrendered in the process of wearing down the attackers, bargaining positions that can be abandoned to reach a settlement. One by one, these lesser interests can be sacrificed to protect the core interest.[1]

And so it was after the 1996 Japanese national election. Before and during the election campaign, the major political parties were loud and unanimous in blaming the Finance Ministry for economic mismanagement and administrative incompetence. It was the broadest, the most intense, and most sustained campaign of political rhetoric against the ministry in the postwar era. Among the voting public there was a good deal of resentment, confusion, and fear, and the politicians were anxious to channel it. The Okurasho was a ready target, and with some reason. It bore chief responsibility for pitching Japan into its first homegrown recession since the war.

After five years in which economic growth had averaged 4.6

percent, the country suffered five years with average growth of 1.6 percent. This represented more than a change in the cycle of economic growth; it was a paradigm shift. In the preceding thirty years, Japan's rate of growth had fallen significantly below 3 percent only once. Now, without warning, it seemed destined forever to inhabit that grim realm of economic mortals.[2] The Okurasho had compounded this with its other failings. These were many, but in the public mind the most serious were the banking crisis and its most upsetting element—the appropriation of public money to solve the jusen problem. And the revelations of corruption among some of the ministry's top-level officials meant that it was not only the ministry's performance that was open to challenge but also its qualifications and motivations. In a few short years, the ministry had stripped Japan of its economic immortality and grubbied its own priestly vestments.

> **The ministry had stripped Japan of its economic immortality and grubbied its own priestly vestments.**

The prime minister both before and after the election, Ryutaro Hashimoto, told the nation in a televised address the day after his reappointment that

> "the economic system that supported Japan for fifty years after the war has come to its serious limit. You are all familiar with this. To rebuild this into an economic and social system suitable for the twenty-first century, the government needs to take immediate steps to work on the core problem, Kasumigaseki reform."

Kasumigaseki is the administrative district in central Tokyo, the seat of all the national ministries. Its centerpiece, of course, and the keystone of the economic system, was the Okurasho. Hashimoto promised his people

> "a complete redesigning of the long-standing administrative systems, and we can never succeed in its implementation without a strong political will."[3]

The politicians pledged themselves to a fundamental reform of the Finance Ministry. The man appointed to draw up the reform plan for the three-party ruling coalition that ran Japan before—and after[4]—the 1996 election, Shigeru Ito, explained why the government was acting. Speaking some four months before the election and while drafting his plan, he said: "We have been under pressure from both within the country and from abroad to change the system. Prime Minister Ryutaro Hashimoto wants to regain international trust. A scandal occurred in which the Okurasho was involved. We cannot keep up appearances of normalcy any more."[5]

■ Plan of attack

What changes did the government have in mind? Mr. Ito explained: "I want to propose fairly drastic revisions. Probably the Banking Bureau, the Securities Bureau and the International Finance Bureau will disappear, at least in their current form." He envisaged giving powers of inspection and oversight of the financial sector to a new division that was to be answerable to the prime minister and not the finance minister. The logic was clear: The ministry had proved that it was not competent to supervise the banks and the financial markets. Its punishment was to lose that function.

Deprived of its fiscal function, the ministry that sometimes described itself as the Mt. Fuji of Japan's bureaucratic structure would be leveled.

Still more ominous for the Okurasho, Mr. Ito suggested that his project team planned to strike directly at the ministry's core power: "There is also a plan for a separate revenue agency that will not handle financial affairs. Then there is the question of what to do with the process of preparing the Budget." This pair of ideas would strip the ministry of its powers to collect revenue and to dispense it through the national budget. The Finance Ministry would lose its fiscal function. This is the source of its moral authority and its political power, its chief instrument of patronage and its most formidable weapon of coercion—as the Hosokawa government had so recently discovered. Deprived of its fiscal function, the ministry that sometimes described itself as the Mt. Fuji of Japan's bureaucratic structure would be leveled. Mr. Ito's task force was considering a plan to transfer the budget-making monopoly from the ministry to the Cabinet, where it could be brought under greater political control.

But the government was not yet finished with the ministry. Mr. Ito said that a separate government panel was to consider changes to the law regulating the central bank. The most important issue here? "To secure the independence of the central bank," said Mr. Ito. This would deprive the Finance Ministry of its power over interest rates by granting independence to its monetary agency, the Bank of Japan.

The sum of all of these proposals—to strip the Okurasho of its powers over financial supervision, fiscal policy, and monetary policy—would devastate the ministry. The loss of monetary and fiscal powers would remove all its instruments of control over the macroeconomy and most of its leverage over the political system. And the loss of the right to supervise the financial sector would seriously diminish its ability to place amakudari in the private sector.

Yet these proposals circulating within the ruling coalition were not particularly adventurous at the time. All the major political parties promised to perform painful surgery on the Ministry of Finance. Probably the most common campaign theme focused on the need to break up the Ministry of Finance into a series of smaller parts, with the hope that this would shatter its concentration of power and solve some of its internal conflicts of interest. This proposal also had the advantage of promising a viscerally appealing satisfaction—the chance for a wronged people to sack a great, arrogant, and unpopular institution. In the tradition of a Japanese saying, when the dog is in the ditch, it should be beaten; in other words, the dog should be attacked when it is most vulnerable. The Okurasho was in the deepest ditch it had stumbled into since the war, and the Japanese people and their political proxies were lining up to beat it.

■ Defensive action

Anticipating the attack, the ministry pursued the Imperial Japanese Army strategy of setting the weight bases in defense.

Setting weight base 1

The Finance Ministry's first action was to put together its own task force and propose a plan for restructuring itself—something akin to a criminal taking charge of his own sentencing and rehabilitation. In appraising itself, the ministry criticized its performance as administrator of the banking system and financial markets; it had been too slow to change, too reluctant to embrace the two fundamental principles of liberalization and transparency. The solution? According to the ministry, the answer to the problem was to separate policy making from the function of inspection and surveillance. This structural separation was to be achieved through internal reorganization. The ministry proposed no transfer of any powers to any outside body and no diminution of its role.[6]

This position was the barest acknowledgment of the case for change, offering a little self-criticism and minimal internal reorganization. Some in the ministry actually preferred a more drastic course. Within the Budget Bureau, the Tax Bureau, and the Minister's Secretariat there was a current of thinking in which the institution was perceived as better off without the Banking and Securities Bureaus; these so-called market-based divisions were seen as debasements of the ministry's larger roles as economic policy maker and fiscal guardian. In this view, the market-based bureaus confused the ministry's mission. And by drawing officials too close to the private sector, these functions created the opportunity for corruption and therefore cast doubt on the integrity of the organization as a whole. In this view,

> **The Okurasho's position was the barest acknowledgment of the case for change, offering a little self-criticism and minimal internal reorganization.**

the Banking and Securities Bureaus should be walled off in a separate institution, thereby severing the gangrenous arm for the sake of the body.[7] This line of thought brought politicians to the same conclusion on the matter of supervision of the financial sector. But the ministry's plan conceded no such point. The first weight base was set, a negotiating position established. The contested ground was far from the core interest.

Setting weight base 2

The Bank of Japan Act of 1942 was enacted in the emergency conditions of World War II and yet remained unchanged fifty-five years later. Governments in the 1960s twice debated the need to revise the act, but both attempts were killed by the Okurasho.[8] This time, however, things looked different. The campaign to make the central bank independent of the ministry had built great momentum and was apparently unstoppable. The concept enjoyed the support of the mainstream of economists and commentators. All the major political parties supported the concept. The Bank of Japan itself openly advocated the idea. The prime minister spoke for the national consensus in announcing the independence of the central bank as government policy.

The ministry did not concede the point but resolutely opposed any meaningful change. The weapon of attack on the ministry on this matter was to be an advisory panel to the prime minister. The Finance Ministry countered; because the relevant law was administered by the ministry, the Okurasho was responsible for drafting any change in the law. The ministry stipulated that any recommendations from the prime minister's panel would have to be considered by the Finance Ministry's own advisory group, the Financial System Research Council, before legislative revisions could proceed. The second weight base had been set.

> **The campaign to make the central bank independent of the ministry drew wide support. The ministry did not concede the point but resolutely opposed any meaningful change.**

Setting weight base 3

In its effort to protect its core base—the monopoly power over writing the national budget—the ministry set yet another forward defense, a third weight base. The ministry's mandarins mounted a major and reinvigorated campaign for keeping discipline in government finances and for containing the national debt, a program of fiscal consolidation. Rather than waiting fearfully for an attack on the main power center, the mandarins of the ministry took the fight right up to the politicians. This instantly transformed the politics and the psychology of the contest.

First, it was a demonstration of the ministry's determination and credentials as fiscal guardian of the nation. The ministry was portraying itself as morally motivated and fully functional. Second, it immediately made the political campaign against the ministry's budget-making powers appear to be just another self-seeking episode in pork-barrel politicking, grasping and opportunistic. Suddenly, the question was not simply, "Can we trust the Ministry of Finance?" Now, it was, "Can we trust the politicians to be more honest than the Ministry of Finance?" It was a much more difficult question. Third, it was a position in full accord with that of the prime minister. This was not entirely coincidental; in his earlier term as finance minister, Mr. Hashimoto was exposed to the full force of the ministry's fiscal rhetoric. In a 1994 book, he had shown that he was a good pupil: "As everyone knows, the outstanding balance of national debt is nothing other than a loan from the generations of our children and grandchildren," he wrote. "Far from being a rich country, with this astronomical debt it owes to its own people, Japan could be counted as the world's greatest debtor country."[9] Essentially regurgitating the Finance Ministry's line, Hashimoto stuck with it through the 1996 election and beyond.

> **"Far from being a rich country, ... Japan could be counted as the world's greatest debtor country."**

The ministry knew that by resharpening its campaign for fiscal rectitude, it would be depriving Hashimoto and his party of any political or policy excuse for changing the system. The campaign bore early fruit. A month before the 1996 election, the Hashimoto government agreed to persist with the long-standing plan to raise the rate of the consumption tax from 3 percent to 5 percent the following April, thereby raising an extra 5 trillion yen ($50 billion) in tax revenue, and to terminate a temporary tax cut worth another 2 trillion yen ($20 billion). What's more, the government also agreed to abandon the practice of boosting the economy through an autumn supplementary budget.[10]

The politics of this campaign were impeccable; the economics were not. Around the end of 1996, ten leading think tanks were forecasting an economic relapse in the coming year. The consensus held that Japan's rate of economic growth was about to fall from an uninspiring 2.5 percent in 1996 to a dismal 1.5 percent the year after. Mainstream private-sector economists argued that this was precisely the wrong time for the government to withdraw fiscal stimulus from the economy. The government needed to allow a self-sustaining expansion to take hold before turning to the task of fiscal consolidation, they argued.

The politics of the ministry's campaign were impeccable; the economics were not.

Prices on the financial markets offered a powerful confirmation of this analysis. "The Government's current fiscal policy is detrimental to the economy," said the chairman of the Japan Center for Economic Research, Hiaso Kanamori.[11] Or, as the Nomura Research Institute's Richard Koo put it: "While the market has returned to reality, the policy debate has not."[12] The *Nikkei* newspaper summarized the consensus criticism on its front page: "The Government is over-eager to cope with 'fiscal crisis' and not sufficiently motivated to rescue the public from 'economic crisis.'"[13] The reason was simple. The policy debate was once more being determined by

"While the market has returned to reality, the policy debate has not."

the institutional priorities of the Okurasho rather than the national need for economic management. But the ministry kept up relentless pressure for continued fiscal tightening. This was the third weight base.

Mounting a low-level skirmish

Throughout this period, the ministry kept up a defensive action in its permanent guerilla-style campaign on another issue—blocking deregulation. Pressure for more deregulation was not really a new part of the anti-Okurasho campaign, but it was approaching something of a climax; economic and market stagnation combined with a steady stream of official reviews were building pressure for deregulation, and a top-level government advisory group, the Administrative Reform Council, was to release its recommendations at the end of 1996. This was bound to arm the deregulators. The ministry was beginning to waver in its perennial resistance but still struck a general attitude of defiance. This was less a weight base set for the defense against the new antiministry campaign than it was a permanent, low-level skirmish serving the perpetuation of its petit-bureaucratic privileges.

Protecting the core base

And so the ministry had set three weight bases to deflect direct attacks on its core base—the power to compile the national budget. But it also took action directly to protect this central interest. It campaigned to have its "main castle" removed altogether from the invasion plans of the enemy.

The Okurasho was assisted by the presence of friends in the enemy camp. Of the ten Liberal Democrats on Mr. Ito's coalition project team for reform of the Okurasho, two were former officials of that very institution.[14] And the ministry had long counted among its political friends both Ryutaro Hashimoto, now prime minister, and his chief political patron and a leading powerbroker in the Liberal Democrat Party, former prime minister Noboru Takeshita.

As we have seen, the historical relationship between the ministry and such top-level Liberal Democratic politicians was symbiotic; the politicians allowed the ministry tremendous freedom in the conduct of its affairs and the pursuit of its interests, and in return the ministry was expected to finance some of their pet projects.

And in this hour of crisis for the ministry, this symbiosis once again came into play, and with telling force. The Liberal Democratic Party members of the project team for Okurasho reform successfully forestalled the group's attack on the ministry.[15] They persuaded the team against any pronouncement on the proposal to strip the ministry of its budget-making function, arguing that this was a matter for consideration after the election. The delay of the decision was, in effect, the death of the proposal. In this way, the political spearhead for reform of the ministry was blunted.

Why? The public argument was presented by the Finance Ministry's vice minister for administrative affairs in mid-1996. Tadashi Ogawa defended the Okurasho's right to continue to be the sole agency for compiling the budget on the basis that it made sense for all "aspects of the economy that have to do with money" to remain under the ministry's jurisdiction "for the sake of efficiency." And, by unifying the Japanese position on these matters, the country would be better able to present a single position at meetings of the Group of Seven richest industrial countries.[16]

The real reasons for the Liberal Democratic Party's decision to abandon the idea were less public spirited. One party official said that its members opposed sharp attacks on the ministry because they depended on it for solving difficult issues of policy, such as the still-unfolding debt crisis. A party staffer explained that many of its politicians were "concerned that excessive attacks on the ministry might affect the amount of budgetary money for their districts."[17] And so, despite the angriest and noisiest push for reform of the Finance Ministry in the postwar

Despite the angriest and noisiest push for reform of the Finance Ministry in the postwar era, the government mounted no direct attack on the main castle of ministry power—the power of the budget.

era, the government mounted no direct attack on the main castle of ministry power. It has proved to be unassailable. The ministry won the concession it sought. And did the Liberal Democratic Party win the concessions it hoped for in return? We will see when we examine the fighting that took place at the third weight base.

■ Engagement and negotiation

With a direct hit on the core base forestalled, the ministry could concentrate its efforts on defending the three weight bases and the ongoing skirmish with the deregulators.

Yielding ground at base 1

At the first weight base, the contest over supervision of the financial markets and institutions, the ministry was obliged to yield some ground. Its record was simply indefensible. Immediately after the 1996 election, the reelected government of Liberal Democrats and their parliamentary allies agreed to set up a new body for inspecting and supervising financial institutions and markets. It would be established in 1998 within the prime minister's office and its head appointed by the prime minister.[18] It was an unambiguous blow to the ministry.

The reelected government agreed to set up a new body for inspecting and supervising financial institutions and markets. It was an unambiguous blow to the ministry.

And yet this loss was mitigated by three factors. First, it was not a core interest of the ministry. Indeed, some officials saw its loss as an advance for the purity and standing of the ministry overall. Second, the ministry was to keep control over policy for the banking and securities industries. It would only surrender the physical function of conducting inspections and could still call the shots in the larger regulatory and operational issues. This would preserve the intellectual end of the event for the ministry. And third, the new body was to work in close consultation with the Finance Ministry. This would provide the ministry with enough assets—information and leverage—to preserve a diminished but solid claim on amakudari positions in the banking and brokerage industries.

Negotiated peace at base 2

At the second weight base, in the struggle over the independence of the central bank, the Finance Ministry was again forced to yield some territory in the face of a determined attack. But it minimized its losses by means of cunning rear-guard action. The prime minister's advisory panel on the issue pronounced the obvious—that the existing law was out of date. It proposed that the government cut some of the main ties binding the bank to the ministry. The panel recommended that the government legislate to abolish the finance minister's broad discretion in issuing instructions to the Bank of Japan. And it proposed to remove the finance minister's power to fire central bank executives merely for holding views that differed from the minister's. These were significant recommendations; in practice, powers bestowed on the Finance Ministry were exercised by the bureaucrats of the ministry. The other important proposal to come out of the prime minister's advisory panel was to have interest rates set by a policy board, whose membership would exclude officials of the Okurasho. The sum of these suggestions amounted to a serious loss of ministry power over interest rates. Even so, the recommendations fell far short of proposing independence for the central bank. They would still allow the ministry to send officials to meetings of the policy board when this was deemed necessary. And if the ministry disagreed with a policy board decision on interest rates, it would have the power to freeze the decision for an unspecified time. The panel's chairman, Yasuhiko Torii, described his group's proposals as nothing more than "the first step to securing the Bank of Japan's independence."[19]

These proposals then went to the Financial System Research Council, an advisory group to the Finance Minister, for further emasculation. This council is convened, sponsored, and guided by officials of the Okurasho. As a result, it generally functions as a mechanism for legitimizing proposals from the ministry itself. As the chairman of another Finance Ministry advisory council remarked, "the biggest problem is that the bureaucrats ultimately steer these various investigatory councils; no matter how many opinions are aired, the debate invariably moves in the direction the bureaucrats think is right."[20]

And so while the council agreed that there should be some increase in the independence of the Bank of Japan—the Finance Minister should indeed lose the right to fire officials of the central bank merely for holding contrary views on interest rates—it maintained that the central bank should still be kept on a fairly short leash. For instance, the council recommended that the "Bank of Japan shall maintain close communication with the government to ensure there is sufficient mutual understanding to secure consistency between the government's economic policy and its monetary policy."[21] Translated, this catch-all clause meant simply that the Bank of Japan should submit to the Finance Ministry's grand plan for the economy.

The council also proposed that the ministry should be able to send officials to policy board meetings whenever it chose. And it said that these officials should not only be able to make proposals for monetary policy but also have the right to ask the board to withhold implementation of any decision on interest rates. And to increase the leverage of these Okurasho officials, the council made a series of other recommendations: the ministry was to retain control of the central bank's operating budget; the central bank was to have no direct contact with the parliament but was to be accountable to parliament only through the finance minister; the central bank was not to open any new offices or branches except with the permission of the finance minister; the finance minister was to have the power to order audits of the bank; he was to have the power to issue instructions for corrections of misconduct by officers of the bank; he retained the right to issue instructions to the bank in a national emergency or in order to maintain an orderly credit system; the bank was only to operate as the agent of the government in any intervention in the foreign exchange market; and, although he was to act on the recommendation of the policy board, it was the finance minister who was to actually appoint all executive directors and advisers of the central bank.[22]

The council's report was a clever piece of construction. In a strict sense, the Finance Ministry's minimal role on the policy board allowed it only limited direct influence over the Bank of Japan's monetary decisions. But set in the larger framework, the Bank of Japan would be so dependent on the Okurasho that the Finance Ministry's will would loom over every conversation, submission, and meeting in the central

In this new arrangement, the Okurasho had limited but *direct* control of the Bank of Japan.

bank. It was certainly not explicit Okurasho control over the central bank, but it was control nonetheless. One indicator of the ministry's success in preserving much of its control is that the Bank of Japan's governor, Yasuo Matsushita, made it clear the proposals would not give the bank the independence it needed.[23] Another indicator is that ministry officials were "quite comfortable" with the new proposals.[24] And in framing the new Bank of Japan Act, the ministry held the ultimate trump card—the actual drafting of the new law was to be done by the Finance Ministry.

A new alliance at base 3

Within three months of the Hashimoto government's return to office after the October 20, 1996, election, the Finance Ministry had agreed to a series of Liberal Democratic Party requests for major new spending initiatives. These included a supplementary budget for fiscal year 1996 of 4.5 trillion yen ($45 billion). This money was to be allocated for public works projects and for compensation packages for farmers who were suffering from hardship. The opposition political parties, the press, and a large body of commentators immediately attacked this decision as a classic example of pork-barrel politics. The leader of the major opposition party, Ichiro Ozawa of the Shinshinto, argued that if the government were serious about fostering economic growth, it would have approached fiscal policy differently; instead of spending extra money on public works, it would have continued the temporary cuts in income taxes. Others pointed out that the government might have postponed the scheduled increase in the rate of consumption tax instead. Outraged that the Liberal Democratic Party had no interest in either the taxpayer or the economy but only in channeling money to its own constituents, three of the opposition parties prepared to demand a revision of the supplementary budget.[25]

Perhaps the most blatant evidence of favoritism, however, was the agreement by the Finance Ministry to approve the Liberal Democratic Party's request to resume a full-scale expansion of the *shinkansen*, or bullet-train system. For nearly thirty years shinkansen projects have been synonymous with the pork barrel in Japanese politics. Expansion of the system had been frozen for seven years because of Japan's fiscal crisis. But now neither the Liberal Democrats nor the Finance Ministry was deterred, it seems, by the cost of the new expansion program of 1.2 trillion yen ($12 billion).[26] Despite this, or perhaps because of it, the Finance Ministry and the Liberal Democratic Party launched a heightened campaign for fiscal rectitude. Just one day before the final decision to go ahead with the new shinkansen program, the Finance Ministry solemnly announced a plan to halt the use of deficit financing by the year 2005.[27] A few weeks later Prime Minister Hashimoto promised, straight-faced, that "there will be no sanctuary when we review Budget expenditures."[28] The proposal to strip the ministry of its budget-making function vanished altogether from the government agenda.

For nearly thirty years shinkansen projects have been synonymous with the pork barrel in Japanese politics.

■ The Big Bang

On November 11, 1996, less than a month after the election, Prime Minister Hashimoto summoned Finance Minister Hiroshi Mitsuzuka to his office at 3:30 P.M. and handed him a document titled "Structural Reform of the Japanese Financial Market: Toward the

Revival of the Tokyo Market by the Year 2001." It was a plan for a sweeping deregulation of Japan's financial markets. The prime minister said that in presenting the plan to the foreign press it should be called the Tokyo Big Bang, an echo of London's Big Bang a decade earlier,[29] when officials deregulated the stock market, dismantled fixed commissions, and opened markets to foreign firms in an effort to ensure London's future role in world markets.[30] The Japanese Big Bang, however, was to be much grander. London's was restricted to the stock market, while Japan's was to embrace all financial markets. The first line of the three-page document said: "Goal—An international market comparable to the New York and London markets by the year 2001."[31]

Tokyo's markets had been comparable in size to the Anglo-American markets in the late 1980s. But cyclical downturn worked in deadly combination with Japan's structural stagnation and over-regulation to relegate Tokyo to second-class status (as described in chapter 6). Japan was in the bizarre position of being the world's biggest creditor yet losing the markets where that money was being brokered. Japan supplied the cash but not the markets. Now, the prime minister was instructing his finance minister that it would be "necessary not only to transform the financial administration into a more transparent one based on the market mechanism, but also to vitalize the Tokyo market through structural reform." He laid out three guiding principles: markets were to be free, fair, and global.[32] The effect of these principles would be revolutionary. They are the precise opposite of the working principles that dominated the postwar financial system: controlled, operated for the benefit of insiders, and local.

And Hashimoto set out the stakes for Japan in achieving the Big Bang:

In order for the Japanese economy to retain its vigor in the coming "aging society," it is essential to secure the supply of funds to newly rising industries as well as to establish a place for efficient asset management. It is equally important to ensure that Japan provides a smooth supply of funds to the rest of the world. . . . Thus the Japanese financial market, which serves as the artery for the Japanese economy, needs to play its true role of optimal resource distribution, as the markets in New York and London do, so that Japanese individual savings of as much as 1,200 trillion yen [$12 trillion] can be fully utilized.[33]

The announcement of the Big Bang was so unexpected, so sweeping, and so authoritative that it stunned the global marketplace. It seemed to be a significant prime ministerial strike against the power and prerogatives of the Finance Ministry, a decisive act of leadership intended to exploit the Okurasho in its weakest moment. But surprisingly, even perversely, the ministry fully endorsed the plan. It was the finance minister who announced the decision to the media and officials of the ministry who conducted the background briefings to explain the prime minister's intentions. In fact, some senior officials seemed positively enthusiastic.

"Sometimes in order to conserve what is good for the country you have to implement very radical reforms."

The director-general of the International Finance Bureau, Eisuke Sakakibara, said:

I would quote a statement by Edmund Burke, a very famous conservative philosopher, that sometimes in order to conserve what is good for the country you have to implement very radical reforms. This is what we are doing, we are going to implement very radical reforms. . . . We have been proceeding with deregulation in a sort of gradualist approach. In a sense I, as an outside philosopher, do not like shock therapy, but here, in this particular case, I think shock therapy is necessary. . . . You could say our awareness has come somewhat belatedly but better late than none; we are now thinking this is the last opportunity for us to revitalize the Tokyo market.

He explained why: "We recognize that the Tokyo financial market has lagged behind New York and London and maybe Frankfurt, we

recognize that Japanese financial institutions have lagged behind.
. . . We would now like to provide the opportunity for Japanese
financial institutions to catch up with their counterparts in Europe
and the U.S. We recognize that one of the reasons for the regenera-
tion of the American economy is probably its financial deregulation." And there was no suggestion that the ministry would try to
stall or sabotage the process. Sakakibara said that "although we have
mentioned the year 2001, this is not to imply that implementation
will be delayed till then—whatever is possible will be implemented
as soon as possible."[34]

When the international investment community grasped the significance of the plan and the fact that it had the ministry's support,
it responded instantly. The slow-
motion, seven-year withdrawal
from Tokyo went into immediate
reverse in the anticipation of a
flowering of opportunity. Within
a month of the announcement of
the Big Bang, international investment banks and brokerages
were planning expansion and reinvestment in their Tokyo operations.[35]

**Within a month of the an-
nouncement of the Big Bang,
international investment banks
and brokerages were planning
expansion and reinvestment in
their Tokyo operations.**

The ministry's embrace of the Big Bang seemed a startling apos-
tasy: an abandonment of the Okurasho's notorious resistance to
deregulation, a departure from two decades of gradualism, and a
contrast with its familiar defiance of inconvenient prime ministerial
declarations. It was also a surprising move by Sakakibara, the intellectual defender of the status quo. What happened?

The ministry emphasized that the Big Bang was the prime minister's initiative, but there were persistent suggestions that the idea
originated in the Okurasho. Pressed on this point, a senior official, a
deputy director-general of the International Finance Bureau, Yuzo
Harada, explained that while "the idea of the Big Bang itself came
from the prime minister," Hashimoto had not been operating in a
vacuum: "One of the prime minister's personal secretaries is a person from the ministry, and it's certainly possible this person talked
to ministry officials, including Sakakibara, in formulating the

plan."[36] There certainly seems to be some ministerial empathy for Mr. Hashimoto. Mr. Sakakibara said that the Big Bang was one of the prime minster's five main pillars of policy, and he admonished skeptical reporters with these words: "The foreign press has always been negative in their evaluation of the Hashimoto government. Somehow you think reform is with [the opposition party] Shinshinto . . . which is not true."[37]

Nor was the Big Bang as disruptive to the ministry agenda as it might seem. Mr. Harada explained that it was a logical extension of a process that had been under way: the International Finance Bureau had been preparing for the total abolition of the remaining controls of foreign exchange since June 1996; this had in turn put pressure on the Securities Bureau to deregulate the markets. The reason? "The deregulation of foreign exchange would remove a privilege from the banks, and we have been hard pressed by the banks, who complain that it's not fair and they want a parallel deregulation in the securities field where they stand to gain."[38] The Securities Bureau had been examining options for sweeping deregulation in the securities markets since September 1996, and a review of remaining restrictions had been due for March 1997. The Banking Bureau had been reviewing banking policy, too. Indeed, many ministry officials had gradually developed the view that a dramatic reform of the financial sector was required.[39] And as a commentator observed, nothing on the list of Big Bang deregulation was new. All the measures had been debated by various ministry panels for a decade or more. What was new was the deadline[40]—and the packaging into a political initiative.

In a sense, the Big Bang is a case of the Okurasho making a virtue of necessity, bundling current reviews into a single, politically salable declaration of intent while retaining the five-year comfort buffer of implementation by 2001. By this time, none of the officials in the top three strata of the ministry will still be working in the Okurasho—they will be comfortably ensconced in amakudari sinecures. And the ministry may benefit substantially in the mean-

> **In a sense, the Big Bang is a case of the Okurasho making a virtue of necessity.**

time. By supporting and perhaps even suggesting the Big Bang, the ministry is giving Mr. Hashimoto a major political asset. It appears that this is part of a bargain, implicit or explicit, for political cooperation with Hashimoto for the institutional protection of the ministry.[41]

■ Damage assessment

In mid-1996, the Ministry of Finance seemed destined to be dismantled. It was held responsible for pitching Japan into an unprecedented era of low growth and macroeconomic misery. The ministry that had helped create the first of Asia's economic "miracles" had now ended it. It was guilty of exacerbating market collapse and banking disaster. It was blamed for perpetrating the jusen outrage on taxpayers. With its credibility already in doubt, the stain of scandal seriously damaged public trust in the institution. The national consensus for reform of the Okurasho seemed irresistible. Even with all its power and prestige, surely it could not stand against the entire nation?

By the second quarter of 1997 it was possible to observe that while the ministry had sustained some damage to its institutional interests, it had withstood the storm pretty much intact—the castle had been protected. The ministry was not broken up, and its core interest and chief source of power—the exclusive right to draw up the national budget—remained intact. In fact,the ministry's mandate to manage fiscal policy had perhaps been strengthened in its new understanding with the Liberal Democratic Party, despite some short-term accommodation of party spending.

A closely related right, the power to make macroeconomic policy for the national economy, was intact. The ministry's degree of sway over the Bank of Japan had been diminished, but it retained significant avenues for influencing monetary policy and other activities of the central bank.

The ministry suffered only one outright loss of any of its functions—the function of supervision of the financial markets—although it retained policy oversight. Yet even here the ministry seems to have immediately recovered the initiative by offering the financial markets up for wholesale deregulation in a Big Bang. In this, it traded some of the minor powers of the regulator for a grander political bargain.

Importantly, the ministry had preserved not only the legal footings for its structure and powers but also the cultural basis of its unity. The systems of recruitment and retirement—the Tokyo University club-type entry and the amakudari exit—were intact. The bureaucratic solidarity these systems support was, in turn, in a position to continue sustaining the Okurasho's ability to master its ministers and control its destiny.

The ministry traded some of the minor powers of the regulator for a grander political bargain.

In sum, it was an impressive exercise in institutional self-preservation. Does this imply that the ministry's victory was the politician's loss? Only if the politicians were serious about breaking up the ministry. And while some were, others were not. The Hashimoto government's real political need was spelled out, perhaps inadvertently, by the man in charge of the coalition's Okurasho reform team, Shigeru Ito, when he told some ministry mandarins the following: "The ministry cannot stay the way it has been. It has to change in a way that is clearly visible to all."[42] The appearance of change, and not the substance of reform, seemed to be the real political imperative.

And so the Okurasho in the 1990s has an impressive record of dealing with political threats. It dispensed with one prime minister, the ambitious reformer Morihiro Hosokawa, by withholding its budgetary powers, and it dealt with the reformist threat from the Hashimoto government by offering the inducement of its budget largesse. In both cases, the ministry used its control of the national budget to shape the political system so as to meet its institutional needs.

■ The way ahead

Some change has already coursed through the ministry in the 1990s. Forces already in place mean that more is to come. The program of financial deregulation—the Big Bang—will diminish the formal extent of its meddling in markets and companies. Each new piece of deregulation will set up pressures for yet more. An internal personnel decision may prove to be even more powerful in bringing about change. The new policy of sending all career-stream recruits— rather than just a third of them— abroad to study will transform attitudes over time. As this younger echelon of officials moves through the institution, they will accelerate the existing trends toward policies based on market forces rather than legal and administrative mechanisms. This has already begun.

The appearance of change, and not the substance of reform, seemed to be the real political imperative.

Yet there is a good case for further reform of the Okurasho. The ministry has consistently put the interests of its elite members, and of itself, ahead of the national interest. Perhaps in a high-growth economy the ministry had enough leeway to serve the nation and itself at the same time. But now that Japan's economy is at the frontiers of economic development, the interests of a club of elite officials too often conflicts directly with the national interest.

Leaving the ministry unchanged would not necessarily be a disaster for Japan. It would simply deliver to the nation a lower level of growth and competitiveness than the country is capable of achieving. Without further change to the ministry, Japan's economic cycle will continue to be influenced by fiscal intrigue at the Okurasho rather than guided by the pursuit of optimum, sustainable economic growth. Monetary policy will continue to be a hostage to fiscal policy. And economic transformation will still move according to the Okurasho's control and influence.

Most proposals for the reform of the ministry propose breaking it into several components to disperse its power and to minimize the opportunity for internal conflict of interests. And this is indeed a necessary condition for meaningful reform. For instance, the Bank of Japan must have the independence to set interest rates according to the needs of the economy and not be bound by the Okurasho's plans for fiscal policy.

And the Cabinet must have the power to fundamentally review

the structure of government finance so that fiscal policy, too, is set according to the needs of the nation and not subject to the Finance Ministry's pursuit of its own power. Similarly, the Fiscal Investment and Loan Program—the zaito system—needs to be reviewed in explicit detail at the cabinet level to address its role in a modern financial and fiscal system and its accumulation of losses.

But a necessary precondition is the strengthening of the Cabinet itself and the role of the prime minister. Under the existing system, cabinet proceedings are choreographed in advance by the bureaucracy.[43] And the main source of advice to the prime minister's office on economic and financial matters is an Okurasho official on temporary assignment. These arrangements have compromised the very core of the system of executive government; the cabinet and the prime minister's office have become extensions of the bureaucracy.[44]

Transferring budget-making functions to an upgraded Cabinet office will not, in itself, guarantee better fiscal outcomes. But at the very least it will improve accountability for failure. And in cases where an administration failed to win support for its budget, the reason would be its failure to win the support of elected politicians—not its failure to win the support of the Okurasho in secret negotiation.

As a general proposition, the separation of the ministry's functions into different and distinct organizations should diminish the opportunity for conflicts of interest, and this applies to its tax and its market-based functions, too.

Such changes will address some of the key structural problems of the ministry. But if only these structural changes are made, then the ministry will only have been rearranged and not reformed. One of the most pervasive themes in the functioning of the Okurasho is the triumph of informal and cultural arrangements over formal and structural ones. It is as important to change the informal and cultural arrangements of the ministry as it is to change the formal and structural ones. In particular, the systems of recruitment and retirement—the Tokyo club entry and the amakudari exit—should be overhauled. Depriving retired bureaucrats of amakudari jobs may translate into a need for dramatic increases in retirement payments to civil servants. If so, this should be done—under the existing system, the costs to the structure and performance of the economy are incalculably larger than any such payment might be. This probably requires a review of the personnel system across the public service.[45]

The ministry, a vital asset in Japan's postwar reindustrialization and reconstruction, has become a liability in the nation's transition to its proper status as a modern economy. And although it continues to trade on its ancient, quasi-mystical origins, its elite status, and fiscal vigilance as sources of moral authority, the Okurasho is not on a divine mission—it is just an institution of the civil service that has lost its way.

GLOSSARY

amakudari
(ah-ma-coo-dah-ri)
Literally "descent from heaven"; the movement of a retired bureaucrat into a high-level private sector position. Also refers to a person employed under this system.

BoJ
Bank of Japan; Japan's central bank.

The Big Bang
Proposal for sweeping financial deregulation; the program aims to revive the Tokyo market by the year 2001.

BIS
Bank for International Settlements, Swiss-based.

bubble economy
The period during the late 1980s when the price of assets rose high above their intrinsic worth. Drawn on a graph, the chart resembled a bubble.

bureau
One of the primary divisions of a government department.

CP (corporate paper)
The issue of corporate debt instruments.

Diet
Japanese parliament.

director-general
The head of a bureau.

EIE International
The small company owned by Harunori Takahashi—focused on building an international tourism empire.

EPA
Economic Planning Agency.

escorted convoy system of banking
Government-supervised cartel whereby a group of banks falls into line with each other and has implicit ministry protection. Also known as *goso-sendan* (go-so-sen-dahn).

FILP	*See zaito.*
G-5	The group of five major industrial democracies—Germany, the United Kingdom, France, USA and Japan.
goso-sendan	see *escorted convoy system of banking.*
Gyokakushin *(gey-yo-ka-coo-sheen)* (begins with a hard *g*, as in *go*)	Administrative Reform Council.
gyosei shido *(gey-yo-say she-doe)*	Administrative guidance, a process of extralegal coercion widely practiced by Japanese bureaucrats, including Finance Ministry officials.
hollowing out	The shift of manufacturing out of Japan as companies sought to escape the high yen.
IMF	International Monetary Fund.
jichiro *(gee-chee-row)*	Worker's union.
jusen *(jew-sen)*	Home loan company; also refers collectively to such firms.
jushin jinchi o shike *(jew-sheen gin-she oh* *she-keh)*	"To set the weight bases," an expression that describes a defensive military strategy used by the former Imperial Japanese Army.
kakaricho *(ka-ka-ree-cho)*	Section chief.
kanpo *(kahn-po)*	Post office life insurance bureau.
karoshi (ka-roe-she)	Death caused by exhaustion from overwork.
Kasumigaseki *(ka-soo-me-ga-seh-key)*	Administrative district in Tokyo, seat of the national ministries.
Keidanren *(kye-dahn-ren)*	Biggest of the big business associations.
kohai *(ko-hi)*	Junior colleague (see also *senpai*).
LDP	Liberal Democratic Party.
LTCB	Long Term Credit Bank.
MoF	Ministry of Finance; often referred to by the Japanese term Okurasho, which literally means Great Storehouse Ministry.

moftan
(mof-tan)

In Japan's national banks, the title of the executive position responsible for closely monitoring the activities of the Finance Ministry. Derived from MoF, the acronym for the Ministry of Finance, and *tan*, which means "responsibility" in Japanese.

MITI

Ministry of International Trade and Industry.

nenpuku
(nen-poo-coo)

Pension Welfare Service Corporation Fund.

Nikkei

The short form of *Nihan Keizai Shimbun*, Japan's major daily business paper.

Nikkei 225

The benchmark index of average prices on the Tokyo stock market; takes its name from the newspaper.

nokyo
(rhymes with Tokyo)

Farmer's co-operatives.

NTT

Nippon Telegraph and Telephone: Japan's dominant phone company.

Okura
(oh-coo-rah)

Treasure-store.

Okura ikka
(oh-coo-rah ee-ka)

Literally, "finance family"; how members of the Okurasho often refer to themselves.

Okurasho
(oh-coo-rah-show)

See MoF.

OTC

Over-the-counter stock market.

pachinko
(pa-cheen-ko)

Slot machine.

PKO

Price keeping operation. Okurasho strategy to manipulate the stock market to support stock prices.

Plaza Accord

Agreement signed on 22 September 1985 at the Plaza Hotel, New York, by the finance ministers of the G-5, pledging to intervene in world foreign markets to push the U.S. dollar down and to hold it there.

Sakigake

New Pioneers Party.

senpai
(sen-pie)

Senior colleague (see also *kohai*).

shinkansen
(sheen-kahn-sen)

Bullet train; also refers to the bullet-train system.

Shinshinto

New Frontier Party.

tanimachi
(tahn-ee-ma-chee)

Name of gifts given to sumo wrestlers by their patrons.

tokkin accounts
(toe-keen)

Special speculative stock-trading accounts popular during the bubble economy through which cash raised at low cost on the stock markets by corporations was put back into stock investments.

vice minister for administrative affairs

The most senior official in a government department.

vice minister for international affairs

Subordinate to the vice minister for administrative affairs; the most senior official responsible for foreign dealings.

wataridori
(waa-taa-ree-door-ee)

Migratory birds.

yakuza
(ya-coo-zah)

Japanese Mafia.

yucho
(you-cho)

Postal savings establishment.

zaibatsu
(zye-baht-soo)

Japan's biggest, most powerful, prewar industrial conglomerates.

zaito
(zye-toe)

Fiscal Investment and Loans Program, a giant public-sector financing system, and the largest pool of funds available to the Okurasho.

NOTES

INTRODUCTION

1. *Asahi Evening News*, 18 February 1994, 1.

2. Morihiro Hosokawa, *Nihon-shinto sekinin aru henkaku* (New Japan party—reform with responsibility), (Tokyo: Tokyo Keiza Shimposha, 1993), 37.

3. *Asahi Shimbun*, 22 April 1994, 11.

4. Eisuke Sakakibara, *Beyond Capitalism: The Japanese Model of Market Economics* (Lanham, MD: University Press of America, 1993). In particular, please note the preface and the prologue.

5. Ibid., chapter two.

CHAPTER ONE

1. Total staff in the Secretariat was 471 in 1992, or 2.1 percent of the Finance Ministry's total staff.

2. Specifically, economic policy making is done by a division of the Minister's Secretariat called the Research and Planning Division. (See Ministry of Finance, *Structures and Functions of the Ministry of Finance*, 1992.) Japan's economy accounted for 16.2 percent of global output in 1993 and more than three-quarters of Asia's output. (See *The World Bank Atlas*, 1995.)

3. The ministry hires twenty to twenty-five new graduates into its executive stream annually. The year 1994 was typical. Of the twenty-one new hires, sixteen had graduated in law and five in economics. Hiring statistics are from the Ministry of Finance (MoF). Asked to list the prerequisites for recruitment, an official of the Minister's Secretariat said that a knowledge of history and society were important but made no mention of economics. The deliberate subordination of economics in policy making is explained by Ryutaro Komiya

and Kozo Yamamoto in *History of Political Economy* 13 (Durham, N.C.: Duke University Press, 1981). This is also reproduced as chapter 9 in Komiya and Ryutaro, *The Japanese Economy: Trade, Industry, and Government* (University of Tokyo Press, 1990). In 1995, there were twelve career-stream Okurasho officials working in its economic policy-making section—the Research and Planning Division—about half of whom held degrees in economics but none of whom was considered a professional economist. There were eight economists in the division on temporary assignment from outside institutions.

4. Ryutaro Komiya and Kozo Yamamoto, *History of Political Economy*, 13 (Durham, N.C.: Duke University Press, 1981).

5. In personal interviews with the author in 1995, Komiya and Yamamoto separately agreed that in the case of the Okurasho, nothing had changed.

6. The finance family, or *Okura ikka*, is a term commonly used in the ministry. This has long been widely known, even outside Japan. For instance, see John Creighton Campbell, *Contemporary Japanese Budget Politics* (Berkeley: University of California Press, 1977), 48–49. Two sometime officials in the ministry (Sakakibara and Noguchi, 1977) described the entire Japanese business world and government bureaucracy as a "quasi-family system existing in a modernized form," a prewar arrangement left untouched by occupation reforms following World War II. The description as a club is recorded by Kevin Rafferty, *Inside Japan's Power Houses* (London: Weidenfeld and Nicolson, 1995), 257.

7. Carol Gluck, *Japan's Modern Myths: Ideology in the Late Meiji Period* (Berkeley: University of California Press, 1989), 55–56.

8. Hirofumi Uzawa in Edward W. Desmond, "How the Mighty Have Fallen," *Time*, 19 February 1996, 15.

9. Gluck, *Japan's Modern Myths*, 179.

10. Sakakibara, *Beyond Capitalism*, 10. Originally published in Japanese in 1990 as The Japanese Model of a Mixed Economy. Dr. Sakakibara, a graduate of Tokyo University, was director-general of the International Finance Bureau at the time of writing.

11. This quote describing politicians as bystanders is taken from a paper Dr. Sakakibara wrote during a sojourn as an academic between ministry appointments, a paper written jointly with an ex-MoF official, Professor Yukio Noguchi. ("Okurasho-Nichigin ocho no bunseki" ["Dissecting the Finance Ministry-Bank of Japan Dynasty"] *Chuo Koron*, August 1977.) Sakakibara's description of the Murayama Cabinet of the mid-1990s as idiots was reported widely in the press—for example, in the *Weekly Bunshun*, 23 November 1995—but denied strenuously by the Finance Ministry.

12. Nobuhito Kishi, *Okurasho o Ugokasu Otoko-tachi* (The Men Who Move the Okurasho) (Tokyo: Toyo Keizai Shimposha, 1993).

13. Recruitment figures are from the MoF.

14. This episode was recorded in the Japanese press—for example, in

Mainichi Shimbun, 7 April 1995, p. 3—and was confirmed in personal interviews with MoF officials.

15. The target figure and other comments were from a personal interview with Hiroshi Watanabe, director of the secretarial division of the Minister's Secretariat, 1995.

16. Ibid.

17. B.C. Koh, *Japan's Administrative Elite* (Berkeley: University of California Press, 1989), esp. 114–123 and 143–147.

18. Komiya and Yamamoto, *Political Economy.*

19. The account of the previous system is based on Komiya and Yamamoto, *Political Economy,* while the explanation of the new system is from a personal interview with Hiroshi Watanabe of the Minister's Secretariat.

20. Koh, *Japan's Administrative Elite,* 168–170.

21. Ibid.

22. *The Shokun,* April 1994.

23. Yoshiaki Miwa, interview by author, 1995. Miwa, a member of the economics department at Tokyo University, is a specialist in industry policy and a member of a government committee charged with the pursuit of deregulation.

24. See Komiya and Yamamoto, *Political Economy.*

25. See also Junko Kato, *The Problem of Bureaucratic Rationality* (Princeton, N.J.: Princeton University Press, 1994), 58–59.

26. Personal interview, 1995.

27. Ibid.

28. This point is recorded by Yoshimitsu Kuribayashi in his book *Okurasho Shukeikyoku* (The Finance Ministry Budget Bureau) (Tokyo: Kodansha, 1986), and by the writer Takao Kawakita in several articles, as in the *Tokyo Shimbun* in January 1981.

29. Personal interview, 1996.

30. This information is courtesy of Takao Kawakita.

31. Of these marriages, forty are listed by Kuribayashi in *Okurasho Shukeikyoku,* chapter 4. Many are also listed by Toshio Toshikawa in *Okurasho: The Secret of Its Power: Who Is the Real Ruler of Japan* (Tokyo: Shogakukan, 1995), 64–75. Toshikawa also adds a new one, taking the total to forty-one. The prime ministers whose families were linked by marriage to ministry officials were Ikeda Ashida (twice), Fukuda (twice), Ohira, Suzuki, and Takeshita. Of these, only one, Takeshita, is still active. Although he no longer holds any formal office except as a backbench member of the Diet, he is probably the most influential politician in the Liberal Democratic Party.

32. Contrary to the widespread belief outside Japan, the lifetime employment system extends only to the industrial elite and the public sector in Japan, covering about 30 percent of the total workforce.

33. Toshikawa, *Okurasho.*

34. Sources include personal interviews with officials; Toshikawa, *Okurasho;* and Koh, *Japan's Administrative Elite.*

35. *The Australian Financial Review*, 25 May 1993, 1, 10.

36. Ibid.

37. Ibid.

38. Kuribayashi, *Okurasho* (Budget Bureau), chapter 2.

39. This work is done mainly in the documentation division of the Minister's Secretariat. Sources include personal interviews with officials and Koh, *Japan's Administrative Elite.*

40. Yoshimitsu Kuribayashi, *Okurasho Shuzeikyoku* (The Finance Ministry Tax Bureau) (Tokyo: Kodansha, 1987).

41. *The Australian Financial Review*, 25 May 1993, 1, 10

42. Personal interview, 1995.

43. Isao Kubota, director-general, Customs and Tariff Bureau, personal interview, 1995.

44. This explanation of the process is based on personal interviews with officials in 1995. The greatest detail was provided by the director-general of a bureau who asked to remain anonymous.

45. Tanaka chose Fumio Takagi over Osamu Hashiguchi. The later episode came about at the insistence of the finance minister, Masayoshi Takemura, that Eisuke Sakakibara be appointed director-general of the International Finance Bureau. The circumstances were unusual because the yen's strength was proving punishing for the economy and the ministry had proved ineffectual in halting the trend. Takemura wanted Sakakibara to deal with this problem. In addition, this pair had an existing personal relationship.

46. This succession plan was recorded in a number of media including, for example, *Tokyo Business Today*, January 1995.

47. Saito was succeeded by Kyosuke Shinozawa in 1995, who was replaced by Tadashi Ogawa in 1996.

48. This episode was reported in the Japanese press (such as *Nikkei*, 15 March 1995; *Japan Times* of the same date; *Asahi Shimbun*, 19 April 1995; and *Asahi Evening News*, 20 May 1995) and confirmed in personal interviews. Saito's parting words to reporters are as recorded by the Knight-Ridder news wire on May 29, 1995.

49. Jiji Press Newswire, 5 January 1996.

50. Koh, *Japan's Administrative Elite*, 145.

51. *The Korea Times*, 24 May 1994.

CHAPTER TWO

1. *Asahi Shimbun*, 28 June 1994. Statistics are from Japan Tobacco, which in 1993 had 82.1 percent of the Japanese cigarette market and 5.4 percent of the world market.

2. MoF.

3. Tax data from Japan Tobacco.

4. *The Australian Financial Review*, August 11, 1994, 1, 12.

5. MoF.

6. Personal interviews with former and serving officials. See also Chalmers Johnson, *Japan, Who Governs?* (New York: W. W. Norton & Co., 1995), 146–151, and Koh, *Japan's Administrative Elite*, 230–240.

7. As recorded by Koh in *Japan's Administrative Elite*, an official who resigns on his own initiative after twenty years' service is paid a lump sum equal to twenty-one times the amount of his final monthly salary. One who leaves at the ministry's request is paid a lump sum equal to 28.875 times his monthly salary.

8. In 1992, for example, 208 amakudari appointments from all national ministries were granted exemptions from the two-year rule. National Personnel Agency.

9. Johnson, *Japan, Who Governs?* 143.

10. Management and Coordination Agency, Toku-Shuhojin Soran *(Special Corporation Yearbook, 1994)* (Tokyo: Management and Coordination Agency, 1994).

11. Labor Federation of Government-Related Organizations *(Seiroren)* annual survey, 1993.

12. Subsidy figure from the *Special Corporation Yearbook, 1994*. Total tax revenue for the general account budget in fiscal 1994 was 53,665 billion yen. MoF. Singapore's GNP in 1993 was $55.4 billion. *World Bank Atlas*, 1995.

13. Bank rankings published by *Worldscope*, 1993.

14. Labor Federation of Government Related Organizations *(Seiroren)* annual survey, 1993.

15. Statistics from *Toyo Keizai* magazine's 1994 amakudari survey. In interviews with former and serving officials, it was pointed out that not all retiring bureaucrats avail themselves of this system—for instance, Makoto Utsumi retired as vice minister for international affairs, took up an academic post, and remained in it. But for the career stream, multiple postministry jobs are generally available.

16. Yamaguchi's finances were reported in the Japanese press and recorded in Rafferty, *Inside Japan's Power Houses*, 260.

17. *Mainichi Shimbun*, 14 January, 1994.

18. In the private sector, *Toyo Keizai* magazine's 1994 survey of 2,220 major firms found that 602 of them employed a total of 1,404 amakudari as directors. The Okurasho supplied more of these—213—than any other ministry. In the public sector, the Finance Ministry had more former officials employed in senior positions—73—than any other ministry, according to a survey by *Yomiuri Shimbun*, 31 October 1994.

19. Personal interview, 1995.

20. Personal interview with Hiroshi Watanabe, director, secretarial division, Minister's Secretariat, 1995.

21. Ibid.

22. Adrian van Rixtel, "Amakudari in the Japanese Banking Industry: An Empirical Investigation," unpublished paper (Tindenberg Institute, Free Amsterdam University), 1995.

23. Sources for the Japan Air Lines episode include *Asahi Shimbun*, 28 November 1994; *Kyodo News Service*, 28 November, 1994; JAL news release, 28 October 1994 ("JAL—Forward Currency Exchange Contracts Disclosure"); and phone interviews with a company spokesman.

24. *Themis* magazine, October 1995.

25. Personal discussion, 1995.

26. Keikichi Honda, economic adviser to the president, Bank of Tokyo, personal interview, 1995.

27. Van Rixtel, "Amakudari in the Japanese Banking Industry."

28. Ibid.

29. Personal interview, 1995. The "colonization" has been much documented and discussed, including in *Mainichi Shimbun*, 7 April 1995, and *Tokyo Business Today*, January 1995.

30. Tokyo Shoko Research, which conducts an annual survey.

31. Tokyo Stock Exchange.

32. Comments by Mr. Yamaguchi and Mr. Nagaoka are from a press conference at the Tokyo Stock Exchange, May 25, 1994.

33. Fair Trade Commission.

34. Sources include personal interviews with Bank of Japan officials. MoF officially describes the rotation of the governor's job as "a kind of coincidence."

35. Cameron Umetsu of UBS Securities in Tokyo used the steepness of the yield curve to measure monetary tightness from 1970 to 1994. As he explains, "Unlike a simple examination of ODR levels or real call rates, this picks up any de facto tightening from yen strength or fiscal retrenchment." He published this finding in several research reports, including his regular "BoJ Watch," 24 November 1994.

36. A former Okurasho vice minister for international affairs, Tomomitsu Oba, was appointed to the Simex board as an adviser. *Nikkei Weekly*, 4 April 1994.

37. *Asahi Shimbun*, published in *Asahi Evening News*, 4 April 1994.

38. *Tokyo Business Today*, June 1994, 13.

39. Bureaucrats are paid salaries equivalent to those of workers in the private sector judged to be of similar seniority under a formula applied to annual salary adjustments. However, senior officials are paid on a separate scale, and this arrangement has fallen prey to public and political pressure; as a result, top officials' pay has fallen slightly behind the theoretical equivalent in the private sector.

40. See, for example, Kent E. Calder, *Strategic Capitalism* (Princeton, N.J.: Princeton University Press, 1993), 66–69, on the persistent strength of Okurasho representation in the Diet.

41. Kuribayashi, *Okurasho* (Budget Bureau).

42. Mr. Miyazawa was finance minister from July 1986 to December 1988. He was some twenty years older than the senior echelon of officials at the time and also headed one of the major factions in the ruling Liberal Democratic Party (LDP). In chapter 1 we saw that he failed to change ministry recruitment policy, and in chapter 3 we will see that he had only very limited success in changing the course of fiscal policy. Mr. Fujii was minister from August 1993 to April 1994. He was a much more junior politician and reportedly had been nominated for the post by the Okurasho itself.

43. Personal interview, 1995.

44. Ibid.

45. *Nihon Keizai Shimbun*, 11 May 1994, 2.

46. Ibid.

47. *Euromoney*, February 1994, 36.

48. *Tokyo Business Today*, May 1995.

49. Special loans were supplied by the Bank of Japan during the 1964 near collapse of the big brokerage firm Yamaichi Securities in 1964, but no actual outlays from the budget were involved.

50. The issue was closely covered by all the Japanese press, including for instance *Yomiuri Shimbun*, 14 March 1995, and (in English) the *Japan Times* of the same date. The widespread indignation at the mildness of the punishment was reported in, for instance, *Yomiuri Shimbun* on 15 March, 1995.

51. *Daily Yomiuri*, 8 September 1995.

52. *Asahi Shimbun*, 12 September 1995.

53. *Daily Yomiuri*, 8 September 1995.

54. Again, this was thoroughly reported in the press, including *Nihon Keizai Shimbun*, 8 September and 29 September 1995, *Asahi Shimbun*, 2 February 1996, and (in English) *Nikkei Weekly*, 11 September 1995.

55. *Themis* magazine, December 1995, and personal interview with vice president of the National Tax Office Workers' Union, Toshiaki Okada, 1995.

56. The reprimand they received was described by the author, Yoshimitsu Kuribayashi, as the sternest disciplinary action taken against an MoF official postwar.

57. The earlier warnings are recorded in the *Yomiuri Shimbun*, 8 September 1995.

58. "Vox Populi, Vox Dei," *Asahi Shimbun*, 10 September 1995.

59. *Nihon Keizai Shimbun*, 11 November 1993, 1.

60. Takeo Fukuda was director-general of the MoF Budget Bureau at the time of the Yamashita Steamship bribery scandal and was prime minister from 1976 to 1978.

61. For example, Takao Toshikawa, editor of several political and financial newsletters and author of a book on the Okurasho. Personal interview, 1995.

62. No legal action had been taken by the time of writing in late 1997.

63. *Mainichi Shimbun*, published in the *Mainichi Daily News*, 12 November 1995.

64. *Asahi Shimbun*, 15 July 1994, 1.

65. *Asahi Shimbun*, 14 July 1994, 1.

66. Personal interview, 1995.

67. Hitoshi Abe, Muneyuki Shindo, and Sadafumi Kawato, *The Government and Politics of Japan* (University of Tokyo Press, 1994), 36.

68. The first anecdote is from the *Nihon Keizai Shimbun*, 26 March 1995, 1, while the inspection tip-off was recorded in the *Sankei Shimbun*, 12 April 1995, 2.

69. Newpis was allowed to sell its stocks in 1978. The Tokyo District Court, under presiding judge Michio Sawada, handed down its judgment in October 1994.

70. The report, *The Market Economy and the Government's Roles*, was quoted in the *Sankei Shimbun*, 9 October 1993, 9.

71. The effects of the changes to the law governing administrative guidance are noted by Ulrike Schaede, "The Old Boy Network and Government-Business Relationships in Japan," *Journal of Japanese Studies* 21, no. 2 (1995): 301, and by the man who drafted the legislation, Yoshio Suzuki, *Ekonomisuto*, 15 November, 1994, 80–83.

72. *Asahi Shimbun*, 9 October 1995.

CHAPTER THREE

1. Ted Rall, "A Sprocket in Satan's Bulldozer: Confessions of an Investment Banker," *Might* (magazine, San Francisco) no. 6 (1995).

2. *Forbes*, 18 May 1987.

3. Robert Zielinski and Nigel Holloway, *Unequal Equities: Power and Risk in Japan's Stock Market* (Tokyo: Kodansha, 1991).

4. *Report of the Research Committee on the Mechanism and Economic Effects of Asset Price Fluctuations*, Institute of Fiscal and Monetary Policy, Ministry of Finance, Tokyo, 1993 (hereafter cited as MoF research committee), 24. Chairman: Professor Emeritus Ryuichiro Tachi, University of Tokyo. The causes of rising land prices—including monetary policy—are also addressed in a research paper by Keizo Takagi, an economist at the Bank of Japan. The paper, titled "The Rise of Land Prices in Japan: The Determination Mechanism and the Effect of the Taxation System," is published in *Bank of Japan Monetary and Economic Studies* 7, no. 2 (1989).

5. Yoichi Funabashi, *Managing the Dollar: From the Plaza to the Louvre* (Washington D.C.: Institute for International Economics, 1988), 17.

6. MoF research committee, 8.

7. Funabashi, *Managing the Dollar*, 12–13, 38, 44.

8. Ibid., 39, 44.

9. Ibid., 61, 230.

10. Ibid., 40.

11. Ibid., 31, 32.

12. Nobuhito Kishi, *Okurasho o Ugokasu Otoko-tachi* (The Men Who Move the Okurasho) (Tokyo: Toyo Keizai Shimposha, 1993). The official was Mr. Yoshino—he had been promoted from director-general of the Budget Bureau to vice minister for administrative affairs.

13. Shigenobu, Hayakawa, ed., *Japanese Financial Markets* (London: Gresham Books, 1996).

14. Budget papers, MoF.

15. Yukio Noguchi, "The 'Bubble' and Economic Policies in the 1980s," *Journal of Japanese Studies* 20, no. 2 (1994): 298.

16. Hayakawa, *Japanese Financial Markets*, 68–75, and Noguchi, "The 'Bubble,'" 298, and the Economic Planning Agency, *Economic Survey of Japan*, 1989.

17. This point is well made by Noguchi, in "The 'Bubble,'" 298, although there are some discrepancies of less than half a percentage point between his percentage figures and those of the MoF. None of these affects the trend or the point. However, where discrepancies exist, I have used the MoF figures.

18. Funabashi, *Managing the Dollar*, 55, 96.

19. Ibid., 53.

20. Noguchi, "The 'Bubble,'" 296.

21. MoF research committee, 2, 69.

22. Merrill Lynch's manager, International Economics, William Sterling, in *Euromoney*, September 1989, 28–29.

23. Christopher Rathke, *The Outlook for Housing*, research report to clients of brokerage firm Hoare Govett, 6 April 1988.

24. Based on market price figures compiled by the Japan Real Estate Institute.

25. MoF research committee, 1.

26. Daniel Burstein, *Yen! The Threat of Japan's Financial Empire* (New York: Bantam/Schwartz Books, 1989), 190.

27. Zielinski and Holloway, *Unequal Equities*, 13, 150. The equity warrant was one of the key mechanisms used, allowing firms to raise about a quarter of a trillion dollars from the stock market at near-zero cost.

28. MoF research committee, 79, and Zielinski and Holloway, *Unequal Equities*, 140.

29. Zielinski and Holloway, *Unequal Equities*, 148.

30. MoF research committee, 79.

31. Senator Lloyd Bentsen made this point in vice-presidential debates in 1988.

32. Personal interview, 1995.

33. The figures are from a paper given by Nomura Research Institute (NRI) specialists in corporate governance, Shigeru Watanabe and Isao

Yamamoto, in Tokyo at a Nomura seminar on 30 September 1994. The quote is from Mr. Yamamoto.

34. Zielinski and Holloway, *Unequal Equities*, 220.

35. Yamamtoto, NRI.

36. Personal interviews with Mr. Takahashi and his staff, Long Term Credit Bank (LTCB) executives and others, 1989–95.

37. Zielinski and Holloway, *Unequal Equities*, 146–147.

38. Burstein, *Yen!* 192.

39. MoF research committee, 13.

40. According to Michael Lewis's book, *How the Japanese Lost the Land War*, as excerpted in *The Sydney Morning Herald*, 18 June 1991.

41. Personal interview, portfolio manager, Sumitomo Life Insurance Co. When the big life insurance companies exercised that mentality in U.S. markets in March 1987 and decided to sell, they were responsible for a disastrous collapse of U.S. bond prices. They off-loaded huge volumes of U.S. Treasury bonds, and yields zoomed from 7.5 percent to 9 percent. And as they shipped their money out of dollars and into yen, the same panic also collapsed the value of the dollar from 150 to 138 yen. The life insurance companies themselves were among some of the biggest victims of their own behavior.

42. The MoF research committee mentions the role of the pack mentality in contributing to the bubble on pp. 26–27.

43. The importance of expectations in speculative frenzy has been well noted, and in this case it has been pointed out by the Economic Planning Agency, *Economic Survey of Japan 1992–93*, 17, and in the report of the MoF research committee, 27–29, 36–38, 62, and 63.

44. Mr. Ozawa's trip was in April 1990, according to *Shukan Gendai*, 25 March 1995.

45. *The Australian*, 15 March 1989.

46. *The Australian Financial Review*, 3 March 1995.

47. Ibid.

48. *Economic Survey of Japan, 1992–93*, 21. The pack mentality has been criticized by, among others, the former governor of the Bank of Japan, Mr. Yasushi Mieno, in a speech to the Yomiuri International Society, Tokyo, 25 March, 1994.

49. Hiromitsu Ishi, *The Japanese Tax System* (Oxford: Clarendon Press, 1993), 345, and the MoF research committee, 40.

50. *Euromoney*, September 1989, 28–29.

51. *Economic Survey of Japan 1992–93*, 21, and Ishi, *Japanese Tax System*, 345.

52. MoF research committee, 40–41.

53. *The Japanese Budget in Brief*, Budget Bureau, MoF, 1995, 61.

54. Noguchi, "The 'Bubble,'" 300.

55. Hayakawa, *Japanese Financial Markets*, 42.

56. MoF research committee, 38–40.

57. From a speech to the Foreign Correspondents' Club in Tokyo, 17 January 1989.

58. Personal interview, 1995.

59. Isao Kubota, "Postmortem on the 'Bubble,'" *Japan Times*, 11 September 1995.

60. Personal interview, 1995.

61. Personal interview, 1995.

62. Personal interview with a former Bank of Japan executive board member, Yoshio Suzuki, 1995.

63. Bank of Japan Economic Research Department, *Money and Banking in Japan* (New York: St. Martin's Press, 1973), 228, cited in Funabashi, *Managing the Dollar*, 61.

64. Personal interview, Yoshio Suzuki, formerly of the Bank of Japan executive board and chairman of the Nomura Research Institute at the time of writing.

65. Personal interview, 1995.

66. Ibid.

67. Noguchi, "The 'Bubble,'" 299.

68. Figures from the Life Insurance Association of Japan.

69. Investment Trusts Association of Japan.

70. Zielinski and Holloway, *Unequal Equities*, 113.

71. MoF research committee, 18.

72. Ibid., 24, 37.

73. Ishi, *Japanese Tax System*, 367.

74. *The Japanese Land Tax System*, research report by the brokerage firm Hoare Govett, Tokyo, 7 March 1988.

75. *Economic Survey of Japan*, 1992–93, 21, and Ishi, *Japanese Tax System*, 367.

76. Noguchi, "The 'Bubble,'" 303.

77. Market prices according to the Japan Real Estate Institute. Note that market prices differ from official prices. For the same period, official price data show Tokyo prices stabilizing rather than falling.

78. *The Japan Real Estate Quarterly*, research report by Merrill Lynch, Tokyo, November 1988.

79. In a speech on 31 October 1994, to the Kinyu Kenkyu-kai association, Mr. Mieno advocated "promoting competition, establishing better risk management by financial institutions, utilizing market-based checking mechanisms, and improving infrastructure for financial institutions."

80. The rules are issued by the Basle Committee on Bank Supervision, made up of the bank supervisors of the Group of Ten richest countries, meeting at the Bank of International Settlements.

81. Zielinski and Holloway, *Unequal Equities*, 180–188.

82. According to Dr. Ishizaki.

83. Takao Toshikawa, *Tokyo Insideline*, 31 January, 28 February, and 31 March 1995.

84. Personal interview, 1995.

CHAPTER FOUR

1. For example, a newspaper survey of business executives in early 1990 found a majority expecting 40,000 points by the end of the year and some predicting as many as 48,000. The most pessimistic expected a fall to 34,000.

2. Burstein, *Yen!* 34–36.

3. Personal interview, 1995. The Banking Bureau was traditionally responsible for negotiations with the Bank of Japan over the course of monetary policy. This role has gradually shifted to the Minister's Secretariat, but the Banking Bureau—through the money market section in its coordination division—is still involved in consultations whenever the ministry wants to initiate a change in monetary policy.

4. Personal interviews with staff at EIE and the Long-Term Credit Bank.

5. MoF research committee, 44–45.

6. Bank of Japan, monthly research report, April 1990.

7. Sources include personal interviews with Bank Bureau officials, *The Economist*, 21 April 1990, and Noguchi, "The 'Bubble,'" 303–304.

8. The diffusion index of the real estate industry's financial position showed a marked tightening from 22 in the three months to the end of March to 14 in the following quarter.

9. The Economic Stabilization Board put the cost of the total wartime economic damage at 99.2 billion yen in 1945 prices. Adjusted for inflation of 19,600 percent, the figure is the equivalent of 19.5 trillion yen in 1995 prices. Cited in Tatsuro Uchino, *Japan's Postwar Economy: An Insider's View of Its History and Its Future* (Tokyo: Kodansha, 1978), 14–15. Inflation is measured by the Bank of Japan's wholesale price index, which stood at 3.5 in 1945 and 687.3 in 1995.

10. For the year of 1946. Uchino, *Japan's Postwar Economy*, 15.

11. E. Philip Davis, *Debt, Financial Fragility, and Systemic Risk*, (New York: Oxford University Press, 1995), 32–100.

12. "Capacity Utilization in Manufacturing," *OECD Economic Outlook*, no. 56 (December 1994): A59.

13. Mieno, speech to the Yomiuri International Society.

14. According to the Japan Development Bank's survey of technological know-how, conducted annually since 1970, as reported in *Nikkei*, 7 August 1995.

15. World Economic Forum, International Institute for Management Development, *World Competitive Report*, as reported in Japan Development Bank research report no. 50, October 1995, and in *Nikkei*, 6 September 1995.

16. Sources are the Economic Planning Agency's 1994–1995 *Annual Report on the National Accounts* and the Tokyo Stock Exchange.

17. Both sets of comments are from personal interviews, 1995.

18. For instance, MoF research committee, 31–36, 51–61.

19. Ibid., 28.

20. *The Australian Financial Review*, 7 June 1994, 1, 12.

21. Ibid.

22. *Bungei Shunju*, February 1994.

23. *Yomiuri Shimbun*, 5 June 1994

24. Hayakawa, *Japanese Financial Markets*, 161.

25. Deutsche Morgan Grenfell.

26. Worldscope, 1992.

27. The ban, effective from March 1990, was much noted in the Japanese press. For example, *Nikkei*, 18 November 1993, and 8 December 1993.

28. For example, *Nikkei*, 11 December 1993.

29. MoF.

30. Mr. Tsushima's remarks are drawn from interviews published in *The Australian*, 27 March 1993, and *The Wall Street Journal*, 19 March 1993.

31. Ibid.

32. Personal interview, 1993.

33. Personal interview, 1995.

34. Deutsche Morgan Grenfell.

35. *The Australian Financial Review*, 27 March 1995, 1.

36. Ibid.

37. *The Australian*, 27 March 1993.

38. Personal interview, 1995.

39. *The Wall Street Journal*, 19 March 1993.

40. Personal interview, 1995.

41. For instance, at an off-the-record dinner, foreign correspondents from *The Wall Street Journal*, *The Financial Times*, and other organs remember Eisuke Sakakibara saying that "we do the PKO and we will continue to do the PKO" to sustain financial order in Japan.

42. Personal interview, 1995.

43. Personal interview, 1994.

44. *The Wall Street Journal*, 19 March 1995.

45. Personal interview, 1994.

46. *Nikkei*, 11 December 1993.

47. *Asahi Evening News*, 27 February 1995.

48. Personal interview, 1995.

49. For example, *Nikkei*, 11 December 1993.

50. Tokyo Stock Exchange.

51. *The Survey of Equities Investment*, published by the National Council of Stock Exchanges. Foreigners were the most aggressive buyers, but they have been set aside for the purposes of this analysis, which considers only Japanese investors.

52. Ibid.

53. The figures, calculated from the accounts of the public funds, were collated by the securities industry.

54. *The Australian*, 27 March 1993.

55. Personal interviews, 1994 and 1995.

56. According to an Okurasho official quoted in the *Mainichi Shimbun*, five of the first six rate cuts in the easing cycle of the early 1990s were initiated by the Finance Ministry. The Bank of Japan had itself sought to make only one. As published in *Mainichi Daily News*, 16 February 1993. In personal interviews, a ministry official confirmed this report, and senior officials at the Bank of Japan, while not confirming it, would not deny it either. The report added that there had been political pressure on the ministry to cut rates.

57. *Shukan Toyo Keizai* (magazine), 5 June 1993.

58. All budget figures are drawn from MoF documents.

59. National Personnel Agency.

60. Van Rixtel, "Amakudari in the Japanese Banking Industry."

61. Personal interview with Isao Kubota in 1995. Mr. Kubota is MoF director-general for Tariffs and Customs, formerly director of research and planning in the Minister's Secretariat.

62. Rall, "A Sprocket."

63. *The Australian Financial Review*, 7 April 1994.

64. MoF research committee, 30.

CHAPTER FIVE

1. Telephone interview, 1996.

2. Of the seven jusen, only the Jutaku Loan Services Co. refused to hire MoF amakudari. The other six appointed MoF men as chairman, president, or senior executive.

3. Personal interview with Tomomitsu Oba, 1995, formerly a senior MoF official.

4. This refers to nonperforming assets. See *Nikkei Weekly*, 29 April 1996. Unofficial estimates put the level of jusen problem loans at 8 trillion yen or more.

5. Prime Minister Tomiichi Murayama and his Cabinet resigned after announcing that 685 billion yen ($6.85 billion) in taxpayers' money would be used to compensate jusen creditors, chiefly the politically powerful agricultural cooperatives. The figure was arrived at in negotiations between the Finance Ministry and the Agriculture Ministry. The Finance Minister at the time, Masayoshi Takemura, later said that he had never been told how the figure was arrived at, Prime Minister Murayama said he had not read any of the official documents on the subject.

6. Telephone interview, 1996.

7. Personal interview, 1995.

8. Personal interview, 1995.

9. Personal interview, 1995.

10. Personal interview, 1995.

11. Figures compiled by commercial banks.

12. Personal interview, 1995.

13. Lending figures from commercial banks.

14. *Nikkei Weekly*, 22 January 1996.

15. Statistics compiled by commercial banks.

16. MoF report, recoded in *Nikkei*, 6 February 1996.

17. According to the MoF and reported in *Asahi Evening News*, 6 February 1996.

18. *Nikkei Weekly*, 22 January 1996.

19. *Nikkei Weekly*, 12 February 1996.

20. Personal interview, 1995.

21. Diet testimony, Lower House Budget Committee, 16 February 1996. The politician was Shin Sakurai. The former official was Masaaki Tsuchida.

22. Personal interview, Sanwa Bank officer, and *Asahi Evening News*, 15 February 1996.

23. Ibid.

24. The plan itself was widely reported, and the estimates of the cost are from UBS securities, Tokyo.

25. From the MoF, as reported in *Asahi Evening News*, 15 February 1996.

26. Miyazawa interview in *Asahi Evening News*, 8 February 1996.

27. *Nikkei*, 29 February 1996.

28. *The Australian Financial Review*, 3 March 1995.

29. Ibid.

30. Ibid.

31. Surveys were conducted by credit industry associations, as reported by James Fiorillo, ING Barings Securities, Tokyo, 24 August 1995.

32. *The Australian Financial Review*, 3 March 1995.

33. The characterization "government-supervised cartel" is from Yoshio Miwa of Tokyo University's economics faculty, personal interview, 1995. The escorted convoy is a characterization used widely by officials, bankers, academics, and analysts.

34. For most of the postwar years, maximum ceilings on commercial interest rates were set by the Bank of Japan under MoF supervision. Short-term loan rates were set by agreement among the members of the National Bank Federation in joint session with officials of the MoF and the Bank of Japan. (Sakakibara and Noguchi "Okurasho-Nichigin ocho no bunseki." When the liberalization of interest rates was completed in October 1994, rates still moved uniformly and deposit interest rates remained at uniformly low levels as a result of agreement among the banks, as pointed out by Shozo Ueda, professor emeritus, Kansai University, in personal interviews and in his paper titled "Disappointing: The Truth of Japanese Banking," published by Ueda, Shozo, 1995. The paper also quotes a senior officer of Sumitomo Bank who concedes that Japan did not yet have "active competition" in this field. The Fair Trade Commission investigated suspicions of collusive rate setting but found no evidence even in cases where a group of banks launched identical products on the same date with identical interest rates.

35. J. Mark Ramseyer, and Frances McCall Rosenbluth, *Japan's Political Marketplace* (Cambridge: Harvard University Press, 1993).

36. Personal interview, 1995.

37. In a speech on 31 October 1994, to the Kinyu Kenkyu-kai, Mr. Mieno said, "It is not the business of the central bank to save all financial institutions from failure. On the contrary, failure of an institution that has reasons to fail is even necessary from the viewpoint of nurturing a sound financial system."

38. Personal interview, 1995.

39. *Nikkei kinyu*, 12 December 1994.

40. The politician was Toshio Yamaguchi, as reported in *Yomiuri Shimbun*, 8 November, 1995.

41. This was the former defense minister, Mr. Nakanishi.

42. *The Australian Financial Review*, 10 March 1995.

43. *The Australian Financial Review*, 3 March 1995.

44. *Mainichi Daily News*, 27 February 1995.

45. Diet testimony, 22 February 1995.

46. *Tokyo Business Today*, May 1995.

47. Widely reported, as in *Asahi Shimbun*, 3 March 1995.

48. *Sankei Shimbun*, 2 March 1995.

49. The contribution, denounced and blocked before local elections, was approved afterward.

50. Personal interview, 1995.

51. *Asahi Evening News*, 29 September 1995.

52. Personal interview, 1995. The economist did not want his name or affiliation disclosed.

53. *Australian Financial Review*, 1 September 1995.

54. *The Asian Wall Street Journal*, 19 June 1995.

55. Text of Moody's announcement, May 11, 1995.

56. Under the earlier definition, only two types of loan were counted as nonperforming: loans to borrowers in bankruptcy or liquidation or reconstruction and loans on which no interest payments had been made for six months. Under the new definition, one more category was added: loans with interest rates reduced to levels below the official discount rate. The definition still excluded other restructured loans and loans that were being only partly serviced. Definitions are from the MoF.

57. The nonperforming loan figures are from the MoF, and the U.S. figure is from *The Asian Wall Street Journal*, 15 June 1995.

58. *The Asian Wall Street Journal,* 15 June 1995.

59. S&P estimate was reported in *Nikkei,* 20 October 1995; Nomura's estimate is from personal interviews, 1995. The Veribanc estimate is from the Kyodo News Service, New York, 28 November 1995.

60. *The Australian Financial Review,* 13 July 1995.

61. *Nikkei Weekly,* 27 November 1995.

62. The ministry's report, titled *Reorganizing the Japanese Financial System* and dated 8 June 1995, set a five-year deadline for the resolution of the problem loans of the banking system. It called for more disclosure and more self-responsibility among financial institutions. It hinted that some failed institutions would need to be wound up, and it promised to create a framework for depositors to begin accepting some risk within five years. But on every point the statement was vague and lacked a sense of urgency, and the Nikkei stock index fell heavily in reponse.

63. *The Asian Wall Street Journal,* 15 June 1995.

64. The negotiations over the Hyogo Bank were reported in *The Australian Financial Review,* 6 September 1995.

65. The Hyogo Bank's business was assumed by a new bank, the Midori Bank, created specifically for that purpose, on October 27, 1995. The new bank's managing director, supplied from the ranks of MoF amakudari, was Minoru Akine.

66. *The Australian Financial Review,* 1 September 1995.

67. Personal interviews with MoF officials, bank analysts' reports, and media reports including *Nikkei,* 21 August 1995.

68. The migration of money was reported in *Nikkei,* 4 December 1995, and 29 February 1996, and the popularity of sales was reported by the *Mainichi Daily News* on 5 December 1995. *Nikkei Weekly,* 12 February 1996, listed the new publications.

69. *Nikkei,* 31 October 1995.

70. Estimate by Yoshinobu Yamada, Merrill Lynch, Tokyo, reported in *Nikkei,* 30 October 1995.

71. *The Economist,* 11 November 1995.

72. *The Australian Financial Review,* 10 July 1995. The same concern was expressed, less colorfully, by the chairman of the Nikko Research Institute, Yasuo Kanzaki, in a paper titled "The Present Status and the Outlook for the Japanese Financial System," at a conference in Tokyo in October 1995.

73. The arrangement, announced by the chairman of the House Banking Committee, Rep. Jim Leach, was reported widely, as in *Nikkei Weekly,* 23 October 1995, and was analyzed in more detail in *Nikkei,* 30 October 1995.

74. Sanyu System Housing Loan Co. *Nikkei Weekly* reported a slightly worse ratio—80 percent—November 27, 1995.

75. MoF.

76. This suppression of information was reported widely within the financial community, and recorded—for example, by UBS Securities property analyst Dan Nielsen—in research reports.

77. *The Asian Wall Street Journal*, 15 June 1995.

78. This refers to *tobashi* schemes—in which banks financed dummy subsidiaries to buy out collateralized assets from troubled borrowers, who then used that finance to repay part of their bank debts—and to sales of problem assets to a company created jointly by the banks, Cooperative Credit Purchasing Corporation (CCPC). Sales of problem assets to this company allowed the banks to realize losses and to recover part of the face value of the loan. This was not a real disposal mechanism, however, because if after five years the CCPC was unable to sell the collateral, it reverted to the bank. At the time of writing, the CCPC had a recovery rate of around 3 percent of the face value of the loans outstanding on its problem assets.

79. Personal interview, 1995.

80. Statistics from bank accounts compiled by Bank of Japan.

81. The value of stockholdings in the banks' accounts rose by 18 percent in the two years to March 1995.

82. Salomon Brothers Tokyo, Japanese equity research report on banks, 13 April 1994, and 23 June 1995.

83. Interviews with commercial bankers.

84. A report by the National Council of Stock Exchanges entitled "The Survey of Equities Investment."

85. *Nikkei Weekly*, 15 January 1996.

86. *Nikkei Weekly*, 11 December 1995. Central bank buying and selling of bonds is a normal part of reserve-supplying operations. However, this particular exercise was exceptional; it was large in volume and designed specifically to bolster bank profitability. In the market, it was dubbed a "price-keeping operation," or PKO.

87. This was implied in the September 27, 1995, report by the Financial System Stabilization Committee of the Financial System Research Council, which said: "In the next five years, it will be difficult to ask depositors of a failing or failed institution to bear the cost of loss." The council, as with most such advisory committees, is used by the ministry to proclaim new policy. The ministry's commitment to phasing out total deposit security after five years was confirmed as new policy in interviews with ministry officials.

88. Personal interview, Sei Nakai, Banking Bureau, 1995.

89. Press conference by Kyosuke Shinozawa, Tokyo, 10 October 1995.

CHAPTER SIX

1. Flows measured by basic balance, 1987 to 1989. The current account surplus during the same three years came to a total of $223.7 billion. MoF statistics.

2. The turning point was 1990 with basic balance close to equilibrium with an outflow of $7.8 billion; the current account surplus in the following four years totaled $451 billion. For more on this subject, see *Economic Survey of Japan*, 1992–93, 30–31. For a more detailed description of capital flows in the 1980s, see Mitsuhiro Fukao, *Bank of Japan Monetary and Economic Studies* 8, no. 2 (1990): 101–165. And for a description including the early 1990s see Toshio Yamasaki, in *Tokyo Ginko Geppo*, May 1993 and (in English) in *Economic Eye*, Autumn, 1993, published by Keizai Koho Center.

3. Japan's authorities do not disclose details of currency intervention. These estimates are compiled by an economist at the Japan Research Institute, Sayuri Kawamura. Her research was published in the institute's *Japan Research Review*, June 1996.

4. Mr. Inoue, deputy director of research, quoted in *The Wall Street Journal*, 7 May 1994.

5. Securities investment figure is from the Life Insurance Association, while the real estate figure is an estimate by the Nomura Research Institute.

6. For example, Shusaku Toda, director, Standard & Poor's, in *Nikkei Weekly*, 23 October 1995.

7. Nomura Research Institute, *Capital Market Trends*, August 1995, 8.

8. Executive at Sumitomo Life Insurance Co, personal interview, 1994.

9. Hayakawa, *Japanese Financial Markets*, 152–153.

10. Kathy Matsui and Hiromi Suzuji, *Portfolio Strategy*, Goldman Sachs (Japan) 26 June 1995.

11. Hayakawa, *Japanese Financial Markets*, 158–162.

12. Josei Ito, quoted in *Nikkei Weekly*, 23 October 1995.

13. Industry talks with the MoF, as described by MoF officials; the cuts were reported widely, as in *Nikkei Weekly*, 15 January and 29 January 1996.

14. *Nikkei Weekly*, 23 October 1995.

15. Budget Bureau, *The Japanese Budget in Brief*, April 1995.

16. *Nikkei Weekly*, 12 February 1996, citing Social Insurance Agency figures.

17. Contributions are counted as the amounts paid in by the employee plus those made on his behalf by employers. In *Look Japan*, September 1995. Professor Ueda wrote that these calculations remained valid. The Sanwa Bank published similar calculations in its Economic Letter of October 1994, where it said that those born after 1986 would receive fewer benefits than they paid in as contributions.

18. Paul Van den Noord and Richard Herd, "Pension Liabilities in the Seven Major Economies," working paper 142, Organization for Economic Cooperation and Development, Paris, France, 1993.

19. Ibid.

20. Sadayuki Horie, "Current Status of the Pension Fund System in Japan," paper and appendix presented in Tokyo on November 11, 1994, on behalf of the Asset Management Research Unit, NRI.

21. Reported in *Nikkei Weekly*, 2 October 1995.

22. Horie, "Pension Fund." European figures are from the European Federation for Retirement Provisions, quoted in *Mainichi Daily News,* 12 March 1995.

23. In March 1993 the Trust Fund Bureau held 97 trillion yen in pension assets.

24. A tiny fragment—138 billion yen—is managed by the National Mutual Insurance Federation of Agricultural Cooperatives.

25. The rate is the interest rate paid on Fiscal Investment and Loans under the Fiscal Investment and Loan Program administered by the Okurasho.

26. Horie, "Pension Fund."

27. Inflation calculated using OECD figures for the GDP deflator in the two countries, 1985–93.

28. This point was made by Ichiro Yamanaka, president of Daiwa International Capital Management Co., in *Nikkei Weekly,* 16 January 1995. This practice was cited by the U.S. Treasury as "the principal obstacle facing U.S. and foreign trust banks in Japan," in *National Treatment Study,* 1994, 345.

29. *The Australian Financial Review,* 17 October 1994.

30. "Changing Demographics and Japan's Pension System," Economic Letter, Sanwa Bank, October, 1994.

31. See for instance, *Nikkei Weekly,* 14 August 1995.

32. Noboru Terada, executive director, Pension Fund Association, personal interview, 1994.

33. *National Treatment Study,* 345–346.

34. This concern was reported in *Nikkei Weekly,* 14 August 1995.

35. Horie, "Pension Fund."

36. *Nikkei Weekly,* 2 October 1995.

37. *Nikkei Weekly,* 14 August 1995.

38. *Nikkei Weekly,* 2 October 1995.

39. Although this may seem to be at odds with the inflow of funds into Japan in these years, it is not. There was considerable outflow of foreign direct investment, but this was far outstripped by capital inflows, so the net position was an inflow.

40. *Tokyo Business Today,* August, 1995.

41. Economic Planning Agency, *Economic Survey of Japan,* 25 July 1995.

42. From a speech to the Economic Club of Detroit, quoted in *The Asian Wall Street Journal,* 22 June 1994.

43. Ministry of International Trade and Industry (MITI).

44. Company plans according to a survey by Economic Planning Agency, reported in the *1994 Survey of Corporate Activities;* actual movement sourced from MITI, and reported in *The Australian Financial Review,* 5 April at 8.9 percent in 1995; forecast by Mr. Fukukawa in *Journal of Japanese Trade and Industry,* July/August, 1995.

45. Peter Boardman, analyst, UBS Securities, Tokyo, as reported in *The Australian Financial Review,* 21 April 1995.

46. MITI.

47. *Tokyo Business Today*, August 1995.

48. Japan Automotive Manufacturers' Association.

49. Boardman, April 1995.

50. *The Australian Financial Review*, 28 April 1995.

51. Mazda announced on April 12, 1996, that it was issuing 144.1 million new shares to Ford, lifting Ford's stake in the company from 24.5 percent to 33.4 percent for a consideration of 52.3 billion yen. The injection of fresh capital delivered control of Mazda to the U.S. firm. *Bloomberg Business News*, April 12, 1996.

52. *Yomiuri Shimbun*, 10 October 1995.

53. *The Australian Financial Review*, 9 October 1995.

54. *Manufacturing Productivity*, published by McKinsey Global Institute, Washington D.C., October 1993.

55. Protection figures are pre-Uruguay Round, and both are expected to fall after the round, for manufacturing to 2.1 percent and for food to 56.1. Martin T. Hertel, K. Yanagishima, and B. Dimaranan, "Liberalizing Manufactures Trade in a Changing World Economy," paper presented to World Bank Conference on the Uruguay Round, Washington D.C., January 1995.

56. *Nikkei*, 29 May 1995.

57. *The Economic Survey of Japan, 1994–95*, estimates that about 80 percent of the Japan-U.S. price gap is attributable to the productivity disparities between Japan's manufacturers and nonmanufacturers.

58. Shunsuke Motani, senior economist, Deutsche Morgan Grenfell Securities, Tokyo, personal interview, 1995.

59. *Asahi Shimbun*, 31 July 1994.

60. "New Frontiers for Reform: Shinshinto's Vision for the Twenty-First Century," (Japan: Shinshinto Political Party, undated).

61. *The Australian Financial Review*, 8 March and 5 April 1995.

62. *Nikkei*, 7 April 1995.

63. *The Australian Financial Rview*, 11 April 1995.

64. This conclusion was shared by the Economic Planning Agency, the Japan Research Institute (the independent research arm of the Sumitomo Bank), and the Institute of Mitsui & Co. for Trade and Economic Studies.

65. Intervention estimates by Sayuri Kawamura of the Japan Research Institute and published in the institute's *Japan Research Review*, June 1996.

66. At a press conference, as reported in *The Australian Financial Review*, 11 April 1995.

67. *Journal of Japanese Trade and Industry* 14, no. 4 (July–August 1995).

68. Quoted in *Nikkei Weekly*, 28 August 1995.

69. Quoted in *Nikkei*, 19 April 1995.

70. John B. Judis, "Dollar Foolish," *The New Republic*, 9 December 1996.

71. Kemper Financial Services bulletin from David Hale to investment staff, 15 August 1995.

72. *The New Republic*, 9 December 1996.

73. *The Australian Financial Review*, 11 April 1995.

74. *Japan Research Quarterly* 4, no. 1 (Winter 1994/95).

75. Japanese Economic Council, *Social and Economic Plan for Structural Reforms, Toward a Vital Economy and Secure Life*, (Japan: Economic Council, 29 November 1995).

76. Hayakawa, *Japanese Financial Markets*, 110–123.

77. Yoshiaki Miwa, "Kinyu gyosei kaikaku," Nihon Keizai Shimbunsha, 1993.

78. Japan Credit Rating Agency, *Financial Digest*, August 1995.

79. The survey is titled *Opinions and Strategies of Foreign Financial Institutions Regarding the Tokyo Money and Capital Markets*, published by the Japan Center for International Finance, December 1995.

80. From a speech by Yasuo Matsushita titled "The Roles and the Challenges of the Capital Market in Japan," delivered to the Capital Markets Research Institute in Tokyo on June 14, 1995, and published in the *Bank of Japan Quarterly Bulletin*, August 1995.

81. *Nikkei Weekly*, 13 November 1995.

82. Benn Steil, *Illusions of Liberalization: Securities Regulation by Japan and the EC* (London: Royal Institute of International Affairs, 1995).

83. Quoted in *Asahi Evening News*, 27 February 1995.

84. *The Australian Financial Review*, 12 July 1995.

85. Ibid.

86. From Mr. Matsushita's speech, "Capital Market in Japan."

87. *The Capital's Future as an International Financial Center*, Metropolitan Areas Development Bureau, National Land Agency, March 1994.

88. Based on an interview with a Securities Bureau official, 1995. The five points are as follows: First, were foreign securities companies abandoning Tokyo? The Finance Ministry's securities bureau decided that the total number of staff employed by such firms in Tokyo was "more or less stable" and dismissed this concern. Second, was the number of foreign companies listed on the Tokyo Stock Exchange falling? The ministry decided that, yes, it was, and listing criteria were eased as a result. Third, was an increasing proportion of Japanese stock trading occurring on the London stockmarket? The ministry found that this was just a mirage—orders placed in London were actually drawing on shares from Tokyo and so generating trading in Japan, not displacing it. Fourth, was the Simex exchange in Singapore taking the lead in trading futures contracts based on Tokyo stock prices? The answer was yes: "This is a real problem," said an official. The ministry would try to address this by cautiously exploring how to develop futures products that would not adversely affect the market. Fifth, was the bond market in Japan losing its vitality? Because of a rebound in bond issues in early 1995, the ministry decided that "there was a problem, but it's already been addressed." The numerical results of the ministry study were collated in an undated paper titled "Discussion about the Hollowing Out of Securities Markets."

89. Personal interviews with the bureau's director-general, Eisuke Sakakibara, 1995 and 1996.

CHAPTER SEVEN

1. Yukio Noguchi, *1940 nen taisei* (The 1940 system) (Tokyo: Toyo Keizai Shimposha, 1995).

2. The quotes here are taken from a discussion between Noguchi and a fellow professor at Hitotsubashi University, Iwao Nakatani, published in *Ushio*, August 1995.

3. Ibid.

4. *Shukan Toyo Keizai*, 8 July 1995.

5. Ichiro Ozawa, *Nihon kaizo keikaku* (Blueprint for rebuilding Japan), (Tokyo: Kodansha, 1993).

6. *Shukan Toyo Keizai*, 8 July 1995.

7. Francis Fukuyama, *The End of History and the Last Man* (New York: Penguin Books, 1992).

8. *Shukan Toyo Keizai*, 8 July 1995.

9. Ibid.

10. Sakakibara's essay summarizing the interim results of the project was published in *Chuo Koron*, August 1995.

11. Hidehiro Iwaki, "A Renovation of Government Regulations: Fostering Market Mechanisms in Japan" (paper presented during a seminar at the Nomura Rearch Institute, Tokyo, Japan, 28 July 1994).

12. Personal interview, 1995.

13. Citing the Economic Planning Agency's *Economic Survey of Japan, 1994*, reported in the *Nikkei*, 27 June 1994, and elsewhere, was only one of many such estimates of the effects of deregulation. Others included the Keidanren's, summarized in *Keidanren Review* no. 147 (December 1994), the Japan Research Institute's, published in its *Japan Research Quarterly* 3, no. 4 (Autumn 1994), and the Sanwa Bank's, reported in the Sanwa Economic Letter, May 1995.

14. *Tokyo Shimbun*, 2 June 1994.

15. As observed by author's assistant during a session on November 2, 1995, in the No. 4 Common Government Building.

16. *The Australian Financial Review*, 25 October 1995. Professor Miwa has also made his views known elsewhere, as in *Nikkei*, 4 September 1995.

17. *The Australian Financial Review*, 28 October 1994.

18. Ibid.

19. Ibid.

20. Ibid.

21. Professor emeritus Shozo Ueda. Of the nonconformist banks, one offered 0.05 percent and the other 0.12 percent.

22. See the *Report on Yen/Dollar Exchange Rate Issues* by the Japanese Ministry of Finance and the U.S. Department of the Treasury Working Group, May 1984, 13–16.

23. The characteristics and descriptions of OTC companies are from *The Australian Financial Review*, 12 July 1994.

24. Sanwa Bank, Economic Letter, February 1995.

25. Statistics from the Japan Securities Dealers' Association.

26. Nobuyori Kodaira, director, industrial finance, MITI, personal interview, 1994.

27. Personal interviews, officials of the Japan Securities Dealers' Association, and MoF Securities Bureau; also reported in part in *Nikkei*, 18 November 1994.

28. *The Australian Financial Review*, 12 July 1994.

29. *Nikkei Kinyu*, 23 August 1995.

30. Published in *Chuo Koron*, August 1977, as "Okurasho-Nichigin ocho no bunseki" ("Dissecting the Finance Ministry-Bank of Japan dynasty"), and condensed in English in *Japan Echo* 4, no. 4 (1977).

31. Senior Japanese politicians, including Kakuei Tahaka, prime minister at the time, were accused of taking multimillion-dollar bribes from Lockheed Corporation. Tanaka's administration was brought down by the scandal.

32. *Shukan Toyo Keizai*, 8 July 1995.

33. Personal interview, 1995.

CHAPTER EIGHT

1. Quoted in Sakakibara, *Beyond Capitalism*, 54.

2. Kumio Fukumoto, *Kanryo* (Bureaucrats) (Tokyo: Kobundo, 1959), 142–143, cited in Karel van Wolferen, *The Enigma of Japanese Power: People and Politics in a Stateless Nation* (New York: A. A. Knopf).

3. The Finance Ministry was hoping to cut the current account surplus by stimulating demand.

4. The likening to a narcotic was reported in the *Mainichi Daily News*, 25 January 1994, and the demonizing was done by Hirohisa Fujii, a ministry official who went on to become a politician, reported by the Kyodo news service, 25 August 1993.

5. Mamoru Ozaki, as reprinted in *Finansu* (Finance), an MoF in-house publication, April 1993.

6. *Nikkei*, 7 February 1994 and 27 June 1994.

7. Correspondence with the author, 19 February 1996.

8. *Sentaku*, February 1994.

9. Correspondence with the author, 19 February 1996.

10. This was widely reported at the time, as in *Sentaku*, February 1994. The MITI vice minister for administrative affairs was Hideaki Kumano.

11. Personal interview, 1995.

12. John Campbell, *Contemporary Japanese Budget Politics* (Berkeley: University of California Press, 1977), 2.

13. *Nikkei*, 18 October 1993.

14. Correspondence with the author, 19 February 1996.

15. *OECD Economic Outlook*, no. 56, December 1994.

16. Defense Agency official, personal interview, 1995.

17. *Nikkei*, 4 December 1995.

18. Hiromitsu Ishi, "Rigidity and Inefficiency in Public Works Appropriations: Controversy in Reforming the Budgeting Process in 1994," *Journal of Japanese Studies* 21, no. 2 (Summer 1995).

19. *Nikkei*, 9 August 1994.

20. *Asahi Shimbun*, 25 November 1994.

21. Ibid.

22. *Yomiuri Shimbun*, 12 February 1995, and *Nikkei*, 14 and 16 February 1995.

23. Mr. Kato's views as reported in the *Japan Times*, 15 March 1995, and Kyodo News Service, as published in *Asahi Evening News*, 3 February 1995.

24. "Dynamic Structuralism: An Application for Politico-Economic Analysis," discussion paper 21, Office of Systems Analysis, Economic Research Institute, Economic Planning Agency, March 1979.

25. The eight objectives are listed in Campbell, *Japanese Budget Politics*, 2, as:
1. Protecting the ministry's autonomy, elite status, and jurisdictional boundaries.
2. Pursuing correct fiscal policies for given economic conditions.
3. Minimizing the size of the total budget in the current year.
4. Getting the budget finished smoothly and in due time.
5. Preserving "balance."
6. Achieving a desirable policy mix in accordance with national priorities.
7. Avoiding future expansions of expenditures.
8. Eliminating wasteful spending and obsolete programs.

26. Junko Kato, *The Problem of Bureaucratic Rationality: Tax Politics in Japan* (Princeton, N.J.: Princeton University Press, 1994). Kato is not alone. Jiro Yamaguchi, a professor of administrative policy at Hokkaido University, for instance, argues a very similar case.

27. According to the 1995 MoF report on the zaito system, its total funds under management were 346.7 trillion yen in 1994. Japan's nominal GDP that year was 475 trillion yen. Its full name in Japanese is *Zaisei Toyushi Keikaku*—the first syllable of each of the first two words are merged to create *zaito*.

28. Two useful descriptions of the development and workings of the system are Kent Calder, *Strategic Capitalism* (Princeton, N.J.: Princeton University Press, 1993), and Yukio Noguchi, "The Role of the Fiscal Investment and Loan Program in Postwar Japanese Economic Growth," working paper 93-34, Economic Development Institute, World Bank.

29. Budget in Brief, MoF, 1995, 3.

30. In the 1993 zaito allocation, 99.8 percent of funds were interest-bearing deposits that required servicing.

31. Noguchi, "Postwar Japanese Economic Growth."

32. *Tokyo Business Today* 63, no. 4 (April 1995).

33. Personal interviews, 1995.

34. Atsushi Miyawaki, *Japan Research Quarterly* 2 no. 2 (Spring 1993). Yoshio Suzuki of the Nomura Research Institute also estimates that about half of total zaito funding is used as a substitute for finance from the general account of the budget; *Tokyo Business Today* 63, no. 4 (April 1995).

35. Personal interview, 1994.

CHAPTER NINE

1. Rafferty, Kevin, *Inside Japan's Power Houses* (London: Weidenfeld and Nicolson, 1995).

2. Ibid.

3. Karel van Wolferen, *The Enigma of Japanese Power: People and Politics in a Stateless Nation* (New York: A. A. Knopf, 1989), 11.

4. Gregory Millman, *Around the World on a Trillion Dollars a Day* (New York: Bantam Press, 1995).

5. Ibid.

6. *Australian Financial Review*, 8 November 1994.

7. Ibid.

8. This does not, however, suggest that the policy is Dr. Sakakibara's alone. U.S. officials say that several officials of the Ministry of Finance have made similar threats in recent years

9. OECD estimates.

10. *Australian Financial Review*, 8 November 1994.

11. Ibid.

12. Ibid.

13. Ibid.

14. Ibid.

15. Interview with an official of the International Finance Bureau, 1994.

16. *The East Asian Miracle: Economic Growth and Public Policy* (New York: Oxford University Press, 1993).

17. Although this comparison is commonly used in the Japanese media—for instance, *Nikkei*, 7 November 1993—it is somewhat specious. Asia is not a country.

18. MoF press release.

19. *Australian Financial Review*, 9 November 1994.

20. Ibid.

21. Japan Securities Dealers Association.

22. *Nikkei,* 20 February 1996.

23. *Nikkei Business,* 31 October 1994.

24. *Financial Times,* 18 December 1989.

25. From a speech to the Foreign Correspondents' Club of Japan, Tokyo, 3 April 1995.

26. From a speech titled "The U.S.-Japan Financial Relationship," given in Tokyo, 20 September 1994.

27. The definition of *savings* in this identity includes not only private-sector savings but savings or dissavings in the government sector.

28. *Shukan Toyo Keizai,* 10 July 1993.

29. *Tokyo Business Today* 62, no. 4 (April 1994).

CHAPTER TEN

1. Junko Kato explains how the MoF used this approach to set the weight bases, or *jushin jinchi o shike,* to negotiate the introduction of consumption taxes in Japan. It abandoned its initial negotiating positions, cutting the rate of tax and amending the methodology for collecting it, in protecting its core priority—the introduction of the tax. Junko Kato, *The Problem of Bureaucratic Rationality* (Princeton, N.J.: Princeton University Press, 1994), 87–92.

2. The rate of real GDP growth in 1986 was 2.9 percent; in each subsequent year it was 4.7, 6.0, 4.3, 5.3, 3.6, 0.3, –0.2, 1.7, and, in 1995, 2.8, according to the MoF. In the preceding three decades, the only time that growth fell below 2.9 percent was in 1974, the time of the first oil shock, when growth fell to zero.

3. Address to the nation by the Prime Minister Ryutaro Hashimoto, broadcast on NHK TV, 9 November 1996.

4. Formally, the coalition between the Liberal Democratic Party (LDP), the Social Democrats, and the Sakigake, or New Pioneers Party, ended with the election. The LDP increased its strength in the Lower House from 211 seats out of 511 in the old parliament to 239 out of 500 in the new, an improvement from 41 percent of the seats to 48 percent. however, the LDP still lacked the numbers for a majority and continued to rely on the two smaller parties for their support on the floor of the parliament to pass legislation. And so the Social Democrats and Sakigake formed an informal alliance with the LDP, outside the government and unrepresented in the Cabinet but cooperating in the parliament. These two smaller parties had been seriously weakened in the election—the Social Democrats' numbers in the Lower House fell from 30 to 15 and the Sakigake from 9 to 2. Their incentive to remain in loose alliance with the LDP was that this delivered them disproportionate influence. The alternative was to have even less influence as minor opposition parties.

5. Mr. Ito's comments are drawn from an interview published in the *Nikkei Weekly*, 8 July 1996.

6. The report by the ministry's internal task force was delivered by the Finance Minister, 18 September 1996, about a month before election and the same day that the leadership of the majority ruling party, the Liberal Democrats, met to confirm a plan to transfer supervision of the financial sector to an independent body. *Nikkei*, 19 September 1996.

7. Interviews with officials in the relevant bureaus, 1995.

8. *Nikkei Weekly*, 18 November 1996.

9. Ryutaro Hashimoto, *Vision of Japan—A Realistic Direction for the Twenty-first Century* (Tokyo: Bestsellers Co., 1994), 42–43. At the time he wrote the book, the gross value of outstanding national bonds was 184 trillion yen ($1.84 trillion). He commented: "This translates into a loan of about 1.48 million [$14,800] from every Japanese person—far too much." By the end of 1996, the total gross value had reached 240 trillion yen, or $2.4 trillion.

10. *Nikkei*, 18 September 1996.

11. *Nikkei Weekly*, 18 November 1996.

12. *Capital Market Trends*, Nomura Research Institute, February 1997, 8–9.

13. *Nikkei*, 26 December 1996.

14. Office of Shigeru Ito.

15. *Nikkei Weekly*, 10 June 1996.

16. Ibid.

17. Ibid.

18. *Nikkei*, 25 December 1995.

19. Reuters News Service, 12 November 1996.

20. Hiroshi Kato, chairman of the Tax Commission and president of the Chiba University of Commerce, quoted in *Tokyo Business Today* 63, no. 10 (October 1995).

21. *Report Concerning the Revision of the Bank of Japan Law*, published by the Financial System Research Council in Tokyo, 6 February 1997.

22. Ibid.

23. Matsushita's views were widely cited; for instance, the *Asian Wall Street Journal*, 26 December 1996, and the *Nikkei Weekly*, 10 February 1997.

24. Conversation with a deputy director of the Finance Ministry, February 1997.

25. *Nikkei*, 6 December 1996, and *Nikkei Weekly*, 27 January 1997. Ultimately, the supplementary budget was reduced to 3.7 trillion yen ($37 billion).

26. *Nikkei*, 6 December 1996.

27. *Nikkei*, 5 December 1996.

28. *Nikkei Weekly*, 27 January 1997.

29. Press briefing by the director-general of the International Finance Bureau, Eisuke Sakakibara, Tokyo, 11 November 1996.

30. "London Stock Exchange Celebrates Big Bang Anniversary," *Focus*, October 1996, www.fibv.com.

31. "Structural Reform of the Japanese Financial Market," provisional translation, as distributed by the MoF, 11 November 1996. According to Sakakibara, this was the document—the "instruction"—Hashimoto handed to Mitsuzuka.

32. Ibid.

33. Ibid.

34. Briefing by Sakakibara to the international media, 11 November 1996.

35. *Financial Times* (London), 10 December 1996. According to the Oxford Analytica Asia Pacific Brief, the institutions planning expansion in Tokyo include Deutsche Morgan Grenfell, Societe Generale, BNP Securities, and the Hongkong and Shanghai Banking Corporation–Midland Banking Group. For unrelated reasons, two South Korean brokerages, Daewoo Securities and LG Securities, and one Hong Kong institution, Peregrine Investment Holdings, are also expanding their Tokyo operations.

36. Personal interview, April 1997.

37. Media briefing, 11 November 1996.

38. Personal interview, April 1997.

39. *Nikkei Weekly*, 18 November 1996.

40. William Dawkins, *Financial Times* (London), 10 December 1996.

41. The *Nikkei Weekly* of November 18, 1996, for instance, reported widespread suspicion that the Big Bang is part of a deal for political cooperation between the ministry and Hashimoto, although the article notes that no hard evidence has been presented.

42. *Nikkei Weekly*, 10 June 1996.

43. The administrative vice ministers of the national ministries meet the day before each scheduled Cabinet meeting. The bureaucrats set the agenda for the Cabinet meeting, debate the issues, make decisions on each agenda item, and then draft the terms of the debate that Cabinet ministers will follow at their meeting. By the time the Cabinet meets, all decisions are made and agreed on at the bureaucratic level. The ministers act out their parts, reading out the prepared notes and going through the motions of executive government, and endorse the decisions made the day before. This is the reason that Japan's Cabinet meetings are extremely brief, typically lasting some fifteen or twenty minutes.

44. An upgrading of the prime minister's powers was being explored by an advisory group in 1997.

45. A review of the options for restructuring of the civil service and its personnel systems was under way in 1997.

INDEX

Administrative guidance, 56–58, 98, 104

Administrative Reform Council (*Gyokakushin*), 209, 213, 244

Administrative vice minister, mission to China, first postwar overseas mission, 228

Advisory Group for Economic Structural Reform, 234

Aera magazine, 134

Agriculture Ministry. *See* Ministry of Agriculture

Agriculture, Forestry, and Fishery Finance Corporation, 35

Aichi, Kazuo, 208

Aida, Yukio, 102, 112, 182

Aiwa Co., 168, 172

All Japan Prefectural and Municipal Workers' Union (*jichiro*), 139

Amakudari, 32–33, 255, 256, 258
  and Bank of Japan, 121
  employment in captive public corporations, 42–43
  employment in the private sector, 42–43, 147
  and estimation of Japanese people, 48–49
  as form of structural corruption, 45

  and Japan Air Lines, 39–40
  and the Minister's Secretariat, 9–10, 38–39
  and Ministry of Finance, 32–46
  movements into speculative, smaller firms, 92–93
  opportunities for increased, as result of recession, 120
  plan to diminish placement in private sector, 239
  positions in the jusen industry, 128, 130
  practiced in all of Japan's national ministries, 37
  process and entitlement, 42–46
  resistance of, in private companies, 40–41
  serious indictment of system of, 130
  and special corporations controlled by Ministry of Finance, 35

Amano, Yoshihito, 123–124

American Stock Exchange, 224

Americans, how to terrify, 177–179

Ampo, U.S.-Japan security treaty, 185, 190

ANA, 70–71, 76

Anzen Credit Cooperative, 134–135

Asahi Shimbun, 45–46, 48, 54
  on Yoshio Nakajima, 51
Asia Club, 21
Asia factor, 228–230
Asia-Pacific Club, 230
Asian Development Bank, 229
Australian, The, 79

Baker, James, III, 69
Balanced budget, doctrine of, 230, 231
Bank cartel, surviving deregulation intact, 197
Bank for International Settlements, 92
Bank of Japan Act of 1942, 241
Bank of Japan, 10, 42, 52, 65, 69, 84,
    91, 137, 158, 174–175, 178, 183,
    223, 228, 247, 249, 255
  and amakudari, 121
  announcing takeover of two Taka-
    hashi-affiliated credit co-ops, 138
  assuring it would supply liquidity to
    overseas operations, 149
  blame for bubble shifted to, by
    Okurasho, 100–101
  and Budget Bureau, 96–97
  easing interest rates in 1983, 62–63
  easy credit policy of, 155
  increasing discount rate, 95–96, 97
  and Ministry of Finance accused of
    massive cover-up operation, 140
  and pressure from Okurasho to cut
    rates, 117
  proposals to grant independence to,
    239, 241, 247–249, 257
  and reservations about easy money
    policy, 85–86
  response to Long Term Credit
    Bank's withdrawal of support for
    EIE International, 135–136
  and rotation of governorship of with
    Ministry of Finance, 44–45
  and supervision by the Okurasho, 85
  and surveillance of jusen manage-
    ment, 129

Bank of Montreal, 180
Bank of Tokyo, 41, 72, 104
Bank of Yokohama, 49
Banking Bureau, 8, 57, 96–97, 124,
    129, 137, 141, 142, 144, 147, 156,
    197, 238, 240–241
Banking crisis, reflecting continuing
    problems in Japan's policy sys-
    tems, 155–156
Banks of Japan, viewed by world as
    Beverly Hillbillies, 193
Banks
  comparative sizes of, 35
  deliberate use of public funds to sub-
    sidize, 155
  selling and buying back stock, 153–
    155
  taking hidden profits, 153–155
  volume as only channel for competi-
    tion by, 136–137
Barclays Securities, 198
Bentsen, Lloyd, 225
Black Monday (stock market crash in
    October 1987), 85–86
Board of Audit, 42
Boeing, 39
Bubble economy of late 1980s, 28, 60–
    94, 134, 137, 142, 156, 173, 180,
    182
  and amakudari, 48–49, 92
  amakudari system not helpful in,
    121–122
  bursting the bubble, 97–98, 166
  collapse of, 188
  cost of burst to life insurers, 159–161
  damage reports on, 98–101
  destruction of wealth greater than
    that of Word War II, 98–99
  and dilemma of banks, 74–75
  effect on Japanese workers, 80–81
  and ego replacing evaluation, 72–73
  and failure to see the obvious, 81–84
  and a fateful obsession, 65–69
  final phase of, 83–84

and frenzy, 69–80
and golf club membership, 62
as good for government finances, 68–69
and "hidden assets," 77
Japan as biggest exporter of money during, 158
the mirage dissolves, 95–122
mismanaged by the Ministry, 87–92
no checks and balances during, 84–87
official post-mortems of, 78
origin of term, 62
and the Plaza Accord, 63–65, 66, 67
presenting opportunities to dine with the devil, 92–94
and purchase of French impressionist paintings, 72
and purchase of Los Angeles real estate, 72
rich country, poor man during, 80–81
signals Ministry missed during, 83–84
Budget Bureau, 8, 21, 38, 51, 65, 66, 96, 123, 203, 211, 212, 223, 240
most authoritative of Ministry bureaus, 208
Budget, closely guarded power of, 208–212
Budget-making monopoly, plan to transfer from Ministry of Finance to Cabinet, 239
"Buffers," 224
Bullet-train system, full-scale expansion of, 250
Bundesbank, 85, 86, 175
Burke, Edmund, 252

Cambridge University, 14
Campbell, John Creighton, 216
Canadian Imperial Bank of Commerce, 35
Capital strike, 225–228

Capitalism, Japan's style consistent with its history, 191
Chase Manhattan, 35
Chemical Bank, 143
Chino, Tadao, 228
Chuo Trust Bank, 104
downgraded by Moody's, 143–144
Clinton, Bill, 1–2, 3, 227, 234
Cold War, 5–6, 188
end of, 187
Post-, 226
Constitution, of Japan, 2
Construction Ministry. *See* Ministry of Construction
Consumption tax, introduction of, 46
Convoy system (goso-sendan), 136, 156, 161
Cornell Business School, 47
Corporate paper (CP), 195
Cosmo Credit Cooperative, run on, 148
Courtis, Ken, 150
Credit co-op industry, increase in amakudari opportunities in, 120
Credit Lyonnais (bank), 180

Dai-Ichi Kangyo, setting up derivatives trading center outside Japan, 181
Daiwa Bank, 156
Damage assessment by the Ministry of Finance, 255–256
Defense Agency, 42, 210
Defensive action taken in 1996 by Okurasho, 240–246
Deliberation Council on the Fiscal System, 211
Deposit Insurance Corporation, 149
Deregulation
in name rather than substance, 198
national debate over, 193
struggle over, 192–196
Deutsche Bank, 150

Diet, 2, 23, 47, 54, 129, 139, 140, 144, 190, 209, 218, 231
and appearance of Harunori Takahashi, 50
described as collection of 300 farmers, 11
former Okurasho members of, 46
and "inherited" seats, 20
and tendency to nepotism, 20
Dutch tulip bulb craze, 62, 122

East Asia, 230
East Asian Miracle, The, 228
Economic Council, 179
Economic Planning Agency, 42, 84, 90, 123, 193, 194, 216
Economist, The, 150
Economists
attitude toward by Ministry of Finance, 4
trouble with, 14–19
in Western countries, 5
EIE International, 75, 79, 134
experience of, with LTCB, 80, 97, 116–117, 120
End of History and the Last Man, The, 189–190
Entitlement, 42–46
Entrepreneur, confession of, 116–117
Environment Agency, 42
Environmental Sanitation Business Financing Corporation, 35
Escorted convoy system (goso-sendan), 136, 156, 161
Euromarket, 179–180
European Union, 232
Export-Import Bank of Japan, 35, 36, 49, 214–215
Exxon, and sale of Manhattan building to Mitsui, 60–62, 77, 90, 121–122

Fair Trade Commission, 10, 42, 44, 177, 197, 233
Faulkner, Mark, 145

Fidelity Investments, 76, 198
Finance Bureau, 38, 125
Finance Corporation of Local Public Enterprise, 35
Finance industry
every aspect of, under Okurasho supervision, 188
most heavily regulated, 192
Finance Ministry. *See* Ministry of Finance
Financial System Research Council, 241, 247–248
Finland, as prudent spender, 209
Fiscal Investment and Loan Program (Zaito), 218–222, 231, 258
Food sector, as notable underperformer, 172
Forbes magazine, comparing bubble economy to Dutch tulip bulb craze, 62, 122
Ford Motor Co., taking control of Mazda, 171
Forest management system, 221
Fourth Wednesday Group (yon sui kai), 39
French impressionist paintings
purchase of, 72
value of, 116
Fuchita, Yasuyuki, 182
Fuji Bank, 84
setting up derivatives trading center outside Japan, 181
Fujii, Hirohisa, 47
Fukada, Takeo, 53
Fukukawa, Shinji, 169
Fukuyama, Francis, 189–191

General Electric, 168
Ghyoten, Toyoo, 41, 223
Goldman-Sachs, 227
Goso-sendan (escorted convoy system), 136, 156, 161
Gray zone, 56–58
Greenspan, Alan, 97

Group of Five (G–5), 63–65, 66, 67, 81
Japan's debt compare with, 99
Group of Seven, 209, 245
Guiness Book of World Records, 60
Gulf War, 98
Gyasei shido, 56–58

Haganuma, Chisato, 107
Hale, David, 178, 225
Harada, Yuzo, 253
Harvard University, 47
Hashimoto, Ryutaro, 132, 140, 173, 214–215, 230, 237, 242–243, 244, 249–256
setting principles for markets to be free, fair, and global, 251
Health Ministry. *See* Ministry of Health and Welfare
Hidaka, Sohei, 112
"Hidden assets," and the bubble economy, 77
Hidden profits, 103–104, 108, 153–154, 159, 160
Hiraiwa, Gaishi, 234
Hiraiwa report, 234–235
Hiroshima, 170
Hitotsubashi University, 185, 211
Hofu, 170
Hokkaido Takushoku Bank, downgraded by Moody's, 143–144
"Hollowing out" problem, 179–182, 183, 184
overcoming problem of, 194
Home-loan company. *See* Jusen
Honda, obliged to buy from inefficient 200-yen sector, 172
Hong Kong, 180, 181
Hong Kong and Shanghai Banking Corporation, 75
Hosenji Temple, 123–124
Hosokawa, Morihiro, 1–2, 4, 26–27, 187, 188, 205–209, 213, 226, 239, 256

advocating a "responsible revolution," 205
and political suicide of government, forced by Okurasho, 205–208
Hotel Okura, 22
Housing Loan Corporation, 35, 127
Hyatt Regency Hotel in Saipan, 75
Hyogo Bank, liquidation of, 145–148, 149

IBM Japan, 94
Imai, Takashi, 173
Imperial Palace in Tokyo, 76
Imperial University of Tokyo, 10
Independent banks, profitability of, 41–42
Indonesia, 194
Industrial Bank of Japan, 60, 146
Inoguchi, Toshihide, and unauthorized bond trading, 156
Inoue, Kengo, 158
Institute for Fiscal and Monetary Policy, 58, 191
Instituts d'Etudes Politiques, 14
Interest rates to be set by policy board, 247
International Finance Bureau, 8, 81, 178, 183, 185, 216, 223, 238, 253, 254
International Monetary Fund, 150, 228, 230
International Trade and Industry, Ministry of, 140, 169, 174, 177, 192–193, 198–199
Ishi, Hiromitsu, 211–212
Ishizaki, Bungo, 79–80, 93–94, 116–117, 135–136
Ishizawa, Takashi, 145, 153
Itami, Juzo, 179
Ito, Shigeru, 238–239, 244, 256

Japan
as an aberration, a "1940 economic structure," 185–187, 191

Japan (continued)
  as an abnormal nation, 187–190
  accused of being mercantilist parasite by U.S., 231–232
  and administrative guidance, 56–58
  Allied occupation of, 11
  and anthropocentrism, 6
  becoming the risk, 123–157
  and cartels, 44
  and the Cold War, 5–6
  Constitution of, 2, 208
  and controls over interest rates, 5
  deterioration of fiscal position contributed to by Ministry's fiscal obsession, 119
  and economic "bubble," 6
  and first homegrown recession, 6
  government of, and concerns over protectionism in 1985, 63–64
  "hollowing out" problem of, 179–182, 183, 184
  land value loss in, 100
  legal retirement age in, 33
  as "most expensive country in the world," 168
  poor levels of investment sophistication in, 164–165
  private-sector banks in, 40–43
  and program of liberalization of financial markets, 18
  real estate value in 1980s, 69–70
  rising price of failure, 158–184
  "special corporations" of, 212–215
  stock market of, 4
  trade surplus of, 232
  troubled pension system of, 161–163
  unemployment rates of, 5
  and use of land, 90–91
  violent crime in, 5
  and wave of hyperliquidity from 1986 to 1991, 61–62
Japan Air Lines, 75
  and foreign exchange loss, 39–40
  overrelying on an amakudari, 39–40

Japan Center for Economic Research, 243
Japan Center for International Finance, 36, 180
Japan Development Bank, 35, 213, 214–215, 219
"Japan, Inc.," 188
Japan National Oil Corporation, 213
Japan premium, on borrowed money in international market, 143, 148, 149
Japan Raw Silk and Sugar Price Stabilization Agency, 212–213
Japan Research Institute, 175, 178
Japan Securities Dealers' Association, 199
Japan Tobacco, 9
  as most heavily taxed company, 32
  president of, 31, 32
Japanese banking problem, and potential to disrupt world economies, 151
Japanese banks, opening all overseas branches in Asia, 229
Japanese capital, reasons for dissatisfaction with, 180–181
Japanese economic system, three features of, 186
Japanese Imperial Army, 186
Japanese life insurance companies and pack mentality, 78
Japanese Mafia (the Yakuza), 179
Japanese manufacturers
  emigrating, 167–174
  managing small miracle of aggressive competitiveness, 168
Japanese stockbrokerage system, dishonest basis of, 101–102
Japanese workers, effect of bubble economy on, 80–81
Jardine Fleming Securites, 143
Johnson, Chalmers, 5
J.P. Morgan, 180
JR Settlement Corporation, 153

Jusen (home-loan company) industry, 123–134
appropriation of public money to solve problem of, 237
and competition from banks, 127
death of the, 124, 155
as "financial garbage cans," 127–129
outrage by taxpayers over, 255
owing large sums to the nokyo, 132
trapped between private and public sectors, 127

Kagami, Nobumitsu, 111
Kakaricho, 47
Kanamori, Hiaso, 243
Kanemaru, Shin, 203, 204
Kanpo, 105, 227
Kansai University, 196
Karoshi, 23
Kasumi Economic Research Group, funding of, 37
Kasumigaseki reform, 237
Katayama Cabinet of 1947–1948, 203
Katayama, Tetsu, 4
Kato, Hiroshi, 215
Kato, Junko, 217–218
Kato, Koichi, 13, 28
Kawai, Noboru, 110
Kawana, Yoshikazu, 169–170
Keidanren, the, 112, 193, 195, 234
Keio University, 13, 167, 171
Kemper Financial Companies, 225
Kim Young Sam, 30
Kinyu Business, 197
Kizu Credit Cooperative, run on, 148
Kleinwort Benson Securities, 109
Kobe, 146
earthquake at, 147
Koh, Byung Chul, 16, 29
Komiya, Ryutaro, 9, 17, 234
Komura, Takeshi, 13
Koo, Richard, 117–118, 225, 227, 243–244

Kosan, Sueno, 128
Kubota, Isao, 82–84, 85, 121, 229
Kubota, Kunio, 93
Kurokawa, Masaaki, conceiving plan to establish California as joint Japanese-U.S. economic zone, 95
Kyocera, obliged to buy from inefficient 200–yen sector, 172
Kyoto University, 13

Land myth exploding, 101
Liberal Democratic Party, 11, 15, 16, 27, 54, 79, 89, 105, 115, 129, 132, 139, 162, 188, 207, 212, 213, 226, 231, 244–246, 249, 250
and business-like symbiosis with Okurasho, 204
and Kiichi Miyazawa, 12, 13
setting up new body to supervise financial institutions, 246–247
Life Insurance Association of Japan, 161
Life insurance companies, 228
"criminal" damage to, 159–161
dumping U.S. bonds, 226
as Okurasho-supervised cartel, 161
poor levels of investment sophistication in, 164–165
strong yen and overseas investments, 175
Lockheed political scandals, 202
Long-Term Credit Bank (LTCB), 78–79, 97, 116–117, 120–121, 134, 135, 138, 139, 145, 146
abandoning EIE, 135–136, 140
resignation of president, 139
seeking out Harunori Takahashi, 75
Los Angeles commercial real estate, purchase of by Japanese institutions, 72
Lower House of the Diet, 46, 187
Budget Committee of, 139

MacArthur, Douglas, 3, 230
Maekawa Report of 1986, 194
Maritime Credit Corporation, 212
Marriage and other intimacies, 19–21
Marxists, 14
Matchmaking service in the Finance Ministry, 9–10
Matsushita
  obliged to buy from inefficient 200-yen sector, 172
  and purchase of MCA, 72
Matsushita, Yasuo, 49, 52, 137, 180, 182, 249
Mazda
  overpowered by yen, 169–171
  taken over by Ford, 171
McKinsey & Co., 172
Meiji, 10
Membership in Ministry of Finance, price of, 22–24
Merrill Lynch, 180
Mieno, Yasushi, 91
Millionaires in Japan during the bubble era, 70
Minister's Secretariat, 8–9, 13, 38, 47, 82, 123, 124, 240
  and amakudari, 9–10
  arranging amakudari posts, 38–39
  and matchmaking service, 9–10, 19–21
Ministry of Agriculture, 176, 211–212
Ministry of Construction, 48, 50, 211–212, 216
Ministry of Finance
  and ability to appoint its own leader, 24–26
  and abuse of position in, 35–36
  action taken following market intervention, 109–110
  address of, 15
  and administrative guidance, 56–58, 98, 104

administrative vice minister of, oldest official, 33
adopting strategy of Imperial Japanese Army, 236–250
and amakudari, 9–10, 32–46
announcing takeover of two Takahashi-affiliated credit co-ops, 138
approach to economics of, 18
approaches taken to stop market collapse, 104–106
arguments for separation of functions of, 258
asking banks to accept responsibility for jusen failure, 132–133
assuming 40 percent of face value would be recovered from bad real estate loans, 152
attacked by major political parties, 236–240
attitude of, toward economists, 4
and available powerful levers for change, 176–177
and Bank of Japan accused of massive cover-up operation, 140
and Bank of Japan, critique of, 200–202
beginning of the end for banking policy of, 134–136
benefiting from the recession, 119–120
blocking deregulation, 244
bureaus of, 9. *See also individual bureaus*
and business-like symbiosis with Liberal Democratic Party, 104
can claim credit for many elements of postwar transformation, 231
claim to origins of, 2–3
and collusion in stock-loss compensation scandal, 102
and concern over consequences of yen appreciation, 174

concern for future generations regarding fiscal policy versus concern regarding pensions, 161
and control of the National Tax Administration Agency, 54
controlling 99 percent of pension assets, 163
damage assessment by, 255–256
and deal with U.S. to adjust the exchange rate, 177
and deepest insight into true motives of, 218–222
defensive action taken in 1996 by, 240–246
defied and competence questioned, from national to local level, 141
delayed response to jusen lending practices, 129–134
easing interest rates in 1983, 62–63
easy credit policy of, 155
engagement and negotiation of, in 1996, 246–250
and entitlement, 42–46
first loyalty to its relationship of patronage, 157
as fiscal guardian of the nation, 242
and fiscal reconstruction victory during the bubble years, 67–69
forcing Liberal Democrats to introduce consumption tax, 204
funding World Bank analysis, 229
and government tax revenues, 68
and guarded power of the budget, 208–212
guiding objectives of, 216–217
"helping" the private sector, 37–42
and Hyogo Bank's liquidation, 147
impressive record of dealing with political threats, 256
and inability to take disciplinary action against elite members, 549–554
indirect directives of, 110–114

indulgence of fiscal obsession contributing to deterioration of Japan's fiscal position, 119
intervention of, beneficial or ethical?, 114–116
and jusen, 29, 125–134
and Kato as enemy of, 13
as liability in the nation's transition to modern economy, 259
lobbied by life insurers for help, 160
location of, 8
loosening of stranglehold on life insurance companies, 167
losing supervision of financial markets, 255–256
management system of, blamed for pension fund losses, 167
"manufacturing the political will of Japan," 208
and marriage and other intimacies, 19–21
media opinion of, 7
merging national budget with zaito system, 221
as "ministry of ministries," 3
mismanaging the bubble economy, 87–92
missed signals during bubble economy, 83–84
and Mitsubishi Bank, 40–42
monopoly of, on proposing and compiling the budget, 203
not mentioned in Constitution, 209
officials' regard for politicians, 11
officials' relationship with Harunori Takahashi, 27
and opportunity to revise its approach to bank supervision, 91
overtime hours at, 21–22
paradoxical appearance of power, 215–218
perception of by others, 6–7
and perversion of due process, 54–56

Ministry of Finance (continued)
plan of attack to reform, 238–240
plan to transfer budget-making monopoly from, to Cabinet, 239
and political careers, 46–48
as political, economic, and intellectual force, 2
and political suicide of Hosokawa government, 205–209
and poll of Tokyo entrepreneurs, 82
and potential to change the structure of the economy, 177
and press campaign against Jiro Saito, 28
and price-keeping operation (PKO), 105, 107, 111, 112, 114–116
price of membership in, 22–24
propping up the property market, 151
protecting cartels instead of reforming pension system, 166
protecting the core base, 244–246, 255
protecting the "main castle," fiscal policy, 96, 118
protecting "special corporations," 212–215
and public anger, 52–54
and punishment of Newpis Hongkong, 57–58
and punishment for troublemakers, 56–58
as "a rather splendid club," 10
and real estate value in Japan, 69–70
real power of, less than it appears, 217
realizes its banking policy is no longer realistic, 136
reasons for delay in correcting jusen problem, 131–132
reassuring overseas bankers, 149
receiving harsh criticism for credit co-ops, 140

and recruitment from Tokyo University, 10–17, 28
reform of promised, 238
refusing to liberalize OTC market, 199
regulation by, causing dissatisfaction with Japanese capital, 180
resisting requests for pension reform, 165–166
response to banks' plan to solve jusen problem, 130
response to Keidanren requests for deregulation, 195
response to LTCB's withdrawal of support for EIE, 135–136
responsible for first recession since the war, 236
retirement system of, and abuse, 34
rewards and punishments at, 31–59
and rewards for allies, 54–56
rewards for faithful service to, 34–37
and rising discount rate, 97
and role as honest guardian of public revenues, 203
and rotation of governorship of Bank of Japan, 44–45
scandal in, 49–54
seniority rule of, 33–34
setting a new policy, 144–146
shadow empire of, 32–34
shifting blame for bubble to Bank of Japan, 101
showing lack of courage, 141–144
special corporations controlled by, 35
staff internal associations of, 21
standard posture of, to resist deregulation, 195
and strength in its solidarity, 25
supervising every aspect of finance industry, 188
and surveillance of jusen management, 129
and suspicion of market forces, 181

and symbiotic relationship with top-level Liberal Democrats, 245
and Tanaka attack on public finance, 204
and tendency to nepotism, 20–21
threatening a capital strike against U.S., 225–228
three recurring mantras of, 181–182
and trade surplus, 232–233
and unwritten contract to its executive stream, 33
on usefulness of market, 4
using administrative guidance to limit real estate lending, 98
versus the stock market, 103–107
viewing final phase of bubble economy, 83–84
wanting to continue increasing consumption tax, 208
withdrawing implicit guarantee of all financial institutions, 138
and yen-busting policy package, 175–176
and zaito system, 218–222
Ministry of Health and Welfare, 162, 166, 167, 194
asking Okurasho for reform of pension system, 165
Ministry of Home Affairs, 3, 186
Ministry of International Trade and Industry (MITI), 1–2, 25, 102, 140, 169, 174, 177, 192–193, 198–199, 207
arguing for 100-yen sector, 193
Ministry of Transport, 176–177, 211–212
Mitsubishi Bank, and amakudari, 40–42
Mitsubishi Real Estate, 76, 77
and purchase of Rockefeller Center, 72
Mitsubishi Research Institute, 171
Mitsui Real Estate Co., 77
and purchase of Exxon building in Manhattan, 60–62, 73, 77, 90, 122

Mitsuzuka, Hiroshi, 250–251
Miwa, Yoshiaki, 17, 179
Miyao, Takahiro, 16
Miyawaki, Atsushi, 220–222
Miyazawa, Kiichi, 12, 13, 47, 67, 69, 84, 132, 214
Mizuno, Masaru, 23–24, 31–32, 33
Moftan, 57
Momura Research Institute, 183
Monetary (interest rate) policy, 117
Money Club, the, 163–165
Moody's Investors Services, 143, 149
Morgan Stanley Japan, 110
Mori Building, 37
Morinaga, Teiichiro, 25
Mr. Jusen (Keiichiro Niwayama), 125–126, 128
Murayama, Tatsuo, 46, 48
Murayama, Tomiichi, 139, 207, 213
Myth of trustworthy bureaucracy, 102–103

Nagaoka, Minoru, 44, 52
Nagaoka, Toshio, and Japan Air Lines, 39–40
Nakai, Sei, 96, 129, 130, 137, 141
Nakajima, Yoshio, 29, 51–53
and close relationship with Harunori Takahashi, 51–52
Nakamura, Yukio, 193
Nakasone, Yasuhiro, 63
NASDAQ, 198
National Australia Bank, 35
National budget, preparation of, 23
National debt, 119
National hospital system, 221
National Land Agency, 42, 183
National Personnel Authority, 34
National rail system, 221
National Tax Administration Agency, 54
National Taxation Agency, deaths due to overwork at, 23–24
Nenpuku pension fund, 166, 167

New Frontier Party (Shinshinto), 175
New Liberal Club, 202
New Oji, 57
New York City Board of Educators,
61
New Zealand, 100
Newpis Hongkong, punishment of by
Ministry of Finance, 57–58
Nihon Keizai Shimbun, 49
Nikkei golf index, 62, 108
Nikkei stock market index, 62, 87, 95,
107, 110
falling, 97, 98, 100, 103, 111
Nikkei newspaper, 243
Nikkei Venture Business Annual 1994,
198
Nikko Research Center, 174
"1940 economic structure," 185–187,
191, 200
Nippon Credit Bank, downgraded by
Moody's, 143–144
Nippon Housing Loan Co., 125, 128,
129, 130, 131
Nippon Life Insurance Co., 72, 111
Nippon Steel, 76–77, 173, 197
Nippon Telegraph and Telephone
(NTT), 70, 88–89
Nippon Trust Bank, 104
Nishibe, Susumu, 190
Nishimura, Yoshimasa, 144–146, 148,
156–157, 197
Nissan Motor Co., 112, 170, 197
closing Zama factory, 169
Niwayama, Keiichiro, 125–126, 128,
129, 130, 132
Noguchi, Yukio, 185–192, 200–
202
and direct assault on the Okurasho,
189
Nokyo (farmers' cooperatives), 131
political clout of, 132
Nomura Research Institute, 73–74,
117, 148, 159–160, 163, 220, 225,
243

Nomura Securities, 95, 102, 107, 111,
112, 170–171, 182
Nonaka, Hiromu, 27–28
Norway, as prudent spender, 209
NTT. *See* Nippon Telegraph and Tele-
phone

Oba, Tomomitsu, 38, 125, 180
Ogawa, Alicia, 154
Ogawa, Tadashi, 29, 245
Ohga, Norio, 172
Ohira, Masayoshi, 204
Oji Paper Company, 57
Okada, Toshiaki, 55–56
Okajima, Kazuo, 123–124
Okuda, Hiroshi, 176
Okura (treasure-store), 3
Okurasho. *See* Ministry of Finance
100- and 200-yen industries, 171, 193
Organization for Economic Coopera-
tion and Development (OECD),
162–163
Osaka, 148, 196
Osaka spinning-industry pension fund,
going bankrupt, 166
Oshima, Hidetoshi, 134
OTC companies, enjoying profit
growth, 198
OTC listings, greatly restricted by
Okurasho, 198–199
OTC Market, 199
Otsuki, Takashi, 124
Overseas Economic Cooperation
Fund, 215
Oxford University, 14
Ozaki, Mamoru, 21
Ozawa, Ichiro, 79, 141, 188–191, 207,
249
and direct assault on the Okurasho,
189

Parking-meter index, 153
Pension assets, 99 percent controlled
by Okurasho, 163

Pension Fund Association, 161, 163
  lobbying Okurasho for removal of
  fund management restrictions, 165
Pension funds, U.S. corporate funds
  compared with Japanese, 164
Pension system problem
  diagnosed extensively, 165–166
  government response to, in 1993,
  162–163
Pension Welfare Service Corporation
  (Nenpuku) fund, 166
People's Construction Bank of China,
  35
People's Finance Corporation, 35, 49
Philip Morris, and tobacco tax, 32
PKO, *See* Price-keeping operation
Plaza Accord, 40, 63–65, 66, 67, 74, 76,
  169
Plaza Hotel, a decoy at, 63–65
Policy debate, being determined by
  Okurasho's priorities rather than
  need for economic management,
  244, 257
Policy Research Council, 13
Politics, a head start in, 46–48
Post Office Life Insurance Bureau, con-
  ducting support buying, 112–113
Postal life insurance system *(kanpo)*,
  105, 114, 219, 227
Postal savings establishment *(yucho)*,
  105, 114–115, 219, 221
Power of Okurasho, paradoxical ap-
  pearance of, 215–218
Price to earnings (PE) ratio during
  bubble economy, 70–71
Price-keeping operation (PKO), 105,
  107, 111, 112, 114–116, 182–184
  public-sector funds invested follow-
  ing launch of, 114
Private fixed investment, as important
  economic indicator, 83
Property market, being propped up by
  Okurasho, 151
Public Finance Law, 204

Public investment, relevance to trade
  surplus, 233–234
Public pension system, 219, 221
Public sector, percentage of amakudari
  officials in, 34
Public-sector funds, investment of, fol-
  lowing launch of PKO, 114– 115
Public Works Subcommittee, 212
Punishment for troublemakers, 56–58

Rall, Ted, 60–61
Reagan Administration, and concerns
  over protectionism in 1985, 63–64
Real estate value in 1980s, Japan vs.
  United States, 69–70
Recession, growing worse, 117–118
Reform, to be guided by Japanese
  ideal, 192
Regent Hotel in Sydney, Australia, 78
Reign of Bureaucracy, 2
Reign of Representative Politics, 2
Rewards for faithful service to Minis-
  try of Finance, 32–37
Rewards and punishments at Ministry
  of Finance, 31–59
Rikkyo University, 56
Riley, Ivers, 224
Rixtel, Adrian van, 43
Roaring Twenties boom, 122
Rogers, Neil, 108

Saitama University, 201
Saito, Jiro, 21, 26–29, 175, 206–207,
  214
Sakaiya, Taichi, 102
Sakakibara, Eisuke, 6, 11, 49, 50, 106,
  177, 185, 189, 190–192, 193, 216,
  226–229, 252–254
  defending the Okurasho, 185, 190–
  192
  maturity or hypocrisy?, 200–202
  1977 article by, 200–201
Sakamaki, Hideo, 182
Sakigate, 162

Sakura Bank, setting up derivatives trading center outside Japan, 181

Salomon Brothers Tokyo, 154

Sanwa Bank, 125, 130, 131, 198
setting up derivatives trading center outside Japan, 181

Sanwa Bank Research Institute, 165

Sato, Mitsuo, and the "ashtray treatment," 224–225

Sato restaurant, 93–94

Savings and investment, examination of, in U.S. and Japan, 234

SBC Warburg Securities, 145

Scandal in the Ministry of Finance, 49–54

Securities Bureau, 53, 109, 112, 183, 184, 238, 240–241, 254

Seike, Arsushi, 167

Sentaku, 206

Shadow empire of Ministry of Finance, 32–34

Shindo, Muneyuki, 56

Shinkansen, full-scale expansion of, 250

Shinozawa, Kyosuke, 21, 28–29

Shinshinto (New Frontier Party), 175, 249, 254

Shukan Shincho, 149

Singapore, 34, 100, 168, 180, 224

Singapore International Monetary Exchange (SIMEX), 45, 224–225

Small Business Finance Corporation, 35, 125

Snoddy, David, 143

Socialists, 162

Sony Corporation, 172, 178

Sony, obliged to buy from inefficient 200-yen sector, 172

Sony, and purchase of Columbia Pictures movie studio, 72

South Korea, 232

South Sea Company bubble, 62, 122

Southeast Asia, 232

"Special corporations," 212–215
taxpayer subsidization of, 212

Standard and Poors, 145

Stock issues in U.S. compared with Japan stock issues, 183

Stock-loss compensation scandal, and collusion with Ministry of Finance, 102

Stock market, being held aloft by two pillars, 105

Sugar Price Stabilization Agency, 212–213

Sumita, Satoshi, 142

Sumitomo Bank, 146
setting up derivatives trading center outside Japan, 181

Sumitomo Real Estate, 77

Summers, Lawrence, 232

Suzuki, Yoichiro, 72, 122

Suzuki, Yoshio, 85–86, 101, 220

Taiwan, 232

Takagi, Masaru, 84

Takahashi, Harunori, 27, 29, 50, 74–75, 78, 79, 92, 116–117, 120, 121, 134, 135, 137, 138–139, 155
and close relationship with Yoshio Nakajima, 51–52
establishing close relationships with aristocracy of Japanese officialdom, 93–94
and Pacific tourism empire, 75, 78–80
and public contempt, 138–139
testifying that LTCB was culpable, 139

Takahashi-affiliated credit co-ops, 137, 138, 142, 144

Takanaka, Heizo, 171

Takata, Shoichi, 153

Takemura, Masayoshi, 27, 28, 50–51, 148, 174

Takeshita, Noboru, 54, 65–66, 214, 230, 245

Tampopo, 179
Tanaka, Kakuei, 12, 26, 204
  and the Ministry of Finance, 12
Tanaka, Shusei, 187
Tanimachi, 52
Tasker, Peter, 109
Tax Bureau, 31, 240
Tax Commission, 215
Taxing Woman, 179
Taxpayer outrage over public monies
  subsidizing failed credit co-ops,
  138
Taya, Hiroaki, 50
Terada, Noboru, 165
Terasawa, Yoshio, 42
Thailand, 194
Tian, Ang Swee, 224–225
Tobacco, increased excise on, 32
Tokkin accounts, 71–72, 88
Tokyo Big Bang, 251–252, 254, 257
Tokyo, cost of living compared with
  New York's, 172
Tokyo Customs House, 50
Tokyo District Court, and repossessed
  real estate, 151–152
Tokyo entrepreneurs, Okurasho poll
  of, 82
Tokyo financial market, 180
Tokyo Kyodo Bank, 138
Tokyo Kyowa Credit Cooperative, 80,
  90, 120, 134–136
Tokyo market, revival of, 251
Tokyo Metropolitan Assembly, 141
Tokyo Metropolitan Government, 138
Tokyo Stock Exchange, 36, 43, 49, 52,
  57, 65, 70, 71, 95–96, 197, 199,
  224
  major problem of, 183
  prices falling in, 97–98, 100, 103
Tokyo, Toranomon Business district
  of, 36
Tokyo University, 5, 161, 166, 185,
  214, 217, 256, 258
  law graduates of, 16

non-Marxist economics at, 15
  recruitment from, to Ministry of
    Finance, 10–17, 28
Torii, Yasuhiko, 247
"Total-war economy," 185, 200
Toyota Motors, 170, 176
  obliged to buy from inefficient 200-
    yen sector, 172
Trade surplus, 230–235
Transport Ministry. *See* Ministry of
  Transport
Troublemakers, punishment for, 56–58
Trust banks
  and new pattern of stock buying
    from 1992 onward, 113
  poor levels of investment sophistica-
    tion in, 164–165
Trust Fund Bureau, 115, 163–164,
  166, 167, 219
Tsukuba University, 16
Tsushima, Yuji, 105–106, 115
200-yen sector, streamlining, 175

UBS Securities, 45, 108, 151
Ueda, Kazuo, 161, 165
Ueda, Shozo, 196–197
United States
  accusing Japan of being mercantilist
    parasite, 231–232
  and the Cold War, 5–6
  and Japan Air Lines, 39
University of Tokyo. *See* Tokyo Uni-
  versity
Unoki, Hajime, 168, 172
Upper House, 205
U.S. Central Intelligence Agency, 111
U.S. Congress, 150
U.S. Federal Reserve Board, 97, 178
U.S. government, asking Okurasho to
  move toward performance-
  oriented system on pension funds,
  165
U.S. House Committee on Banking
  and Financial Services, 150

U.S.-Japan intervention to push the dollar higher, 178
U.S. savings and loan crisis, 145
U.S. Secretary of the Treasury, 69
U.S. Securities Exchange Commission, 125
U.S. Treasury, 177
U.S. Treasury bonds, sell-off of, 227
Utsumi, Makoto, 81–82, 230

Van Wolferen, Karel, 224
Veribanc, 145
Virtual regulation, 196–197

Wakatsuki, Mikio, 175
Wall Street, 70
Waseda University, 13
Watanabe, Michio, 54–55
Watanabe, Takeshi, 230, 231
Wataridori, 36
Welch, John, 168
World Bank, 228, 229, 230
World War II, reconstruction after, 2, 19

Yamaguchi, Mitsuhide, 36, 38, 43–44, 65, 66
Yamaichi Securities Research Institute, 84
Yamakawa, Tetsufumi, 227
Yamamoto, Kozo, 9, 17–18, 25, 47
Yamamoto, Yadahiro, 102
Yasuda Fire & Marine Insurance, 73
Yasuda, Hiroshi, 53
Yasuda Trust Bank, 104
Yen
  appreciation of, 159
  overpowering Mazda, 169–171
Yen-Dollar Committee, 197
Yokohama Specie Bank, 41
Yoshino, Toshihiko, 84
Yoshino, Yoshihiko, 66, 67, 234–235
Yucho, 105

Zaibatsu industries, 3
Zaito system (Fiscal Investment and Loan Program), 218–222, 231, 258
  hidden losses within, 222
Zama, 169

 # ABOUT THE AUTHOR

Peter Hartcher is an award-winning journalist who specializes in the affairs of the Asia-Pacific region. He lived in Japan from 1986 to 1989 and from 1992 to 1995. During those years, he witnessed and chronicled one of the world's great episodes of economic madness—the Bubble Economy—and its disastrous consequences.

Hartcher was first sent to Tokyo as a correspondent for *The Sydney Morning Herald,* and later went on to become the *Herald's* national bureau chief and chief political correspondent. He later returned to Tokyo as a correspondent for the *Australian Financial Review.* Hartcher is now based in Sydney, Australia, as the *Australian Financial Review*'s Asia-Pacific editor. He has won the highest accolade in Australian journalism for his investigative reporting on regional affairs while working at the *Review.* He has been consulted by multinational institutions and called to give testimony to his country's parliament as an expert witness on Asian economies. He has co-authored a book on doing business in Asia and is a leading analyst of Asian economies.